THE BATTLE OF
THE ALMA

THE BATTLE OF
THE ALMA

First Blood to the Allies in the Crimea

Ian Fletcher
and
Natalia Ishchenko

Pen & Sword
MILITARY

First published in Great Britain in 2008 by
PEN & SWORD MILITARY
an imprint of
Pen & Sword Books Ltd
47 Church Street
Barnsley
South Yorkshire
S70 2AS

ISBN 978 1 84415 672 6

A CIP catalogue record for this book is
available from the British Library.

Printed and bound in Great Britain
by Biddles

Pen & Sword Books Ltd incorporates the imprints of
Pen & Sword Aviation, Pen & Sword Maritime, Pen & Sword Military,
Wharncliffe Local History, Pen & Sword Select, Pen & Sword Military Classics,
Leo Cooper, Remember When, Seaforth Publishing and Frontline Publishing.

For a complete list of Pen & Sword titles please contact
PEN & SWORD BOOKS LIMITED
47 Church Street, Barnsley, South Yorkshire, S70 2AS, England
E-mail: enquiries@pen-and-sword.co.uk
Website: www.pen-and-sword.co.uk

Contents

List of Illustrations

Lord Raglan, 1788–1855, commander-in-chief of the British Army in the Crimea.

General François Antoine Certain Canrobert, 1809–1895. Commanded the French 1st Division at the Alma.

Marshal Leroy de Saint-Arnaud, 1801–1854, commander-in-chief of the French Army.

Sir George Brown, 1790–1865, commander of the British 2nd Division.

Prince Alexander Sergeevich Menshikov, 1787–1869. Commander-in-chief of the Russian Army at the Alma.

The Duke of Cambridge, 1819–1904. Commanded the British 1st Division at the Alma.

'The United Service.' *Punch* magazine's view of the new spirit of cooperation between the old enemies.

Another cartoon from *Punch*, this time following the Allied victory at the Alma.

The Brigade of Guards attacking the Great Redoubt during the Battle of the Alma.

The Battle of the Alma, after a print by Dupray.

The battlefield shortly after the end of the fighting. The Great Redoubt can be seen on the right.

The defile at Almatamack through which Bosquet's troops passed to begin the battle.

Another section of the drawing by Hamley, showing the ground to the west of the Sevastopol road.

The defile at Almatamack, from the viewpoint of Bosquet's troops as they began moving up.

The battlefield of the Alma today. A view looking east from a position just south-east of Almatamack.

The river Alma today, just to the east of Almatamack.

The river Alma today, looking east, at a spot where the 2nd Division crossed.

A British infantryman's view of the Great Redoubt as seen from a position just to the south of the river Alma.

The obelisk and battlefield memorial inside the Great Redoubt today.

The memorial to the Vladimirsky Regiment, inside the Great Redoubt.

List of Maps

Introduction

On the afternoon of 20 September 1854, around 100,000 British, French, Russian and Turkish soldiers came together to fight what was the first real battle on European soil for almost forty years. Turkey declared war on Russia in 1853, and when Britain and France did the same the following year the long peace which had existed in Europe since the Battle of Waterloo in 1815 finally came to an end. The Battle of the Alma was not the first battle of the Crimean War. Indeed, the Turks and Russians had been at each other's throats along the Danube even before Britain and France entered the fray. But it was, however, the first battle to be fought on the Crimean peninsula, and, for the British Army at least, was its first since that memorable day back in June 1815.

On 20 September 2004, the 150th anniversary of the battle, we sat on the stone wall close to the site of the Great Redoubt on the battlefield of the Alma and looked out across the fields that sloped away towards the river Alma itself. It was difficult to imagine the scene that would have met our eyes if we had sat on the same spot 150 years earlier. In 2004 the day was hot and sunny, and isolated groups of tourists strolled aimlessly around in the sun. How different it was on the same day in 1854, when the ground would have been strewn with the bodies of dead, dying and wounded British infantry, their red coats ripped aside by Russian shot fired from the redoubt.

It was a pity that no large-scale commemorative event took place on the anniversary of the Battle of the Alma, although this was understandable given the very high-profile events that were to take place just over four weeks later at Balaklava on the occasion of the 150th anniversary of what must surely be one of the most famous episodes in British military history. It was a shame that the anniversary of the Battle of the Alma appeared to have passed by unnoticed, as did that of Inkerman, as these were the two bloodiest battles fought by the British Army in Europe between Waterloo and the First World War. It was especially so with the Alma since it proved to be the only pitched battle in the Crimea fought in the open field, unlike Inkerman, which, although far bloodier, was effectively the parrying of a Russian strike against the Allied siege lines.

By coincidence, 2004 was not only the 150th anniversary of the Battle of the Alma. It saw the 300th anniversary of the Battle of Blenheim, fought on 13 August 1704, and we could not but reflect on the fact that, had the Duke of Marlborough been present at the Alma, he would have been perfectly capable of commanding the British troops as they advanced towards the Russian positions in their long red lines. The other great duke, Wellington, would have had no problem either. Indeed, the British Army was commanded by one of his old lieutenants, Lord Raglan, whilst many other senior commanders had also served under him. The point is that though many historians consider the Crimean War to have been the first of the modern wars, there is little doubt in our minds that, whilst this is partly true, it was certainly the last of the old wars, for the Battle of the Alma was fought in the same manner that scores of battles had been fought over the previous century and a half. So, we have ample scope to discuss a period in military history when, in many ways, the old gave way to the new.

There has been much written before about the Battle of the Alma, not least in the general histories of the Crimean War. In Britain, Kinglake's epic *Invasion of the Crimea* covered the battle in great depth, whilst other contemporary works did so to a lesser extent. There have also been several Russian and French accounts of the war which contain chapters on the battle. But works dedicated solely to the Battle of the Alma have certainly been surprisingly few and far between. The same can be said about Inkerman, the real bloodbath of the Crimean War. Only the battle at Balaklava has ever been tackled on a regular basis. Hence the idea of a new history of the battle, one that is told from both sides, Allied and Russian.

Perhaps the most enjoyable part of our research was visiting the battlefield itself, something which we have done on numerous occasions, in both summer and winter. Indeed, we have stood in the Great Redoubt in sweltering heat. We have also visited the battlefield in temperatures well below zero, when it has been covered with deep snow. We have walked the entire length of the field, from the mouth of the river Alma at the coast, as far as the extreme right flank of the Russian position. Only by doing this can you really get a feel for what it was like for the men on both sides on that memorable September day.

A feature of our version of the battle is the number of eyewitness accounts, for only the Russian, British and French soldiers who survived the battle really knew what happened there. In telling their story we have retained original spellings, and have kept the translations of Russian and French accounts as raw as possible and have not attempted to polish them too smoothly so as to detract from their immediacy. Only dates have been changed, at least those in the Russian accounts, for they were still using the old calendar, which was twelve days adrift of that used throughout the rest of Europe. For example, the battle invariably appears in Russian accounts as taking place on 8 September. This is the only real alteration made to the Russian accounts.

x The Battle of the Alma

The Crimean War has certainly enjoyed something of a revival during the last few years following the 150th anniversary events, but it still continues to give off 'bad vibes', to use the words of one major British publisher who refused to have anything to do with the Crimean War. This, of course, has much to do with the conditions during the terrible winter of 1854–5, and with the widespread disenchantment in Britain, and indeed within the army at the Crimea, at the management of the campaign. All of this was yet to come, however, when the Battle of the Alma was fought on a warm, sunny day in the autumn of 1854.

Ian Fletcher and Natalia Ishchenko

Chapter 1

A Rupture with the Russians

The Crimean War is almost unique in that it has provided generations of historians with a rich source of material on how wars begin. It also demonstrates to political historians how wars can and should be avoided, for it was a war that was a long time in coming. For almost four years politicians around Europe, and particularly in Britain, France, Russia and Turkey, could see the conflict looming on the horizon but they appear to have been helpless in stopping the slow drift towards war, which seemed inevitable once France decided to revive its ancient rights in the Holy Land in 1850. The war is also possibly unique in that not only were negotiations going on prior to the outbreak of war, as politicians and diplomats sought to find a way of avoiding the conflict, but conferences and peace talks were ongoing throughout the war, from the very beginning in 1854 right up to the early days of 1856. Indeed, one might say that the war is unique in having been fought out simultaneously in two very different theatres: in atrocious conditions in the Crimea itself and around various comfortable conference tables throughout Europe. As a result there are literally thousands of documents which provide a wonderful insight into the causes of the tragedy that was the Crimean War. Needless to say, we have no intention of going into too much detail.

On the face of it, the Crimean War may be traced back to Czar Nicholas I and his attempts to achieve Russian supremacy in the Black Sea and access to the Mediterranean. But in order to do this Russia had first to control the Bosphorus and the Dardanelles, the straits which led into the Black Sea. Having failed by peaceful means, Nicholas was given the chance to control the straits following the defeat of Turkey in 1828 and the consequential Peace of Adrianople. But although the peace deprived Turkey of much of the Black Sea coastline, it still did not give Nicholas command of the important straits.

Three years later Nicholas was given a second opportunity following a revolt against the Turks by the Egyptian pasha, Mehemet Ali. Instead of helping Mehemet, Nicholas decided to assist the Turkish sultan, Makhmud, and in 1833 sent a Russian squadron, under the famous Admiral Lazarev, to support the Turks. It was a shrewd move, intended to draw the previously suspicious empires closer. Indeed, the Turks now looked to Russia as a future ally, the consequence being the Unkiar–Skelessi Treaty, which permitted Russian warships to traverse the Bosphorus and the Dardanelles. These straits were now effectively closed to the warships of other countries, something which gave cause for much consternation in London and Paris, which began to seek ways of breaking the influence which Russia enjoyed with Turkey.

In 1839 Mehemet rebelled once again, at which various powers, including Britain, Austria and Prussia, sprang to the Turks' assistance in an attempt to court favour. The Russians did likewise. Two years later, the London Convention resulted in the loss of many of Russia's gains from the Unkiar–Skelessi Treaty, in addition to which the Turks, having now apparently resolved their problems with the Egyptians, felt they no longer needed to depend on Russia for future support. In fact, they regarded it more as a burden, and so looked elsewhere for support and assistance in ridding themselves of Nicholas' influence. This was achieved by the middle of the nineteenth century, largely as a result of French and British help.

Needless to say, Nicholas was not prepared to accept the situation lying down. He knew full well that the Ottoman Empire was in a state of some decline, and the prospect of having two foreign powers, Britain and France, take advantage of the situation so close to the southern borders of his own empire barely warranted thinking about. It was vital, therefore, that Russian influence over Turkey was reasserted, either by diplomacy or war, the latter being the favoured course of action. The problem was that, as yet, Nicholas had no legitimate reason for taking up arms against the sultan's armies.

That was, however, until a minor squabble arose in the Holy Land between two sets of monks. The dispute was over certain religious rights relating to the possession of the keys to the Church and Grotto of the Nativity in Bethlehem, and to the maintenance of the Church of the Holy Sepulchre in Jerusalem. Under the conditions of a treaty, known as 'the capitulations', drawn up in 1740, France had become recognized as the protector of the Latin church in eastern lands, which included custodianship of the Holy Sepulchre. The privileges enjoyed by France had long since ceased to be of any real concern to the French, but the struggle between Mehemet Ali and the sultan in the 1830s enabled Christians to visit the Holy Places for the first time in centuries. As the czar was nominally the protector of Christians in Turkish dominions, Nicholas naturally began to develop a keen interest in Turkish affairs once more. But in 1850 France, taking note of the situation in Turkey and keen to deny Russia a foothold in Turkish domestic affairs, decided to revive its claim, a move that did not go down too well with its Russian rivals. Remarkably, this trivial and seemingly insignificant little quarrel would escalate into something far more serious than a dispute between two sets of monks supported by France and Russia.

The apparently innocuous religious quarrel very soon became the excuse for a major struggle between French and Russian diplomats for influence on the Turkish Empire. The initial dispute was not over the rights to worship in either Orthodox or Catholic churches, since neither was prohibited. The whole sorry business came down to the ungrounded, petty and litigious old dispute between Greek and Catholic monks over who must repair the broken dome in Jerusalem and who must possess the keys to the Bethlehem cathedral, which was not even locked with the keys anyway. There was also a dispute about what star to put in the Bethlehem cave, Catholic or Orthodox. These discussions were absurd even to the most ardent theologian. But for Nicholas I the 'struggle for the Holy Places' was a very advantageous and popular cause, and he was quick to seize upon it. With the help of this slogan he began a radical revision of Russian–Turkish relations, although to the rest of Europe it was clear that it was a becoming a battle of wills between the French emperor, Napoleon III, and the Russian czar.

As the situation worsened, both Nicholas and the French emperor sought to harness public opinion, although it required the best diplomatic skills to convince Europe that their respective cause was both legitimate and right. It was a tricky business. On one hand, Napoleon was only too aware that his aggressive attitude might well resurrect the old alliance between Russia, Britain, Austria and Prussia, for it was this same alliance that had defeated his uncle Napoleon I back in 1815. On the other hand, Nicholas tried to court Europe by stating he was under pressure from his own people, who were growing ever more worried about the religious situation in Turkey.

With the prospect of armed conflict a distant but nevertheless real prospect, Nicholas began to weigh up his options. Of the four major powers in Europe, he considered both Austria and Prussia as allies. France, however, presented a threat, but would Napoleon III really risk his somewhat shaky grip on the throne in an armed struggle against Russia? Nicholas thought it unlikely. This left only Britain as the one great danger. It was the one great industrial power in the world, with great resources and, more important, great financial means at its disposal, with a large army and navy. War against Britain must be avoided at all costs. In the event, Nicholas came up with an astonishing idea which he hoped would both allay British fears of Russian expansionism in the Black Sea and Mediterranean, and prevent any conflict between the two empires.

Britain, ever empire conscious, might be lured into his web of intrigue by the attraction of protecting the overland route to its possessions in India. Nicholas' idea might shock the British, but he hoped they would give it serious consideration. There was, after all, little to lose. And so, between January and February 1853, Nicholas had several meetings in St Petersburg with the British ambassador, Sir George Hamilton Seymour, during which he broached the subject of the state of the Ottoman Empire. He pointed out – if it ever needed pointing out – that Turkey was 'a sick man', and that they must consider the probable future collapse of the Ottoman Empire. Britain and Russia, he said, should make arrangements beforehand in order to avoid any disputes over territories that would inevitably follow. It was a proposal akin to disposing of a sick man's belongings before he was actually dead.

Seymour was somewhat shocked by the bluntness of Nicholas' approach and by what he was proposing. Moldavia and Wallachia, having already formed a separate state, should continue to exist under Russia's protection, whilst Serbia and Bulgaria should be allowed to do the same. Nicholas then moved on to Egypt. All too conscious of its importance to Britain, he suggested that Russia would not oppose any move by Britain to take control of the country, adding that Crete might also become a British possession. Seymour listened in stunned surprise as Nicholas reeled off his proposals, and wondered what the response would be in London when he reported back to his political masters.

The reaction in London was, predictably, hostile. The government was quick to see the dangers of allowing Russia control of the Bosphorus and Dardanelles, and the prospect of seeing the Black Sea turned into what virtually amounted to a 'Russian lake'. Such domination would allow the huge Russian Army to operate close to the Turkish borders and would almost certainly result in a Russian conquest of Turkey. With Turkey swallowed up, Russia would be able to control Persia and, more important from a British point of view, the overland route to India. The concern in London may easily be imagined.

Nicholas' mistake was in refusing to believe that Britain would form an alliance with its old enemy, France. It was something the British government was well aware of. Indeed, the British did their best to convince him that this would be the likely result should Nicholas move against Turkey. Despite letters written to him personally – rather than sent through official channels – and the goading and provocations of British ministers, Nicholas simply did not appreciate the fact that he was driving Britain closer to France.

Napoleon, on the other hand, found his hand strengthened when he finally won the argument over the Holy Places, following which he personally performed the ceremony of passing the keys to the Jerusalem and Bethlehem churches to the Catholic bishop, something which he did with 'provocative ostentation'. It was something which left Nicholas feeling more isolated, although it did not deter him from pursuing an aggressive course of action against Turkey, for in February 1853 he sent the 66-year-old Prince Alexander Menshikov to Constantinople, the object of his mission being the reinstatement of Orthodox Church privileges in the Holy Places. Significantly, he was also to demand a protective treaty similar to the Unkiar-Skelessi Treaty, something which Menshikov was to negotiate in secrecy.

Menshikov's mission, which lasted until 21 May, was a disaster from the very moment of his arrival in Constantinople. His aggressive approach was apparent from the very beginning, when he arrived in a Russian warship. Totally devoid of diplomatic skills, the antagonistic Menshikov succeeded in doing little but upsetting his hosts. He displayed neither respect nor any protocol, his aggressive manner belonging on the battlefield rather than the chambers of the Ottoman emperor. His skills at the negotiating table were less than impressive also, with the far more able Turkish delegates having little trouble in fending off his every move and demand.

Menshikov was also up against the British Ambassador to the Porte (the Turkish government), Lord Stratford de Redcliffe. Known to the Turks as 'the Great Elchi', Redcliffe was an experienced diplomat and a man with enormous influence within the Porte. Indeed, there was no man living outside Turkey who knew more about the affairs of the Ottoman Empire and of its society. The Russian envoy's demand that Nicholas be recognized as protector of all Christians in the Turkish dominions was met with polite but firm rebuttal by both de Redcliffe and the French ambassador, De La Cour. Turkey could not allow a foreign power to wield such influence within the sultan's realm, although it would nevertheless strive to remove any disadvantages the Christians might have endured and would address any grievances they might have. This response was endorsed on 20 May at a conference of the British, French, German and Austrian ambassadors. Menshikov's proposal that Turkey conclude a protective treaty with Russia along the lines of the Unkiar-Skelessi Treaty was also flatly rejected. The embittered Menshikov, suspicious in particular of British motives and believing that Turkey was merely a puppet controlled by the British hand, then broke off both negotiations and relations, and sailed away from Constantinople on 21 May.

With Menshikov having achieved nothing for his master, Nicholas raised the stakes by informing the Turks that unless they accepted the proposals put forward by Menshikov he would send Russian troops across the Pruth river and into the Danubian Principalities of Moldavia and Wallachia. In fact, even as negotiations were going on, Nicholas was ordering Prince Gorchakov to prepare his IV and V Corps for the invasion. Such a move had already been anticipated by Britain and France, however, which sent their fleets to Besika Bay, at the entrance to the Dardanelles, which assembled there on 14 June. Eighteen days later Gorchakov crossed the river Pruth and invaded Moldavia and Wallachia. War was now closer than ever.

Despite the gloom and the prospect of war, efforts still continued to be made in London, Paris and Constantinople to block the seemingly inevitable road to war. Austria, too, did its best to help avert war and a conference was held in Vienna with all the major powers in attendance. Austria, in fact, sided with Britain and France, supporting Turkey in its stance against Russia. Notes flew back and forth between the various countries, but as each formula for peace was proposed and then rejected, either by Turkey or Russia, war appeared more inevitable than ever. The most significant of all the communiqués was the famous 'Vienna Note' of 31 July 1853, thrashed out between Britain, France, Austria and Prussia, and put before the czar for his approval. This note, which in effect bound Turkey to the conditions of the 1774 treaty of Kuchuk-Kainardji, and to the Adrianople Treaty of 1829, was certainly advantageous to Russia but not to Turkey. Indeed, when the conditions were known to Czar Nicholas he accepted the Vienna Note, giving all concerned renewed hope that a conflict could be avoided. However, they had not considered the influential and crucial views of the British ambassador, Lord Stratford. Furthermore – and more remarkably – none of the four powers had bothered to consider Turkey's views on the Vienna Note. It was a great error.

Despite the requests from London to Lord Stratford that he recommend the acceptance of the note to the sultan, the 'Great Elchi' could not hide his true feelings, and when he presented the note to the sultan he did so with a heavy heart, knowing that it would not be in Turkey's interests to accept it. Nevertheless, he did what was required of him as a representative of the British government. He did his duty and urged its acceptance. Lord Stratford pointed out to the sultan that all four of the major powers supporting Turkey recommended acceptance of the Vienna Note, and that even Czar Nicholas had agreed to its terms. He also urged the sultan to come to a speedy decision as a delay might prove dangerous to Turkey. But what Lord Stratford did not do was venture his own private opinion, and it was this that the sultan and the Porte really wanted to hear. His opinion was not forthcoming, but the Great Elchi's look and silence said more than words could ever express.

The Porte studied the Vienna Note carefully before, somewhat predictably, adding some amendments. On 19 August the Porte made it known that unless its amendments were added it would be unable to accept it. Inevitably, these alterations proved unacceptable to Russia. The lengthy negotiations between Britain, France, Austria and Prussia had been in vain. Given the fact that they had not sought the views of the Porte this is not surprising. The sticking point once again was Turkey's refusal to grant Russia protective rights over the Orthodox Church in the Turkish Dominions. The negotiations had come full circle. The disputants were back where they began, and with little hope of a settlement war was now virtually inevitable.

Another important factor that was leading Europe along the road to war was public opinion. Anti-Russian feelings were already beginning to stir in Britain and France, but in Turkey public opinion was in effect driving the country to war. Indeed, Turkey may well have been dubbed 'the sick man of Europe' but its people were demonstrating that there was plenty of life left in the country yet. They were beginning to tire of the manner in which foreign powers were seemingly sitting round discussing their future, whilst the presence of Russian troops in the Danubian Principalities was viewed as a great affront to Turkish honour and prestige alike. Demands for action to be taken against the Russians grew louder by the day. Of course, the cries for a war against Russia were made in the full knowledge that Turkey had the support of both Britain and France, but public opinion and feeling in Turkey should not be underestimated. Whipped into a frenzy by religious leaders, the Turkish people's clamouring for action would not be assuaged, and on 4 October 1853 Turkey went ahead, despite frantic diplomatic activity, and declared that, unless the czar withdrew his troops from the Danubian Principalities within two weeks, a state of war would exist between the two empires, and with neither side willing to back down the Crimean War can be said to have begun.

Nicholas' refusal to withdraw his troops from the Pruth river and the subsequent declaration of war by Turkey left the British and French governments in little doubt – as if there ever was any – that war with Russia was inevitable. And yet, even at this late hour politicians made frenzied efforts to prevent the conflict. But all the time the other nations' priorities seemed to be steering Europe on a course which led to war. Napoleon III, his grip on the French throne already somewhat shaky, looked to use the crisis to enhance

French prestige abroad and with it his own estimation in the eyes of the French people. He had lived in exile for some years in England and knew full well how public opinion often influenced British policy making. Therefore, he began to put pressure on Britain to move its fleet forward from Besika and through the Dardanelles, a move which would undoubtedly gain the approval of the British people. The British prime minister, the somewhat reticent Lord Aberdeen, regarded such a demand as premature but, fearful of flying in the face of public opinion and coming under increased pressure from the French ambassador, Count Waleski, he gave in and ordered the fleet to move through the Dardanelles, which it did on 22 September. Such a move was in breach of the 1841 Straits Treaty and, indeed, no sooner had the move begun than the Russian ambassador, Baron Brunnov, protested, citing the very treaty. The protests were waved away, however, at which Count Nesselrode, Russia's foreign secretary, simply sighed and virtually gave up all attempts at averting war. It was as if, he later said, the British government had 'a settled purpose to humiliate Russia'. There was nothing left now for Russia, and so Czar Nicholas ordered the Black Sea Fleet to put to sea.

Despite Turkey's declaration of war, Count Nesselrode still harboured hopes that the conflict could be restricted to the Danube. Indeed, on 31 October 1853 he issued a circular to various Russian ambassadors to the effect that although Turkey had declared war Russia would refrain from any hostile response unless Turkey made any offensive move first. The circular had possibly been issued to parry any move that Britain or France might have considered, and to demonstrate that Russia was not the instigator of war. It was a faint hope, however, for when Omar Pasha began offensive moves along the lower Danube, the Russians were left with no option but to reply, and reply they did in devastating style.

On 24 November 1853 Admiral Pavel S Nakhimov, sailing in his flagship, the *Imperatritsa Mariya*, along with two ships of the line, chanced upon a Turkish flotilla which was taking refuge from bad weather in the port of Sinope, which lies on the southern shore of the Black Sea, about 340 miles east of Constantinople. The Turkish ships were carrying supplies and weapons to troops in the Caucasus and were, therefore, a legitimate target for Nakhimov. Fortunately for the Turks, Nakhimov turned and sailed away, leaving the Turkish ships to breathe a sigh of relief in the port. Their relief was short-lived, however, for six days later, on 30 November, Nakhimov returned, this time bringing with him four more ships of the line and two frigates. These were more than a match for the Turkish flotilla, which consisted of seven

Theatre of operations in the Black Sea.

frigates, one sloop, a steamer and some transports that sat helpless inside Sinope. Nakhimov opened fire without warning, sending a succession of explosive shells into the mass of shipping that sat at anchor. Things grew worse for the Turks when Admiral Kornilov arrived with three steam-powered warships to join in what soon became a very one-sided battle. The punishment continued for just over an hour, during which time around 4,000 Turkish sailors were lost. Only one Turkish ship, the *Taif*, managed to escape the inferno that raged in the harbour. This ship, commanded ironically by an Englishman, sailed off to Constantinople to deliver the news to a shocked sultan.

We may well imagine how the news of the attack was received in both London and Paris when it reached the two capitals on 11 December. Indeed, it was greeted with horror. It was not so much the fact that thousands of Turkish lives had been lost but rather that British honour had been stained. Britain had pledged to protect Turkey, but the Russians had simply sailed across the Black Sea and had dealt a crushing blow against the Turkish navy. It was a real slap in the face for the two western powers. The question was asked up and down Britain: where was the 'Nelson touch' when it was needed? A similar reaction was felt in Paris. Like Britain, France had pledged its protection to Turkey and thus Sinope was seen as an affront to French martial prowess. Predictably, there was outrage amongst the French and British people, who quickly clamoured for revenge. In Britain the call for action to be taken against the Russians was loudest in the pages of *The Times* newspaper, a call taken up by the population, much to the relief of Napoleon III, who had hoped for such a reaction, one that would drive Britain closer to France and closer to war with Russia.

Despite the clamour in both Britain and France for action to be taken against Russia, the British government still wavered. Whilst France seemed intent on hostilities, Aberdeen's government continued to seek a peaceful settlement to what had become known as 'the Eastern Question'. But Napoleon's demands for action were relentless. He proposed that Britain and France should send their fleets into the Black Sea and force all Russian ships, save for merchantmen, to return to port. He also stated that if Britain would not follow this course of action then France would go it alone. The reaction to this in London can be imagined, for there was only one thing worse than a Russian-dominated Black Sea, and that was a French one. This Britain simply could not allow. And so, despite efforts in London and Paris, and in Vienna, where envoys from Britain, France, Austria and Prussia met to try to find an answer to the 'Eastern Question', war drew ever nearer. Lord Aberdeen, coming under increasing pressure from both his own cabinet and the French, finally bowed to the inevitable and gave orders for the British fleet to sail out into the Black Sea.

On 12 January 1854 Czar Nicholas was informed at his palace in St Petersburg that British and French ships of the line had sailed from Constantinople with the intention of forcing all Russian ships, save merchantmen, to return to Sevastopol and other ports along the northern shore of the Black Sea. War between Britain and France and Russia was now closer than ever. On 6 February, Nicholas recalled his ambassadors from Paris and London, whilst Britain and France recalled their respective ambassadors from St Petersburg soon afterwards, and by the middle of the same month British troops were being earmarked for Malta and from there Constantinople. Three days after recalling his ambassadors, Nicholas issued a proclamation:

We have already informed our beloved and faithful subjects of the cause of our misunderstanding with the Ottoman Porte.

Since then, notwithstanding the commencement of hostilities [with Turkey], it has not ceased to be our sincere desire, as it is also still our desire, to put a stop to the shedding of blood. We indulged the hope that time and reflection would convince the Turkish Government of its delusion, engendered by crafty instigations, in which our just demands, founded on Treaties, were represented as an attempt against its independence, concealing projects of aggrandizement. But our expectations have hitherto been in vain. The English and French Governments have taken up the cause of Turkey, and the appearance of the combined fleets at Constantinople served as the encouragement to the stubbornness of the Porte. Finally, both the Western Powers, without any previous declaration of war, have taken their fleets into the Black Sea, declaring their intention to protect the Turks, and to forbid our ships of war a free navigation for the defence of our coasts.

After such an unheard-of proceeding on the part of civilized Governments, we recalled our embassies from England and France, and suspended all political relations with these Powers.

And thus England and France have ranged themselves by the side of the enemies of Christianity against Russia fighting for the orthodox faith.

But Russia will not alter its divine mission, and if enemies fall upon its frontier we are ready to meet them with the firmness which our ancestors have bequeathed us.

Are we not now the same Russian nation of those deeds of valour to which the memorable events of the year 1812 bear witness? May the Almighty assist us to prove this by deeds! And in this trust, taking up arms for our persecuted brethren professing the Christian faith, we will exclaim with the whole of Russia, with one heart, 'O Lord our Saviour, whom have we to fear? May God arise, and His enemies be dispersed.'[1]

On 27 February 1854, with all possible diplomatic solutions having been submitted and rejected, Britain and France finally issued an ultimatum to the czar of Russia. The ultimatum called upon Nicholas to agree – within six days of its delivery – to the withdrawal of all Russian troops from the Danubian Principalities by 30 April. If no reply was forthcoming or if Nicholas refused, Britain and France would declare war on Russia. Sadly, but perhaps predictably, Czar Nicholas did not deem the summons worthy of reply. In fact, it was not until 19 March that Nesselrode finally let it be known that Nicholas had refused the ultimatum. And with that, the great peace that had lasted in Europe since the Waterloo campaign of 1815 was shattered. And few were left in any doubt as to why the Allies were going to war, following a speech given by Napoleon III to the Chambers, on 2 March 1854:

The time of conquests is passed for ever. So let no one come again and ask us what we are going to do at Constantinople. We are going there with England to defend the cause of the Sultan, and, nevertheless, to protect the prescriptive rights of Christians; we are going there to defend the freedom of the seas and our just rights in the Mediterranean. We are going there with Turkey to help her keep her rank from which they seemed to be trying to degrade her, to assure her frontiers against the preponderance of a neighbour too powerful. We are going there, in short, with all those who desire the triumph of right, of justice and of civilisation.[2]

On 27 March, Emperor Napoleon announced to the Senate and to the Legislative Assembly that France was at war with Russia. In London the same day, Queen Victoria addressed Parliament, informing it that negotiations with Russia had been broken off. The following day, Britain also declared war on Russia.

Chapter 2

The Allies Go to War

The politicians and heads of state had had their say. Now it was down to the armed forces. The British Army, or rather the Army of the East as it was officially known, originally consisted of four divisions, the 1st, 2nd, 3rd and Light Divisions, numbering just short of 23,000 men, with the 4th Division, a further 6,431 men, following behind. In addition, there were two brigades of cavalry, the Light and Heavy Brigades, the former commanded by the notorious Lord Cardigan and the latter by the somewhat eccentric James Scarlett. The cavalry as a whole was in turn commanded by Lord Lucan. The first troops left England in February 1854, bound for Malta and Constantinople and thence for Varna in Bulgaria. Camps were to be established here before the final passage across the Black Sea to the Crimea.

Some forty years had passed since the British Army had gone to war in Europe to take on a European power. Many of its senior officers still found it hard to believe they were going to fight not against the French, but alongside them as allies. It was quite remarkable. At Blenheim 150 years earlier, Marlborough's army had handed the French Army of Louis XIV its first great defeat, after which it went on to inflict further miseries on it at Ramillies, Oudenarde and Malplaquet. There then followed decades of conflict with the French throughout the rest of the eighteenth century, fighting across almost every continent, until by the time Napoleon came along at the end of the century, Britain and France were deeply entrenched as inextricable foes. It all came to a climax at Waterloo in 1815 when, after defeating several of Napoleon's marshals in the Iberian Peninsula, the Duke of Wellington – with a little help from his Prussian allies – finally put paid to the emperor himself. Since then there had been no conflict but much suspicion of the neighbours across the English Channel.

The long peace brought about a slow decay in the British Army. Years of war against Napoleon had taken their toll and all the British people really wanted now was peace. The army consequently slipped well down the order of priorities in the post-war years, with public health, prison and social reforms, education and a general increase in interest of all things scientific taking precedence. The great duke himself didn't help, his 'Torres Vedras' mentality opposing all army reform. Little wonder, therefore, that when the duke died in 1852, the British Army is said to have breathed a sigh of relief. The problem was that even with Wellington gone it was too late to do much to rectify the major ills within the army. 'The day of reckoning for all the follies ... was now close at hand,' wrote Fortescue, the historian of the army.

'We all went back to our bad old ways,' commented one veteran after Napoleon's defeat, and he was right, for with no campaigns being fought, save for colonial affairs in South Africa, Afghanistan and India, the army slowly became a pale shadow of its former self. Old generals lingered on, whilst the sort of generation of young, gifted officers with whom Wellington was blessed simply failed to materialize. Instead, when war was declared on Russia, Horse Guards simply trotted out the old school of elderly generals, most of whom were now well into their sixties and seventies.

Commanding the Army of the East was 66-year-old Fitzroy James Henry Somerset, who, after Wellington's death in 1852, had been raised to the peerage and given the title Lord Raglan. He had served his country faithfully for the greater part of the century to date, largely as secretary to Wellington. He had seen a great deal of action in the Peninsula and at Waterloo, where he lost his right arm: as it was being carried off by the surgeon, Raglan called out to have it brought back so he could remove the ring his wife had given him. He learned to write with his left hand, something he was to do proficiently over the next forty years. And that was the basic problem: he had never commanded a force in his life. In fact, it is not too harsh to say the only thing he had ever really commanded was a desk. Now, at a relatively advanced age, he was being trotted out once more for the last hurrah of the old Peninsular generals, for he was not alone in the ranks of very senior generals. Commanding the Light Division was Sir George Brown, another veteran of the Peninsular War, who had been wounded at the Coa in July 1810. Sir Colin Campbell, commanding the Highland Brigade, had fought in Spain also, as had Sir De Lacy Evans, who commanded the 2nd Division. Evans had at least seen action during the inter-war years, taking part in the Carlist Wars in Spain, whilst yet another veteran of the Napoleonic Wars, Brigadier General Thomas Strangways, of the Royal Artillery, had been present with the Rocket Troop at the Battle of

Leipzig in 1813. Perhaps most remarkable of all the appointments was Sir John Burgoyne, of the Royal Engineers, who was born when the American colonies still belonged to King George. Burgoyne had first seen action way back in 1800.

It is indeed quite astonishing that the British Army of 1854 possessed no generation of gifted young officers at relatively senior level, the likes of whom Wellington had commanded in the Peninsula. The youngest divisional officer in the Crimea, Prince George, the Duke of Cambridge, was 35 years old, but he had seen no active service whatsoever, and owed his position more to rank than ability. With no real experience within the ranks of the younger officers, command would be in the hands of men such as Raglan, Brown and Evans, all of whom ought to have been looking forward to a well-earned retirement. Instead, they were to undertake a campaign against a potentially formidable enemy, at a very late stage of the year and in a country about which very little was known, save for the fact that the winters could be very hard indeed. It was a recipe for disaster. But the root cause of the malaise of the British Army was far more complex than just the problem of ageing generals.

The British Army had slipped well down the political agenda during the inter-war years between 1815 and 1854. Things were not helped by an increasing awareness in Britain of social problems which the nation felt it could finally get to grips with now that the spectre of Bonaparte had been lifted. The Poor Laws, public health, education, industry and a general upturn in interest in things social, spiritual and scientific, let alone a general support for pacifism, left the army lagging way behind when it came to the nation's priorities. For example, an indication of the army's low importance is reflected in the relatively low number of government select committees that sat between 1830 and 1850. No fewer than fifty-eight select committees sat to discuss prisons and prison reform; fifty-one concerned themselves with health matters, forty-four with education and thirty-two with conditions in factories. Only twenty-three select committees sat to discuss the army during these years, there being very little support or even interest in army reform amongst members of parliament. Royal commissions, too, came and went, mainly concerned with conditions in factories or with children's welfare, or they came hot on the heels of strikes and civil and industrial unrest. In the meantime, army reform was generally ignored. As one historian put it, 'nobody signed petitions or burned hayricks in the cause of army administrative reform.' And even when a group of Radical MPs tried to gain support for army reform their pleadings were ignored, for although they genuinely believed in reform the reputation they had acquired through chasing extremist policies – plus their constant complaining over all sorts of different issues, something which had become 'a wearisome irritation' – left them isolated and generally ignored.

But even the Radicals, despite their good intentions, appear to have missed the whole point of reform. As the population of England passed the 20 million mark in 1850, so there came with it a greater appreciation and value of human life, something which the Radicals tried to see extended within the British Army. This move towards greater humanitarianism was all well and good, but it came nowhere near addressing the wider problems. For example, Joseph Hume, a Radical, and one of the more vocal advocates of army reform, championed the abolition of flogging in the army, but failed to appreciate the more deep-rooted problems concerning the well-being of the British soldier. Indeed, given the poor conditions in the army it is little wonder that men were reluctant to take the queen's shilling. Low pay, a lack of amusement, poor diet and a harsh system of discipline based on floggings did not give men much incentive to enlist.

The age-old arguments that, despite the poor pay and conditions, things were much worse for civilians did not stand up to scrutiny either. The pay of a private soldier was just seven shillings a week, but when deductions had been made for messing and general maintenance he was left with barely threepence a day. There were just two meals a day, at seven-thirty and twelve-thirty, with nothing in the evening, save what the men could afford for themselves. It was an unhealthy profession, for whilst the death rate per thousand civilians was nine, the rate for infantry regiments of the British Army was eighteen, and the rate in the cavalry was eleven. In the Brigade of Guards it was as high as twenty per thousand. The death rate in the army from tuberculosis was five times higher than the rate amongst civilians. Given the bad conditions in army barracks this is not surprising, for the average allowance of air for a soldier in barracks was 400 cubic feet, compared with the average 1,000 cubic feet for a convict in a prison cell. Worse still, in some barracks and in at least five military hospitals it was 300 cubic feet. Little wonder, therefore, that the army found great difficulty in attracting recruits from anywhere other than the lower depths of British society, often the dregs from the gutter who were despised rather than pitied. Indeed, given the conditions in Victorian Britain, it is quite remarkable that the soldier was able to sustain himself throughout what was to prove one of the most harrowing campaigns he had ever fought.

The lack of professionalism in the army was apparent even during the early days of the war. Indeed, Frederick Stephenson, of the Scots Fusilier Guards, was quick to point out the mismanagement by Horse Guards of the arrangements made for the troops at Malta:

Between you and me, I do not think matters have been well arranged at the Horse Guards. Excepting the Guards, no brigade has been put together yet. Hardly any of the Staff have come out, although the whole of the infantry of the Expeditionary Force has not only been at Malta for some considerable time, but has actually gone off to the seat of war, leaving their Brigadier-Generals and Staff to follow them at some later time, instead of those officers being the first to land and superintend the disembarking and first settling down in a foreign land of their respective brigades. Some 15,000 troops are now at Gallipoli, not brigaded, and with the exception of Sir George Brown and a staff of five officers, there is only one Brigadier-General (besides the Colonel of Engineers) to look after them all. I cannot tell you how we all long to be off, and how we look forward to Lord Raglan's arrival to have our forces arranged and handled by a true master hand.[1]

And it was not just a lack of organization as regards staff officers that concerned British officers. Another Guards officer, George Higginson, was worried about the lack of arms, ammunition and basic equipment. Given the fact that war with Russia had been likely for many a month, Higginson's comments illustrate the depth of mismanagement at Horse Guards:

But where was our *matériel* for this expedition? The utmost activity in the arsenals barely sufficed to provide guns. The recently-adopted Minié rifle could not be supplied in sufficient quantity to equip the infantry with the most important arm available for modern warfare. Clothing, shoes, general equipment – all had to be ordered in desperate haste; consequently regiment after regiment was hurried abroad ill-prepared for immediate service, and, from the outset, distrustful of the authorities at home to whom they were entitled to look for support and due provision. Hesitation as to our destination still appeared to linger in the counsels of the Ministry. I remember remonstrating on being informed that a 'slop' shirt, to be worn over the uniform aboard ship, was the only article of extra clothing granted to the men of my battalion on embarking. I received the half-whispered reply, 'My dear fellow, you will probably not go beyond Malta!' In short, the gravity of the situation had not been realised by those in authority, and in these, the first stages of the campaign, the army suffered accordingly.[2]

Despite the lack of reform generally in the British Army, attention had been paid to certain aspects of the men's equipment, particularly the introduction of a new rifle, the Minié. For almost 150 years the British infantryman – save for those in the Rifle Brigade – had been armed with a smoothbore flintlock musket, the fabled Brown Bess, which had swept many a Frenchman from many a bloody European battlefield. Flintlocks had given way to percussion weapons, although the basic weapon was still the same – only the firing mechanism had changed. But at the outbreak of war Horse Guards decided to introduce a new weapon, the Minié, a rifle that was destined to play a key role in the coming war with Russia. When the British Army landed in the Crimea, every infantryman – save for Cathcart's 4th Division, which retained the smoothbore musket – was armed with the new rifle.

A contemporary report gave a full description of the Minié, which was to have a profound effect on the outcome of the Battle of the Alma:

A most effective small-arm, the invention of Captain Minié, of the French army, has been substituted in the Queen's service for the old musket. The experiments upon this weapon have been some time in progress, and many improvements upon the original design have been adopted.

The effect of rifling the bore of a gun with grooves which make a spiral curve round the interior surface is, as is well known, to communicate a rotary motion to a ball discharged from it; and the revolutions of the ball round its own axis correct any tendency to diverge from the line of aim. The difficulty in attending the use of the rifle in warfare arises from the necessity of the ball fitting so tightly as to form itself into the grooves within the barrel; and consequently very considerable force and much time are required to drive it down upon the powder – even a mallet is frequently employed for this purpose. The invention of Captain Minié consists, not so much in the introduction of any new principle into the rifle, as in the ball used. The ball is not spherical, as those used for the musket and old-fashioned rifle, but a cone – or rather cylinder, terminated at the fore end by a conical point – and hollow at the base. In this hollow, which is also slightly conical, is a metal plug. This ball is slightly less than the bore of the rifle, and passes down to the breach with the greatest facility. The hollow base of the ball rests upon the powder and receives the first effect of its explosive force. The consequence is that the metal plug is forced into the conical hollow, and expands the sides of the ball so as to force them into the grooves of the gun, and the ball is then projected with the usual effect of the rifle. The gun itself is a well-proportioned weapon; the grooves resemble 'flutings', and have a very slight spiral curve. The exterior of the barrel is fitted with sights, most accurately made, and graduated to suit calculated distances. The charge of powder is much smaller than that used for the musket; but one effect of the resistance caused by the rifling of a gun is to obtain much greater projective force from the same quantity of powder. The *vis motus* of a ball so greatly increased in weight by its elongated shape, aided by the less resistance of the air to such a missile as compared to a spherical ball, carries it to a prodigious distance. The Minié rifle will throw a ball at random upwards of a mile; at 1200 yards a very fair aim can be taken; at 800 yards it tells with much accuracy; and at 600 or 400 it is most deadly.[3]

The Minié certainly did great service during the early months of the war, but barely had it been introduced than it was replaced by the lighter Enfield rifle. This, of course, was after the Battle of the Alma, an action where the Minié was used to great effect.

The French contingent sailing to the Crimea, the Armée d'Orient, initially numbered around 37,500 men, although this would rise dramatically during the next few months to almost 120,000, a number which equated to almost one-fifth of the entire strength of the French Army. Napoleon III was indeed fortunate because he had at his disposal the second largest army in Europe, which by the summer of 1855 would rise from its 1850 strength of 439,000 to 645,000. At the time of the Crimean War it was far more professional than the British Army; perhaps one commentator put it best when he wrote that the British Army was commanded by gentlemen, the French by officers, many French officers having risen from the ranks. Its senior officers were certainly much younger than their British counterparts, with none of them being over 55. It is true that the French had greater recent experience of war, but this was not against regular European opponents, for their most recent active service had been in Algeria, where they had waged war, largely of an irregular kind, against hordes of tribesmen. Much is often made of this difference between the British and French, where British experiences of war between 1815 and 1854 are often dismissed as being against 'lesser' opponents, such as Indians, Kaffirs and Pathans. These, however, were no less fierce than the Algerians. The difference was, however, that only one battalion of British infantry sent to the Crimea had seen recent action and, to use a modern phrase, 'understood battle procedures'. The French, on the other hand, knew them very well.

Algeria had been colonized by the French in 1830, after which Marshal Bugeaud had embarked upon a systematic policy not only of scorched earth but also of intimidation and extreme violence against the civil population. Indeed, the campaign in Algeria may not have provided the French with the sort of training which would be useful against regular European armies, but it did give them a hard edge in battle, something which the British lacked. It also gave them an experience that would stand them in good stead when it came to the dirty, gritty fighting in the trenches during the siege that was to come at Sevastopol.

Commanding the French Army was 53-year-old Marshal Jacques Leroy de Saint-Arnaud, a veteran of the war in Algeria. A tough fighter, he was largely responsible for paving the way in 1851 for Louis Napoleon to become emperor as Napoleon III. Indeed, Saint-Arnaud was made a marshal of France the following year. But despite his experience and reputation, he was a sick man by the time he reached the Crimea and, indeed, was not to survive long, dying of cholera not long after the Battle of the Alma. Saint-Arnaud was not alone amongst the senior French officers in having fought in Algeria, for his future successor, Canrobert, had seen action there, as had the man who would in turn succeed him, Pélissier. Generals MacMahon and Bourbaki were amongst other senior French officers who had fought in Algeria. Finally, the commander-in-chief of the French Army was Napoleon III himself, and although he never set foot in the Crimea he certainly made sure his influence was felt there, particularly throughout 1855. Indeed, as his uncle, the great Napoleon himself, had attempted to run the Peninsular War from Paris, so Napoleon III tried to run things from the French capital also. This would later infuriate the French generals in the Crimea, as he was no military genius. Fortunately for the Allied cause, his influence was kept to a minimum largely by the wily Pélissier, who for as long as he could pretended not to receive any of the numerous telegrams that came down the cable from Paris.

The French threw a vast number of men into the campaign. Indeed, so weak did the British become following the winter of 1854–5 that the beleaguered Raglan asked his allies to take over the right of the British attack at Sevastopol, his own men being too few to maintain the siege lines. However, all that was yet to come, for when the two Allied armies sailed for the Crimea they did so as equal partners, if somewhat uneasy ones. After all, the two nations had been enemies for at least as long as anyone could remember, and now they were expected to fight alongside each other in a spirit of mutual cooperation. The unease was clear to everyone, and despite the many speeches and statements that were made by both sides in support of the common cause, few could hide their true feelings. George Higginson was one:

> But another unforeseen source of difficulty seriously affected the harmonious action of the two armies of the Allies. No *entente*, however cordial on the surface, could remove altogether the belief that French and British soldiers looked upon each other rather as foes than as friends. Traditions of the Peninsula and Waterloo had not died out; the colours of every regiment in the British force recalled the battles and campaigns fought against those we then considered our hereditary enemies. It would be idle to pretend that our simple-minded rank-and-file regarded the under-sized red-legged, quick-witted *fantassins* as comrades with whom they were destined to share the dangers and the glories of the battlefield. Far be it from me to suggest that the *entente* was not preserved by the upper ranks on both sides with absolute loyalty; though from time to time accident or inadvertence did reveal traces of the old rivalry which had not yet been laid to rest.[4]

One of the reasons Lord Raglan had been given command of the British force was his skill and tact in dealing with the French, not to mention the fact that he spoke French fluently. His years of experience as secretary to the Duke of Wellington certainly stood him in good stead. Nevertheless, even Raglan could not help falling into the age-old trap born of years of experience fighting the French. Higginson again:

> When on my way home in 1856, I dined with the British Ambassador in Paris, Lord Cowley, who told me of an incident he had witnessed in 1854 at the great conference in Paris between the French Minister of War and the marshals, Lord Raglan, the Duke of Cambridge, and their

respective staffs. Lord Raglan pointed to the map illustrating the respective positions likely to be occupied by the Allies, and twice indicated with his finger certain places which might be occupied by *l'ennemi*, evidently forgetting for the moment that *l'ennemi* should have been substituted *nos amis* or *nos allies*. Our revered commander-in-chief was evidently back for the moment in the days when he rode side by side with the Duke of Wellington at Waterloo and lost an arm.[5]

There is one final point to make about the generals on all sides in the Crimean war: they looked not forward to the future but back to the days of Napoleon. Indeed, the Russians continually looked back to 1812 and drew inspiration from their defeat of Napoleon, even after the fall of Sevastopol in September 1855. Moscow fell in 1812 and still Russia defeated the French. And thus, in 1855, they claimed that Sevastopol was not the end of Russia and they would go on to prevail. In the event, things turned out differently. France likewise looked back to the glory days of Napoleon and was desperate to revive the days of Marengo, Austerlitz and Wagram. The British generals, meanwhile, simply considered what Wellington would have done in their situation and allowed the events of the Peninsular War to dictate the manner in which the war was fought. It is certainly the case that Raglan, having lived and worked in the duke's shadow for well over forty years, based many of his major decisions on what he had experienced in the Napoleonic Wars.

By the end of May 1854 the majority of the Allied troops had reached their bases in Turkey, one at Scutari and the other at the Gallipoli peninsula in the Dardanelles. Whilst the Allies were idling away their time here the Turkish Army, under its commander, Omar Pasha, was engaged in a fierce struggle on the Danube. Indeed, it was partly as a result of this that Britain and France had entered the war. The Turks had declared war on the Russians in October 1853 and had been carrying on a fight in the Danubian Principalities of Wallachia and Moldavia ever since.

Omar Pasha was a very amenable and capable man who had quickly gained the respect of his allies. Born in Croatia, Michael Lattas, to give him his original name, served in the Austrian Army before leaving for Constantinople, where he joined the Turkish Army. His rise to prominence within the sultan's army was mainly due to patronage secured during his time at a military school in Constantinople. His marriage to one of the richest heiresses in the city also helped him. Given the extent of the sultan's empire and the upheavals, both military and political, that wracked the empire, it is not surprising that Omar

Pasha was so active. Blessed with such important patronage and with military skills to match, it was not long before he was serving on the Danube, and within a few short years he was appointed commander-in-chief of the Turkish Army. As the situation in the east became increasingly volatile, Omar Pasha found himself at the heart of operations in the Danubian Principalities, Moldavia and Wallachia, monitoring a situation that grew increasingly worse until, in 1853, hostilities finally broke out between Turkey and Russia.

Now, with the British and French in the Dardanelles, it was time for him to seek their assistance in driving the Russians back across the Pruth river and out of Wallachia and Moldavia. A council of war was duly convened on 18 May at Omar Pasha's headquarters at Shumla, 50 miles west of the Black Sea port of Varna, with both Saint-Arnaud and Raglan in attendance. During the five-hour meeting, the two commanders listened to Omar Pasha's impassioned plea for help, given largely in broken English:

> I have almost the certainty of beating the Russians, if they should attack me, but is it possible that the French and English, who are upon Turkish territory at Gallipoli, within twenty days march of Varna (or twenty-four hours by sea), will leave me blockaded here, deprive themselves of the assistance of a fine army which can fight well, and allow us to be crushed by the Russians, when, united, we might drive them to the other side of the Danube, and save Turkey?[6]

Saint-Arnaud was certainly impressed by Pasha's speech, so much so that he promised to send troops to Varna in order to march north against the Russians besieging the fortress of Silistria. Upon his return to Scutari, Raglan also decided to send troops, two divisions, in fact, to help. However, no sooner had the British troops got themselves ready to march than Saint-Arnaud changed his mind and decided to deploy his men in a defensive position behind the Balkan hills in case of any Russian incursions south. We may well imagine Raglan's frustration at this, given the unlikelihood of this actually happening. However, it did not stop the Allies steaming north to Varna, where they disembarked.

Ironically, events elsewhere were to dictate the Allies' next course of action, for no sooner had the Allies got themselves ready to march north than news arrived on 24 June that the Russians had lifted the siege of Silistria and were marching away from the Danube. This unexpected development was largely as a result of Turkish aggression and Austrian threats of intervention on the side of the Allies. Whatever the case, it meant that the war on the Danube was as good as over. The news that the Russians had pulled back came as a dreadful disappointment to British officers who were fully expecting to meet the Russians in the field. Robert Lindsay, of the Scots Fusilier Guards, was one of them. He was also none too impressed by the Turkish officers:

> The news was a great disappointment, but we hear they are in great force on the other side of the Danube. Whether this is true or not we have no means of knowing here. I saw Omar Pasha today coming in from Shumla to Varna. He was in an open sort of britzka, with four artillery horses, and behind him followed a carriage with his wife, I suppose, a pretty-looking woman. He is about sixty, I should think, very spare and a good-looking face. He speaks German, Italian and a little French. The defence of Silistria has been the most gallant thing done for a long time; the whole defence was managed by two Englishmen, Butler and Nasmith. Butler, who is since dead, seems to have been a fine fellow; he exposed himself incessantly to the continual fire of the enemy and seemed to have a charmed life, not knowing a word of Turkish, but by his conduct and coolness showing such an example to the Turks that they said they would follow him everywhere. The continual work they had, digging in order to countermine the mines of the Russians, was most harassing, but the Turks burrowed like moles, and were so docile and brave. The fact is that the lower classes of Turks are very fine fellows, but the upper classes are a tyrannical, degraded set of rascals who pillage and cheat everyone they dare; everything from the chief of the boatmen to the higher officers of State is to be purchased, and the man who has robbed and cheated the longest and most successfully buys himself the best berth.[7]

There were few men better qualified to make an assessment of the ordinary Turkish soldier than James Henry Skene, part of the British diplomatic contingent under Lord Stratford at Constantinople. He had seen the Turks at close quarters in the Turkish capital, and sailed to the Crimea when the Allies moved forward. His opinion of the Turks appears to be in keeping with many of the eyewitness accounts written during the campaign:

> The Turkish troops were so badly fed and so irregularly paid, that they used to come about the English and French camps, begging for scraps

of food. When English sailors went from their ships to the Naval Brigade at the front, they would capture three Turkish soldiers apiece, ride on the shoulders of one, and drive the others before them with a long whip, to relieve the first when he should get tired. The poor Turks would then get a few biscuits as payment of their eight miles' stage and return to Balaklava perfectly satisfied. They were so inefficiently officered, that when Lord Raglan obtained from Omar Pasha four battalions of them to hold the four redoubts which he constructed to strengthen the lines above Balaklava, their officers gave the order to fly before the attack of the Russian General, Liprandi, who thus took the sixteen English field pieces entrusted to them.[8]

With no prospect of action on the Danube, the Allies could now turn their attention to the real object of the game, the capture and dismantling of the Russian naval base at Sevastopol. But even as thoughts turned to the impending invasion, the Allied troops were attacked by another more deadly and invisible enemy that swept through the camps 'like the sword of a destroying angel'. Cholera had struck. The plague is said to have been brought into Varna from Marseilles in a transport ship, although with the disease at large throughout Europe generally in 1854, one specific source is hard to identify. Cholera had been rife throughout England in 1854, reaching a peak in the summer months. Indeed, 26,722 people died from the effects of cholera and diarrhoea during the three summer months, with 11,777 dying in London alone.[9] Whatever the source, it spread quickly and silently through the Allies' camps. The French had been suffering for a while before the British troops began to be struck down. Up until that point Raglan's men had been suffering from cases of diarrhoea but nothing more serious. Even so, diarrhoea was bad enough, particularly given the heat and unpleasant conditions within the British camps.

William Russell was correspondent for *The Times* and would become famous for his vivid dispatches from the theatre of war. Commenting on the diarrhoea, Russell wrote:

> The quantity of apricots ('kill Johns') and hard crude fruit which were devoured by the men, might in some degree account for the prevalence of this debilitating malady. The commissariat bread was not so good at first, and speedily turned sour; but the officers took steps to remedy the evil by the erection of ovens in the camp. As the intensity of the

sun's rays increased, the bread served out to us from the Varna bakeries became darker, more sour, and less baked. As a general rule, the French bread was lighter and better than our own, and yet they suffered as much from diarrhoea as our troops.[10]

Robert Lindsay was highly critical of the medical arrangements at Varna, once cholera struck. Writing on 15 August, he said:

The cholera has been fearful; though I came up to the fleet when the worst was over the men were still dying on all sides; in four hours a man in the rudest health was reduced to almost a skeleton, his face quite sunk in and black. The poor tars behaved beautifully, nursing and reading the Bible to the sick till the last moment. A good many were saved by the tremendous way they were rubbed by their messmates during the cramps. Very differently were our poor fellows treated in a close tent under a scorching sun with no alleviations for their pain: very few of those that were taken recovered, though the loss in the Army is not so great as in the Navy. Those who had the misfortune to get into the hospital at Varna never came out, attended on by rascally old pensioners who got drunk on the brandy and wine provided for the sick. Nothing is worse managed than our Medical Staff. Ambulance cooks entirely wanting, officers scarcely able to leave their beds starting to try and ride into Varna, fifteen and twenty miles, rather than remain in the scorching heat of a tent. Had not the General lent me his cart I should never have got to Varna, and the heat of a tent with the sun upon it is enough to drive one mad.[11]

Given the unhealthy conditions in and around Varna it came as something as a relief to everyone when the decision was finally taken to put to sea and make for Sevastopol. Indeed, as Lindsay wrote, 'the idea of active service has acted like a charm on everyone.' Accordingly, on 24 August thousands of British, French and Turkish troops began to muster ready to go aboard the transports that would take them east across the Black Sea to the Crimea. The business of embarking the troops was not an easy one, nor would be the disembarkation once the army reached the Crimea. In order to avoid any confusion, a long and very complicated set of orders was issued relating to the embarkation at Varna and the landings in the Crimea. The instructions ran to twenty-one points:

1. The invasion of the Crimea having been determined upon, the troops will embark in such ships as shall be provided for their conveyance, which will rendezvous at Baldjik, and proceed with the combined fleets to their destination.

2. In an operation of so much difficulty it is essential that the arrangements made should be attentively considered and thoroughly understood by the officers who are responsible for their execution, and should be strictly carried out without any alteration or the exercise of discretion by any subordinate officer. Otherwise confusion would ensue, and the worst consequences might be apprehended.

3. When the troops are directed to land they are to enter the boats in the order in which they stand in the ranks.

4. They are to sit or stand, according as they may be desired; and when once placed are to remain perfectly still, as well as silent.

5. They are to take their knapsacks with them, but not on them, and on leaving the boats they will either put them on, or place them on the beach in the order in which they stand, according as they may be directed.

6. The blankets will, in the first instance, be left on board, folded and labelled with the regimental number of each soldier.

7. The regiments will form in contiguous columns, at quarter distance.

8. They will not load until they have landed, and not then until they are ordered.

9. The spare ammunition (first reserve) will be disposed of as directed in the accompanying memorandum, and will be in charge of an officer of the field train department.

10. The horses provided for the service will be landed after the troops have disembarked.

11. Three days' bread and three days' salt meat, ready cooked, are to be carried both by officers and men, and the men will have their canteens filled with water.

12. The water-bags will also be landed and placed with the reserve ammunition, and the horses appointed for them, if they can be taken, of which there is at present some doubts, will be got on shore as soon as possible.

13. It is necessary that officers should take on shore, in the first instance, such articles only as they can carry themselves.

14. The servants of officers are not only on all occasions of service to

be present under arms with the regiments to which they belong, but they are to carry no more than any other soldier, and they are to mount all picquets and guards with their masters.

15. Mounted officers alone will be entitled to batmen.

16. The medical staff attached to the divisions and brigades will land with them.

17. The batteries will land with the divisions to which they are attached, as well as the sappers similarly situated; and the latter will bring with them a due proportion of entrenching tools.

18. The Light Division will land first. Four companies of the 2nd Battalion Rifle Brigade will be attached to each of its brigades, and will form the advance.

19. The First Division will follow, then the second, then the third, and the fourth.

20. The cavalry will be ready to land; but will not disembark until they receive special directions to do so. They will take with them three days' corn and forage.

21. Provision will be made by the naval authorities for the disembarkation of a due proportion of the horses of the officers of the staff, and these officers are recommended to take upon their horses three days' corn and forage.[12]

The orders went on at length about the procedures for landing in the Crimea. It was all designed to ensure a trouble-free embarkation and disembarkation, and, it should be said, everything appears to have gone off very well indeed. However, unfavourable winds prevented the flotilla from sailing and it was not until 5 September that the ships were finally able to put to sea. It was, wrote Surgeon Munro of the 93rd Highlanders,

A wonderful sight that mighty fleet, even while lying at anchor; but when it got under weigh and steamed out into the open sea, spreading out in long, parallel lines, and covering the face of the waters as far as the eye could see, it appeared to be magnified one hundredfold. The light-armed war-ships led the van, and on either flank hovered the mighty leviathans, which, with their huge hulls, immense spread of canvas, and tiers of guns, inspired us with confidence in their power to protect, and at the same time reminded us of the old homely smile of hens gathering their chickens under their wings.[13]

John Astley, of the Scots Fusilier Guards, was equally impressed by the sight of the great armada putting to sea. His battalion embarked upon the ship *Kangaroo*, bound for the Crimea:

> We started at last at 6 a.m. this morning, and a wonderful sight it was, to see each steamer tow her two transports round a sort of pivot out of the harbour, and get clear out to sea – no easy matter, as so much room is taken by the ships in swinging round. I hardly saw a single collision, though one or two hawsers broke, but were soon made snug again. The line-of-battle ships waited till we were well out of the bay, and they covered our flanks in case the Russians should dare to molest us; and if only the elements keep propitious, as they do now, we shall be at our landing place in about four days, they say. It would be a different matter should it blow, as the tow ships would be a great drag on us. We go along steadily as I write, and I don't feel a bit sick, which is a great pull, as I should like to land with all my energies at concert pitch. I fancy the 'Ruskies' are in an awful stew, and if their glasses are good enough to see the little lot that is coming to pay them a visit, it will by no means make them easier.[14]

Sergeant Timothy Gowing left one of the most famous accounts of the Crimean War, certainly from a ranker's perspective. Gowing, a 20-year-old from Halesworth in Suffolk, had enlisted in the Royal Fusiliers three months before his twentieth birthday, stirred by tales of his regiment's deeds in Spain, particularly Albuera. Gowing, '6ft. high, very active and steady', had sailed from Varna on 7 September with his regiment and, like many others, was mightily impressed as the fleet put to sea:

> We were now off, and it was a grand sight. Each steamer towed two transports; a part of the fleet was in front, a part of it on either side, and part behind us. We had some eight hundred ships of various sizes, and it seemed as if no power on earth were capable of stopping us. The Russian fleet might well keep out of our way. This voyage was truly a source of delight to the proud and war-like feelings of a Briton. As each ship with her consort steamed majestically out of the harbour of Varna, the hills on either side echoed for the first time with the loyal strains of England and France. The bands in a number of ships played 'Rule Britannia,' 'God

Save the Queen,' and the French and Turkish national anthems. We dashed past the huge forts on either side of us, with the Turkish, English, and French flags floating proudly to the wind, and the guns at each fort saluting us.[15]

The Allied flotilla was finally steaming out into the Black Sea, 'bidding defiance to the Russian Fleet'. The great expedition to the Crimea was under way at last.

Chapter 3

Across the Black Sea

Despite the deterioration in his health, Marshal Saint-Arnaud could still be relied upon to stir his men and remind them of their duty. Indeed, when the French officers boarded the ships that would spirit them away across the Black Sea they did so with another of his dramatic announcements ringing in their ears:

> The hour has come to fight and to conquer! Generals, Colonels of regiments, Officers of all arms! You will inspire your soldiers with the confidence with which my heart is filled. Soon we shall, together, salute the three united flags, floating upon the ramparts of Sebastopol, with our national cry of *Vive l'Empereur*![1]

The fleet certainly looked impressive enough as it set out across the Black Sea. George Higginson, of the Scots Fusilier Guards, recorded his impressions as his ship, the *Kangaroo*, set sail:

> At five our anchor was up and our steam fizzing away impatiently, but it was half-past six before the signal was given to take up our respective stations ... Then the scene did indeed become glorious! Away went countless steamers searching for their 'tows' like passengers for their carpet bags and, having found them, proceeded to 'tie the knot' and puff leisurely to the rank to which their division was told off. The transports, which, as you know, are some of the largest and finest of our commercial fleet, seemed almost to disdain the aid of the 'fire engine', and showed symptoms of anxiety for a separation from the tow rope, thinking, no doubt, that the breeze, which was fair from the south-west, would be sufficient to keep them in their respective places. But Admiral Lyons was inflexible, and the huge *Agamemnon* went doubling in and out among the smaller fry, whipping up one and shoving back another, till the line was formed.[2]

One of the main concerns amongst the senior Allied officers was the safety of the fleet. There was always the chance that the Russians might come out from Sevastopol and attack the ships out in the Black Sea, but this was never an option, certainly not as far as the Russians themselves were concerned. The Russian strategy was based firmly on allowing the Allies to land and dealing with them then. Given the strength of the Allied fleet the Russians would have stood little chance against it anyway. Thus, the Allies were allowed to continue their 'cruise' across the Black Sea towards the Crimea unhindered.

The major issue as far as the Allies were concerned was, of course, the choice of a landing site. A meeting had been held, in fact, on 8 September whilst the fleet was at sea. The meeting, held on board the French ship *Ville de Paris*, was attended on the British side by Admiral Dundas, Colonel Sir Thomas Steele, Raglan's military secretary, and Colonel Hugh Rose, the liaison officer, whilst the French representatives were admirals Hamelin and Bruat, and Colonel Trochu. Raglan himself was not able to attend the meeting on account of the rough sea which prevented him – with his one arm – from boarding the French ship. Saint-Arnaud was not present either because of his poor state of health. It is hardly surprising that, given the absence of both the commanders-in-chief of the British and French armies, that no decision was made, although the original choice of a landing site, at the mouth of the Kacha river, was considered by all to be unsuitable. In the meantime, Raglan suggested a reconnaissance take place the next day.

The sea was much calmer when, at six o'clock on the morning of 9 September, Admiral Lyons' ship, the *Agamemnon*, with Sir George Brown on board, steamed alongside the *Caradoc*, with Raglan and Burgoyne, the ship being joined soon after by the French steamer *Primoguet*, carrying Colonel Rose, Admiral Bruat, colonels Trochu and Leboeuf, and generals Canrobert, Tiry, Bizot and Martimprey. The *Sampson* joined the reconnaissance to cover the other three ships. The small flotilla arrived off Sevastopol at daylight on 10 September, running close to the shore, so close in fact that Admiral Lyons exchanged greetings with a Russian officer who bowed in return. The flotilla cruised along the coast as far as the harbour of Balaklava before returning north, round Cape Chersonese, and past Sevastopol for a second time. It then continued north, passing and reconnoitring the mouths of the Belbek, Kacha, Alma and Bulganak rivers.

Somerset John Gough Calthorpe was one of the staff officers on board the *Caradoc* as it steamed out towards the Crimean coast. He left by far the best account of the reconnaissance, which included a view of Sevastopol and also a first look at what would prove to be the site of the Battle of the Alma:

> Soon after four a.m. steam was up, and we started for Sevastopol, going thirteen knots. At a quarter to five a.m. we first caught sight of the town, or rather the fortifications, which looked like a small white spot on the

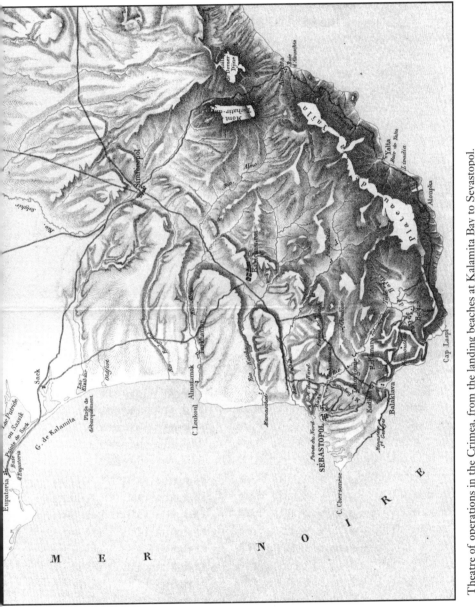

Theatre of operations in the Crimea, from the landing beaches at Kalamita Bay to Sevastopol.

horizon: it was not yet day and we were five miles off; twenty minutes later we were within two miles and a half; and, as day broke, the town with its beautiful harbour appeared before us, each moment getting more distinct, and every house and window lighting up with the morning sun. It reminded one of a scene at a diorama, as it got clearer and clearer. Sir Edmund did not think it prudent to go any nearer, as, if they fired and hit the 'Caradoc,' as they did the 'Fury,' we might possibly go down; for the 'Caradoc' is built of iron, and therefore, if struck by a heavy shot, a whole plate might probably be knocked out, which would have been very awkward. We remained for upwards of half an hour gazing at the scene before us, with an interest deeply excited by the thought that there lay the prize for which we were to fight, the great object of the ensuing campaign. The fortifications looked of immense strength, and appeared to bristle with guns. Our being there did not apparently cause any commotion, although probably the early hour prevented people from being about in any numbers. We counted twelve large ships of war in the great harbour, but we could distinctly see the masts of many more in the inner harbour and Dockyard Creek. All this time the 'Sampson' and 'Prémoget' were within half a mile of us, and the great 'Agamemnon' three miles off, so as not to frighten the Rooshens, I suppose. About 6 o'clock we turned round, and steamed S.E. to the Cape Chersonese, on the extremity of which is the lighthouse ... .

The coast from Sevastopol to the cape is generally a low cliff, with a beach; the cliff varies in height from three to fifteen feet; the ground rises gradually, but to no height; it appeared undulating ground, like low downs. It was proposed by some one that a landing should be effected here, as the natural harbours north of the cape appeared admirably adapted for the purpose, as doubtless they were. But this was at once put aside, as being far too near Sevastopol, and might have risked an action before the troops could be all landed. This, of course, is to be avoided if possible.

There were two or three camps nearer the town, but apparently for few men; I should say 5000 quite the outside. On our turning northwards, as we passed again near the town, we observed a vessel getting up its steam, but otherwise our appearance did not seem to cause them any uneasiness. Steamed N.N.E. on to the Belbec river, nearing the land all the time. The mouth of the Belbec presented the same objections as Cape Chersonese, on account of its proximity to Sevastopol: indeed, probably within range of some earthen batteries on the heights of the northern side of the harbour. About half a mile beyond this there was a small camp of infantry, not more than one battalion – possibly 1000 men. We next arrived off the Katcha river, which appeared in many respects well adapted as a landing-place. This was the spot originally chosen by the reconnaissance made by Sir George Brown two months ago. The naval men, both English and French, objected to it, as the bay was far too small for our enormous flotilla. No doubt they are perfectly right; if the ships are in the least crowded there will be endless confusion. We then steamed on to the Alma river, 18 miles by the coast from Sevastopol. We found on both banks largish camps: the one on the southern side appeared to be chiefly artillery; the other, on the northern side, infantry, – perhaps 6000 men, but two and three miles inland we could see several other camps, quite as large as these nearer ones. There are high cliffs all the way from Sevastopol to the Alma river, say of 80 to 100 feet, except at the mouths of the Belbec and Katcha rivers, when on either side of both rivers the ground gradually slopes down to the sea-shore. At the Alma river we stood in quite close to the shore, within half a mile, and two small boats were sent in, to take soundings, from the 'Caradoc.' They went within a quarter of a mile of the shore, and found five fathom water, – deep enough for anything. Seeing some sort of commotion going on in the Russian artillery camp, it was thought better to sheer off, especially as we were within easy range, and had nothing wherewith to return the compliment, should they fire at us.

From the river Alma, all the way to Eupatoria, about 25 to 30 miles, the coast is quite low, and anywhere practicable for landing. The only doubt is about water. From all accounts there appears to be a great want of it all along this part of the coast. It was finally decided that the landing should be made about seven miles north of the little stream dignified by the name of the river Bulgânak: the English to land on the strip of land between the sea and Kalamita salt lake; the French just south of them, at a place I can't spell or write, but which signifies in English 'Old Fort,' from an old ruined tower, which the Tatars are pleased to call a fort.[3]

With the reconnaissance having been successfully carried out, opinions were expressed as to the various merits and drawbacks of the suggested landing sites. General Canrobert continued to favour the Kacha, whilst the British officers argued against it. At length, Burgoyne was introduced to the French officers, upon which he proceeded to explain why the Kacha was a bad choice. Not only was it too narrow, but Russian troops had been seen encamped there and on the Alma river, but none north of the latter. There was little doubt also that garrisons would be found at Simferopol and Bakhchisarai, which could threaten the Allied rear if they landed at the Kacha and got into difficulties. Canrobert, on the other hand, said that if the Allies landed north of the Alma they would most likely have to fight three battles, on the Alma, Kacha and Belbek rivers, before they could approach Sevastopol. This was true, stated Burgoyne, but he considered it highly unlikely that, if the Russians were soundly beaten at the first river, the Alma, they would contest the others. It would take less than a month for Burgoyne to be proved correct. In the meantime Raglan made his final decision as to the landing site. It would be a fair distance north of the Alma, on a wide expansive beach that lay just south of Eupatoria. The generals leaned over and peered at the map in order to find out its name. Given the caution expressed by many officers and worries relating to the late timing of the campaign and the lack of intelligence about the Russian forces and the Crimea generally, it is strange that no comment survives on the ominous name of the landing site. It was Kalamita Bay.

Even as thousands of Russian troops made their way towards the river Alma, hundreds of Allied ships closed in on Kalamita Bay until on the afternoon of 13 September the distant coastline of the Crimea finally came into view. It was a tense, dramatic moment, as Lieutenant Colonel Charles Townsend Wilson, of the Coldstream Guards, recalled:

> The first glimpse of the Crimea. Out the black waters emerges the sandy coast of mysterious Taurus. A moment – never to be forgotten! – fire flashes in the dullest eye, the most leaden hearts leap; not a smock-faced ensign but glows with the martial rage of the old war-horse, that smelleth the battle afar off![4]

The Allied armada surged onwards, and by the evening of 13 September final preparations were being made for the landing the following morning. The French were particularly anxious that nothing should go awry, and that evening General Canrobert, along with the chief of the general staff of the French Army, General Martimprey, took himself off on one final reconnaissance of the shore, checking the line of approach and making sure that no Russian troops had moved into the area. All being as they hoped, the two returned to the fleet which lay in wait beneath a clear, calm night, the sea barely moving save for a very gentle swell caused by a slight breeze. With the Crimean coast before them, thousands of Allied soldiers began to look to their equipment in preparation for the coming disembarkation.

Each of the British troops had been issued with rations of 1lb of meat, 1lb of bread, 2oz of rice, 1³/₄oz of sugar, 1oz of coffee, and half a gill of rum, for which 4¹/₂d was paid. The ration for a cavalry, artillery or staff horse was 10lb of corn and 12lb of hay or straw, whilst baggage animals were allowed 8lb of corn.[5] Charles Townsend Wilson described his own preparations:

> We crammed into our haversacks the following items; in the way of sustenance – salt pork, biscuit, rum, and tea, for three days' consumption; of clothing – two pairs of socks, two towels, a couple of handkerchiefs, a shirt; of comforts – a tooth-brush, comb, knife, fork, and spoon (the three last set in the same handle, as contrived by Messrs. Mappin), a 'tot' or tin mug, a bit of soap; such – with the addition of the cloak rolled so as to be worn like a hoop across the shoulder while on the march; a 'Colt' stuck into the Turkish sash; and a 'Dolland' slung anywhere out of the way – constituted the catalogue of 'kit' deemed requisite in most instances; here and there, indeed, some peculiarly robust lieutenant, confident in the brawn of his back and the thickness of his calves, might have been observed putting up a more extensive wardrobe, and a load of extra *comestibles*; but alas! Men so athletic and self-reliant were exceptions to the general rule.[6]

Unfortunately for the rank and file, orders were issued forbidding them to take their packs ashore. This was a decision which was felt acutely amongst the men. It was also a decision that was to cause great controversy later on, particularly during the inquiry held after the troubles experienced by the British Army during the bitterly cold winter. Wilson was quick to comment – somewhat critically as usual – on the decision:

> With regard to the soldiers' necessaries, the worthy Adjutant-General was induced to sanction an unfortunate arrangement. Instead of allowing things to take their natural course – i.e., letting Giles pack his little matters in his knapsack, as he had always been used to do – orders were issued that every man was to wrap up a pair of shoes, a pair of socks, a shirt, and forage cap in his blanket and great coat! Thus was formed a big shapeless bundle, which could not fail to wobble uneasily on the victim's back, to heat him, to gall him, to squeeze curses out of him. The knapsacks themselves, with diverse articles of the soldier's private property were to be left behind on shipboard; but in whose keeping, nobody would say.[7]

Wilson went on to add cryptically, 'I can defend myself from my enemies, but God help me from my friends.'

In defending himself against criticism at an inquiry before a board of officers, held at the Royal Hospital, Chelsea, Sir Richard Airey, the quartermaster-general, explained the basis of the decision, suggesting it was largely on account of Lord Raglan's own wishes, which was all very convenient since Raglan was dead by the time the inquiry was held. Airey claimed that, when the army was on board ship crossing the Black Sea, it suffered so much from the effects of cholera that men were being thrown overboard all the time. He added that it was hoped the men would recover and improve their health at sea, but this didn't happen. Instead, even those who escaped serious illness looked barely capable of 'their usual exertions'. He went on:

> Lord Raglan was very anxious about the failing strength of the men, and when we got off the Crimean coast, he thought it advisable to let them land in as light marching order as possible. In Bulgaria we had had occasionally to march short distances, and change the ground, and change the camp, but not to march more than five or six miles; yet the men had become so much reduced from the excessive heat of the summer, that, even in those short marches, it had been found necessary to relieve the soldier of the burthen of his knapsack by having it carried on pack-animals or in the arabas of the country; and now, when about to land in the Crimea, the enfeebling sickness having continued during the voyage, the men were fully incapable of much bodily exertion as they had been in Bulgaria. On the other hand, the men, in a state of great physical weakness, were going to bivouac for the first time in the open air, and Lord Raglan thought it of great importance to them that they should not be without their blankets, and he determined, therefore, that – our soldiers, not being able to carry their great coats, their knapsack and the blanket – the knapsack, rather than the blanket, should be dispensed with. Accordingly, a direction was given to the effect that the men might leave their knapsacks on board ship; but they were to land both with their greatcoats and blankets, and in the latter they were to roll up a change of things – a spare shirt, a pair of socks, and a pair of boots.[8]

The trouble with this arrangement was the difficulty the men experienced not so much in having to wrap their belongings in their blankets, but being able to march comfortably with the blanket wrapped around them. Indeed, giving evidence to the select committee held in March 1855 to look into the state of affairs of the army in front of Sevastopol, Sergeant Thomas Dawson, of the Grenadier Guards, stated that it was much easier to have the knapsack than a bundle wrapped around the body. When asked which was heaviest, the pack or the rolled-up blanket, Dawson answered quite simply, 'The bundle,' and added:

> On a march a man can bring his elbow to a level, and ease his shoulders, by lifting the knapsack up, but these bundles they could not, and they were so heavy behind; they were much worse than the knapsacks.[9]

Sergeant Dawson went on:

> I could have carried my knapsack better with the coat and blanket than the bundle, because, with my arm behind, I could have eased up the knapsack at different times, whereas as it was, it hung so heavily that there was no easing it; we could not ease it in a march.[10]

Charles Wilson also pointed out, writing in his memoirs, that the heavy wooden frame of the knapsacks had been discarded weeks earlier, and that the weight of the knapsack would have had little effect on the men's ability to march.

Colonel Charles Windham, an officer on the staff of the 4th Division, took a different view and saw little problem with the soldiers carrying their belongings wrapped in a blanket:

> I have walked underweight, and have carried my own provisions for many days, and I am sure that, provided you took a blanket, and put in it a spare shirt, a pair of shoes, and towel, you might leave your knapsack and great-coat behind you for a fortnight.
>
> A great-coat is a great-coat and nothing more, but a blanket is a blanket and great-coat too, and when men lie down together in twos and threes, they can, with good blankets, make themselves comfortable; at least, I always found this to be the case in my hunting trips in North America, where I have gone through more real hard work than falls to the lot of most men.
>
> The knapsack appears to be a thing to which officers are peculiarly wedded; which can easily be accounted for by their never having carried them.
>
> If they ever had to do so, they would avoid them as studiously as

gypsies, pedlars, and trappers do.

Any weight, in fact, that cannot be shifted is painful for a man to carry; and as a blanket, rolled lengthways and slung over the shoulder, will carry all that a man can want for a fortnight, I cannot see the use of loading him with more. When going on sentry duty he would leave his trifling effects with his comrade, and use the blanket as a great-coat; when in his tent, his blanket is his bed.[11]

Nonetheless, orders were orders, and so the knapsacks were discarded and gathered together ready to be left aboard ship. In the meantime, officers continued to see to their kit, safe in the knowledge that they, at least, had the benefit of haversacks into which they could stuff what they considered essential items. John Astley, of the Scots Fusilier Guards, was careful in his choice of items. He was also lucky enough to get round Raglan's order by having a servant smuggled aboard ship:

I have been getting my kit in order today, and mean to carry my three days' salt pork and biscuit, some brandy, my cloak, two revolvers, and several useful things on my belt round my waist, the two greatest treasures being an axe and a frying pan; and having smuggled a Greek servant on board, he will carry my knapsack with a change of clothes in it, my blanket and waterproof. I have also put some writing materials in my haversack.[12]

The landing site itself, a mixture of sand and shingle, was 4 miles long and flat, and formed a sort of causeway between the sea and two salt-water lakes. The French and Turks were to land to the south, with the British troops landing to the north. It was still dark when, at half-past two in the morning, two rockets were sent arcing into the air from Admiral Hamelin's flagship, the *Ville de Paris*, as the signal for the final push towards the beaches. The signal was answered by the British naval commander, Admiral Dundas, whereupon the fleet slowly but steadily began to move towards the shore. It was, as the French historian Bazancourt wrote:

a magnificent spectacle, when the first rays of day ascended the horizon, to contemplate the fleet, – the most splendid which has ever crossed the seas, – proceeding in silence towards the place of landing. There are long files of ships of all sizes, extending illimitably over the waters of the sea. All are filled with soldiers, whose bayonets shine in the first rays of dawn.

It is a town, floating and animated, which transports a human exodus from one shore to the other. The coast is before us; the beach, silent and deserted, appears to await these thousands of beings, to receive from them life, movement, and tumult. Officers, soldiers and sailors, all have their eyes fixed upon the shore.[13]

The priority as far as the Allies were concerned was to get their men safely ashore as soon as possible and get on towards Sevastopol. Speed was essential, for many of the Allied commanders were only too aware of the 'desperate undertaking' which the invasion of the Crimea represented, with the Allies taking on a campaign with what can only be described as sketchy intelligence. They knew very little of the country, its people and the difficulties that accompanied such a campaign. Furthermore, with the campaign being undertaken late in the year they also knew that if Sevastopol did not fall within a few months they would be faced with a prolonged siege which would obviously last throughout what would almost certainly be a very harsh winter. It was vital, therefore, that the Allied commanders, Lord Raglan and Marshal Saint-Arnaud, got their men ashore as soon as possible in order to begin the advance south.

Almost 250 ships had anchored off shore, ready to begin the landings themselves. Finally, at seven o'clock on the morning of 14 September, the boats were dropped into the water and the Allied troops clambered into them before waiting for the signal to begin the short trip that would carry them over the final few hundred yards to the shore, where they would disembark. In addition to the boats which would carry the troops to the beaches, large barges had been built by the French in Constantinople and towed to Varna, where they had been tested. They were then towed to the Crimea, ready to begin transporting the artillery ashore. Each one was capable of carrying two guns and their carriages, with one piece being placed at the front and one at the rear. Between them stood twelve horses with their equipment and drivers, numbering eighteen men. Each gun could be made ready for firing within ten minutes of landing on the beach. The British did not use barges but instead tied two boats together and laid a platform across the two on which they placed their guns.

The arrangements for the landings were complex, at least by the standards of the day. Gone were the days when British troops simply jumped into small boats that spirited them ashore on some foreign country. Now, with two large armies disembarking on a relatively small beach, fairly complex arrangements were made in order to avoid any confusion. After all, it was dangerous enough to be landing on foreign soil with a hostile army possibly waiting in the wings. Any confusion and disorder amongst the Allies in the face of such opposition might prove fatal.

General George Bell, a veteran of the Peninsular War, was aboard the transport *Alfred the Great*. The entry in his journal for 10 September 1854 contained the orders for the disembarkation:

> Eight pages of printed regulations are published for instruction. First rendezvous – anchoring off the enemy's territory, and disembarking the army and material, under the orders of Sir Edmond Lyons by G.C.B. Signed, Dundas, Vice Admiral and Commander In Chief. It is a long programme, and, to landsmen, complicated; but we soldiers have only to obey orders. I hope no link in the chain will be broken. The final signals are: for the boats to assemble round ships. To disembark infantry and artillery, one black ball at the fore of the *Agamemnon*; two black balls, to form line abreast, three black balls, advance in line; four black balls, to land. Lord Raglan to be on board the *Caradoc* steamer. Every division has its distinguishing flag, viz First Division, blue, triangular blue; second division, White, triangular white; the third division, red, triangular red; Fourth Division, red, with white fly triangular either; Fifth Division, cavalry and blue, with red fly triangle; Light Division, checked flag. All boats carrying infantry to have in their bows, eighteen inches square. Paddle-boats of *Spitfire*, *Triton*, *Cyclops*, and *Firebrand*, to land regimental staff officers. To precede to sea by signal tomorrow. It appears that 308 boats, of different sorts and sizes, will dash off at once with troops, to land in front of the enemy, and against all opposition.[14]

Even at this late hour, all eyes were fixed upon the beaches, watching for any signs of activity, lest the Russians suddenly appear to oppose the landings. The look-outs in the ships peered through telescopes whilst those in the boats themselves looked ahead, trying to spot Russian troops, but the beaches seemed deserted. Despite this, Admiral Hamelin thought it prudent to dispatch four boats armed with Congreve rockets towards the shore, just in case there was any trouble. A frigate and two steam tenders, along with the *Descartes*, the *Primauguet* and the *Caton* were similarly sent ahead with orders to get as close to the shore as their draught would allow in order to bring their guns to bear. Then, at ten minutes past eight o'clock, and with no sign of any Russian activity on the beach, the long-awaited signal for the final push to the beaches was given by Admiral Hamelin.

Chapter 4

Summer in Sevastopol

The spring of 1854 was unusual for the Crimean peninsula. The fields usually began to turn green from February, and the bushes and trees to blossom. But May had come and the fields were still bare, with hardly a hint of green to be seen. The trees were in leaf but as yet there were no flowers. The starlings came late in April, as did thick fogs, which were no good to anyone. Snow still lay thick on the mountains and it would be some time before it disappeared. The mornings and evenings were cooler than usual, and people never ventured outside without warm clothing. Vineyards were subjected to dry, unseasonable frosts, whilst the herds of cattle suffered also from the cold. It was indeed a strange spring.

In the great Crimean naval base of Sevastopol, meanwhile, the people had other things on their mind besides the weather, for thoughts of the approaching war hung as heavy as the fogs that settled and drifted across the great harbour that separated the northern or Severnaya side of the town from the Korabel'naya, which lay to the south of the water. The war had been a long time in coming, and up until now the people had read and heard little of the war save for news of fighting on the Danube. Even Nakhimov's exploit at Sinope seemed an isolated incident. But now, with news of British and French troops encamped across the Black Sea at Varna, the war was coming closer.

Sevastopol was inhabited mainly by military and naval personnel who made up the bulk of the 40,000 or so population. Indeed, the streets were awash with long-tail-coated men striding purposefully along the wide streets. An English visitor to Sevastopol in 1852, Laurence Oliphant, was struck by the martial appearance of the town, and recorded it in his journal:

> The town is, in fact, an immense garrison, and looks imposing because so many of the buildings are barracks or government offices. Still, I was much struck with the substantial appearance of many of the private houses; and, indeed, the main street was handsomer than any I had seen

since leaving Moscow, while it owed its extreme cleanliness to large gangs of military prisoners, who were employed in perpetually sweeping. New houses were springing up in every direction, government works were still going forward vigorously, and Sevastopol bids fair to rank high among Russian cities. The magnificent arm of the sea upon which it is situated, is an object worthy the millions which have been lavished in rendering it a fitting receptacle for the Russian navy.

As I stood upon the handsome stairs that lead down to the water's edge, I counted thirteen sail of the line anchored in the principal harbour. The newest of these, a noble three-decker, was lying within pistol-shot of the quay. The average breadth of this inlet is one thousand yards; two creeks branch off from it, intersecting the town in a southerly direction, and containing steamers and smaller craft, besides a long row of hulks which have been converted into magazines or prison-ships.[1]

In the late spring of 1854 the stern expressions of the military and naval personnel were more grim than usual, for Russia was at war with two of the greatest powers in the world, Britain and France, and their beloved town had become the unwanted object of the Allies' attention. It was a mystery to them how Russia had got itself into such a position, but politics were for the higher echelons of Russian society, the diplomats and their emperor, Czar Nicholas I. The officers and men of the Black Sea Fleet and the Imperial Russian Army were there simply to defend their homeland and do their emperor's bidding. There was no use in worrying, not now that war had been declared. And so life went on.

The soldiers and sailors in Sevastopol regarded themselves as one great family. During the summer months they were either at sea training or were out patrolling the Black Sea, so their families remained in the town. They had no country houses. They were very proud, and justifiably too, for barely six months earlier their ships had sailed across the Black Sea to Sinope where they had completely destroyed a Turkish fleet which was supposed to have been protected by the British and French navies. Admittedly the Turkish fleet was at anchor at the time, but it was, nevertheless, a glorious moment in Russian naval history, as it was every bit a slap in the face for the Allies. Indeed, the attack at Sinope had largely been responsible for driving France and Britain to war, particularly with public opinion almost forcing the Allied governments' hands.

Now, with Admiral Pavel Stepanovich Nakhimov at their head, they stood ready to sail at a moment's notice in order to do battle with the Allied navies.

When they were not on duty, the naval officers could enjoy any one of several relaxing pursuits in Sevastopol, not least of which was reading in the magnificent officers' library, considered to be the equal of any of the best libraries in Europe both in terms of its interior and exterior decoration. Its collections were just as fine. Indeed, only recently Czar Nicolas had enriched its collection by presenting it with an oil painting by the artist Pavlov, depicting an action on 5 November 1853 when the Russian steamer *Vladimir*, under the command of Vice-Admiral V A Kornilov, captured the 10-gun Egyptian steamer *Pervas Bakhri*, a ship that was subsequently renamed the *Kornilov*.

There was also a great theatre where troupes of Russian actors gave performances three times a week. The town enjoyed visits from troupes of actors from countries such as Italy and Spain, who performed in the theatre, built in 1843, at the bottom of Boulevard Height. There were, of course, numerous religious and other festivals. In April, for example, the empress's birthday was marked with a Te Deum in St Nicholas Cathedral, in all the other churches in Sevastopol, and on board all the ships of the Black Sea Fleet. It ended amidst a blaze of cannon fire as the ships gave their salute. All the ships were decorated with flags and multicoloured pennants for the occasion. In the evening a drama, written by a Mr Kukolnik, was performed. Called *The Battle of Sinope*, it was specifically written for the naval holiday in Sevastopol.

But there was little escaping the fact that Russia was at war, and that Sevastopol would be the main target for the Allies. The situation was brought sharply into focus in mid-April when a flotilla of Allied ships was spotted on the horizon, causing crowds of people to go flocking to the harbour to try to see what was going on out to sea. Everyone expressed their desire to see a battle brought on, confident as they were in their leaders' abilities, but the Allied ships disappeared over the horizon, obviously judging it too risky to try the mettle of the Russian shore batteries, that is, of course, if it were ever their intention to close with them. The people of Sevastopol dispersed, jeering the Allies, and laughing, considering it to be amusing that the most powerful fleets in the world were limiting themselves to chasing small defenceless boats with crews of three to five men, all in the cause of defending Turkey. And even when they did come in closer the Allies behaved even more shamefully, flying flags which were obviously not their own, sometimes Austrian and even

Russian flags, just to try to deceive the coastal battery commanders. Count Nikolai Golitsyn, watching from the shore, was even moved to write that the Allied fleets should be compared to pirates – they were certainly not acting as one would have expected. Indeed, the majority of the watchers on the shore did not know whether to simply laugh or wonder why such actions were being resorted to.

There were few finer places to build a naval base than Sevastopol. The base was situated on the south bank of Sevastopol Bay, which itself was 4 miles long and about half a mile wide. The bay was known as the roadstead, or Sevastopol road, the south side of which was marked by a series of inlets or bays, one of which, the Yuzhnaya (or South Bay), was a mile long and during the Crimean War was capable of accommodating virtually the whole of the Black Sea Fleet. The Yuzhnaya effectively divided the town of Sevastopol, with the Gorodskaya (old or main town) to the west and the Korabel'naya faubourg to the east. Another small bay, the Korabel'naya (or Dockyard Creek), flowed to the east of the Yuzhnaya, close to the roadstead. The other large bays, from west to east, were the Karantinnaya (Quarantine Bay), the Artilleriiskaya (Artillery Bay), and the Kilen-bukhta (known as the Keeling or Careenage Bay or Bight).

The beginning of the nineteenth century had seen much industrial development in Sevastopol. In 1812 and 1813 several plants and factories were built, including saltpetre and lime plants, brickyards, bakeries and so on. In addition, there were 202 shops and two markets, with two major fairs being held every year. At the beginning of the second quarter of the nineteenth century Sevastopol was the largest city in the Crimea with a population of 30,000. The largest proportion of these were, of course, naval and military personnel, most of whom endured severe drilling, strict discipline, hard work, bad food and beatings, all of which were common for the sailors and soldiers. The civilian population fared little better, which gave rise to much discontent. In June 1830 the first mass demonstration of working class people and sailors against the government took place. In fact, Sevastopol was in the hands of the insurgents for four days before the czar's government finally regained control, putting down the demonstration with great cruelty.

In 1834 Admiral M P Lazarev was appointed commander of the fleet and the Black Sea ports. Under his leadership five stone fort-batteries, which defended Sevastopol from the sea, were built. He also undertook the task of refitting and reorganizing the Russian fleet. Although Lazarev was himself an outstanding naval officer, he was fortunate in having round him a group of similarly gifted and honest men, including admirals Nakhimov, Kornilov and Istomin, who were to emerge as three of the great heroes of the siege of Sevastopol. During Lazarev's tenure as commander of the Black Sea ports, trade continued to increase in Sevastopol. In 1838, for example, 170 vessels laden with different goods came to the port. The number of merchants increased also. In 1831 there were twenty merchants in the town, which by 1848 had risen to eighty-three. Most of these provided the fleet with flour, meat, cereals, salt and firewood. There were also some 280 different shops, including 46 'pottery establishments'. Naturally, the construction of sea fortifications, the admiralty, sea fronts, the new docks and numerous other buildings in the centre of the town helped swell the population, with thousands of people arriving looking for work. Indeed, by 1853 the population of Sevastopol had increased to 47,000, and the number of houses to 2,810, all of which were built in forty-three streets and four squares.

In the 1820s two pipelines supplied Sevastopol with its water, although only one supplied the people, the other being used strictly for the admiralty and the fleet. The pipes fed from natural springs, however, and failed to supply the town with sufficient water. By 1846 the situation had improved to the extent that Sevastopol boasted forty-eight wells. As we shall see, the water supply was to prove an important factor during the siege which took place during the Crimean War. The first medical establishment in Sevastopol was the Naval Hospital, built between 1790 and 1791, and capable of housing 200 patients. However, it served only the naval and military officers and their families, and the Sevastopol aristocracy; the overwhelming mass of the population in the town had to call upon the services of just one other doctor, who was also responsible for the condition of the markets, bakeries and shops. It was a thoroughly unsatisfactory state of affairs.

The quality of education was not much better, although efforts to improve the situation were made during the second half of the nineteenth century. In 1826 a School of Sea Cadets for 100 pupils was opened, and two years later the civil district (*uezd*) opened a special school for 40 pupils. During the following eight years other schools were opened, including schools for sailors' daughters, a parish school and a private finishing school. In 1846 it is recorded that there were only 13 teachers and 404 pupils, of whom 74 were girls. The arts and sciences were not neglected. In addition to it being the premier naval base in the Black Sea, Sevastopol was second only to St Petersburg as the centre of naval sciences in Russia. In 1842 the navigational charts of the Black and Azov seas were published, whilst on land important excavations were made of ancient Chersonese. In 1822 one of the first naval libraries was opened in Sevastopol.

But what of the defences of Sevastopol? Although several batteries had been constructed under Admiral Lazarev between 1835 and 1837, it was not until the outbreak of the Crimean War that any real consideration was given to the city's defensive batteries. On the northern side of Sevastopol, the Severnaya, were built the Konstantinovskaya and Mikhailovskaya batteries, and on the southern part the Aleksandrovskaya, Nikolaevskaya and Pavlovskaya batteries. Simple earthwork batteries were constructed also – the no. 5 Battery in Appolonova ravine, no. 8 and no. 10 near Aleksandrovskaya Bay, and no. 4 on Severnaya. The batteries in Sevastopol were named after their commanders or builders, and were numbered according to the order of construction. At the time of Turkey's declaration of war, the batteries were armed with some 533 guns, each battery consisting of between 34 and 105 guns, the calibres of the guns ranging from 12-pounders right up to heavy 36-pounders, in addition to which there were various calibre howitzers and mortars.

The first real fortifications had been built between 1807 and 1811 under the supervision of the engineer Major General Garting, and were constructed on the Severnaya. The walled fortifications housed 47 guns and could accommodate a garrison of almost 4,000 men. These were hardly likely to thwart an enemy attack, however, and so plans were drawn up for the construction of more fortifications in 1834 by the Engineering Department and revised in 1837 following an inspection by Czar Nicholas himself. The plans involved the building of eight bastions connected by a defensive wall and ditch, and extending from the Kilen-bukhta, south to Bastion 3 and then north, running to the west of Gorodskaya and up as far as the Sevastopol Road. This would protect Sevastopol from attack from the south. Seven of the bastions were known simply by numbers, the eighth being the Malakhov Hill.[2]

The worsening situation and the likelihood of war with Britain and France prompted the Russians to begin improving the works. In January 1854 the Svyatoslavskaya battery for seventeen guns was built on the western side of Careenage Bay and was named after the ship *Svyatoslav*, whose crew had built it. At the same time were erected the Dvenadtsatiapostol'skaya (Twelve Apostles) battery between the Panaitova ravine and Hollandia Bay, and the Parizhskaya (Paris) battery on the nameless cape which separated

Sukharnaya Bay and Hollandia Bay. Behind Konstantinovsky fort a new battery, named after its builder, Colonel Kartashevsky, was built, and Volokhov's tower, along with its battery, was built by Daniil Volokhov in twenty-one days and at his own expense.

Given the apparent strength of the defences, the people of Sevastopol could certainly feel confident in the abilities of their town and its garrison to resist the invaders should they try to attack from the seaward side. The great problem was, however, that the Allies fully intended to attack from the landward side, against defences which were virtually non-existent at the time of the Allied landings. Even the seaward defences were not so strong as they first appeared, as Oliphant observed:

> Nothing can be more formidable than the appearance of Sevastopol from the seaward. Upon a future occasion we visited it in a steamer, and found that at one point we were commanded by twelve hundred pieces of artillery; fortunately for a hostile fleet, we afterwards heard that these could not be discharged without bringing down the rotten batteries upon which they are placed, and which are so badly constructed that they look as if they had been done by contract. Four of the forts consist of three tiers of batteries. We were, of course, unable to do more than take a very general survey of these celebrated fortifications, and therefore cannot vouch for the assertion, that the rooms in which the guns are worked are so narrow and ill-ventilated, that the artillerymen would be inevitably stifled in the attempt to discharge their guns and their duty.[3]

Oliphant then went on to point out the lack of defences to the landward side of Sevastopol:

> But of one fact there was no doubt, that however well fortified may be the approaches to Sevastopol by sea, there is nothing whatever to prevent any number of troops landing a few miles to the south of the sea, in one of the six convenient bays with which the coast, as far as Cape Kherson, is indented, and marching down the main street (provided they were strong enough to defeat any military force that might be opposed to them in the open field), sack the town and burn the fleet.[4]

Various plans for improving the defences had been put forward and agreed upon, but actual construction was another matter. Indeed, very little work was carried out, and even as the Allied fleet came gliding towards Sevastopol in September 1854 frantic efforts were under way to try to improve – and in some cases even begin – the fortifications. The construction of Bastion 7 had only just begun, whilst only a defensive wall had been erected on the ground laid out for Bastion 5. On the site where it had been intended to build Bastions 1, 5 and 6 only barracks had been constructed, whilst on Malakhov Hill there was just a fortified tower. In some places the fortifications were connected with simply a thin and unstable defensive wall. The plan of the Engineer Department was far from perfect. For example, although Malakhov Hill, some 97 metres high, rose above the height of Bastions 1, 2, 3 and 4, it was nevertheless lower than some of the heights which surrounded those bastions, such as Vorontsov's Hill and the Careenage Heights.

Despite rumours of war, summer in Sevastopol had passed by peacefully, with soldiers like the Polish Captain Hodasevich enjoying 'a gay time of it in the town – balls, theatre, promenades on Sundays and holidays, when the band played on the boulevards.'[5] Work went on as usual in the naval dockyards, the theatres were full, businesses continued to trade as they had always done and, generally, the people went about their lives blissfully ignorant of the storm looming over what was to them a very distant horizon. But soon, as August turned to September, rumours began flying everywhere. Stories began to circulate in Sevastopol that an Allied fleet had been sighted off the Crimean coast, whilst other, wilder, rumours claimed that there had even been an actual landing. Neither was true, of course, but they certainly increased the tension and even excitement amongst both the civilian and military population in Sevastopol. There was much bravado amongst the young men who were eager to get to grips with the enemy. Many months had passed since war had been declared by France and Britain, whose armies were known to be making their way across the Black Sea in fast ships, whilst even longer had passed since war had been declared by Turkey. The politicians had had their say. It was time for the issue, whatever it was – for there were few amongst the czar's army and navy who knew why the Allies were coming – to be decided on the battlefield or out at sea.

With rumours of an Allied fleet making its way across the Black Sea, security was stepped up along the western coast. Cavalry patrols were dispatched from Sevastopol to maintain observation between the already established chain of posts and semaphore stations that ran north from the city, whilst vigilance was increased generally along the coast. Perhaps because of this, more false alarms continued to sound. For example, on the evening of 11 September, 66-year-old Prince Alexander Menshikov was attending a ball given by the officers of the Borodinsky Regiment, when a messenger reported that the Allied fleet had arrived and was preparing to land its cargo of troops. Menshikov, who had entered service in the Russian Army three years before Napoleon's invasion in 1812, was the commander-in-chief of the Russian Army in the Crimea. He was also the man whom Nicholas had sent to Constantinople to negotiate with the sultan the previous year, a mission that went terribly wrong from the start, largely because of Menshikov's arrogant, overbearing manner. He was, in short, totally unfitted to perform the sort of diplomatic skills required to bring about a possible solution to the so-called Eastern Question. He would also prove somewhat inadequate when it came to commanding an army in the field, although that was still some way off. The report that an Allied fleet had been sighted was, characteristically, dismissed by Menshikov as yet another false alarm. But as the days passed it became obvious that the arrival of the enemy fleet was imminent, and Russian telescopes regularly scanned the horizon in anticipation of the expected armada.

Finally, at ten o'clock on the morning of 13 September, two enemy men-of-war were spotted from an observation post in Sevastopol. Then, shortly afterwards, the watchers on the hills saw several plumes of smoke rising from beyond the horizon, the tell-tale sign that an enormous fleet was heading towards them. The alarm was raised immediately, and throughout the after-noon a constant stream of messages was received at Menshikov's headquarters from the semaphore station at Loukoul, stating that the enemy fleet was heading in the direction of Eupatoria.

Captain Hodasevich recorded a mixture of emotions amongst the Russian officers who now realized they would soon be facing the enemy at last, after so many months of waiting:

> Many of the younger officers expressed extravagant joy at the idea that God had given our enemies over into our hands; the soldiers were also rejoiced at the news; they were burning with impatience to meet the enemy face to face, as well as for a change in their monotonous lives. Some few of the officers became sick, and required to be sent to the hospital, but the number of these was small. I must say that I looked forward to fleshing my maiden sword with pleasure, and hastened towards the enemy with my comrades.[6]

With news of the arrival of the Allied fleet now having been finally confirmed, all was hustle and bustle in Sevastopol as officers began leaving to join their regiments, soldiers, sailors and marines began to prepare for battle, and hastily arranged conferences were held on putting into place measures that had been discussed for the defence of the town. Hopefully, such measures would not be needed, for Menshikov had declared that his army would have little trouble in defeating the enemy once they had landed. Nevertheless, more shrewd officers, such as Edward Todleben, who was to prove one of the heroes of the defence of the town, immediately began drawing up plans to build up the virtually non-existent defences around Sevastopol, for in the event that Menshikov's promises could not be made good it was unlikely that the defences, in their present state at least, would be able to withstand an enemy attack. And so, plans were set in motion to begin improving them, which would involve large numbers of the civilian population, including women and children, who would take on much of the manual work of digging, fetching and carrying, in the absence of the soldiers who were even now leaving to confront the enemy.

But what of Menshikov's plans? Having decided not to oppose the Allied landings he was left with few options. He could either remain in Sevastopol with his troops in order to deal with the Allies' attack on Sevastopol or he could march out to meet them. The problem was that if he decided upon the former course of action and remained in Sevastopol, Menshikov risked having his army bottled up by the besieging Allied forces. The obvious course of action was to simply put his forces in the path of the Allied advance towards Sevastopol. This meant deciding where to position them, for four rivers barred the way towards Sevastopol: from north to south they were the Bulganak, the Alma, the Kacha and the Belbek. The first of these was little more than a large stream, with little or no features of any strategic importance. The Belbek was simply too close to Sevastopol for comfort, whilst the Kacha, like the Bulganak, offered little advantage topographically. The obvious choice was to make a stand astride the river Alma, where the ground to the south of the river made for a fine defensive position.

In the meantime, Menshikov busied himself in moving his battalions north towards the Kacha river. It was a decision that had not been taken without a great deal of thought, for there were many who thought the enemy had sailed towards Eupatoria only in order to lure the defenders away from Sevastopol. Once the army had marched north they feared the Allies would simply use their fast steamships to sail south to an undefended Sevastopol. After all, it would take Menshikov's men far longer to achieve the same distance by simply marching. It was indeed a strong possibility and was an example of one of the advantages which the Allied fleet had over the somewhat antiquated ships of the Russian navy. It was for this very same reason that Menshikov decided from the outset not to oppose the Allied landings, however. Ironically, it might have proved his best course of action. Given the haphazard manner in which the Allies landed in the aptly named Kalamita Bay, it is likely that a minimal degree of resistance offered by the Russians would have been enough to have derailed the landing operation. In the event, Menshikov allowed the Allies to land unopposed, choosing instead to meet them in the field. Whether the British and French generals ever considered racing their ships down to an undefended Sevastopol is doubtful. The strategy was certainly never adopted.

Menshikov himself was confident of throwing the invaders back into the sea, no matter what strategy they employed. On 3 December 1853 Czar Nicholas had written to him, letting him know in no uncertain terms that he was relying on his commander to stop the Allies in their tracks. If the Allies chose to attack Sevastopol by sea, he was confident of dealing them a great blow. If, on the other hand, the Allies landed their troops with a view to attacking by land, he still expected Menshikov to defeat them:

> If the English and French enter the Black Sea, we should not fight with them [i.e. engage at sea]. Let them taste our batteries in Sevastopol, where you'll meet them with a great salute they probably are not expecting. I am not afraid of their landing but if it happens we could repulse it even now. In April we'll have the whole 16th division with its artillery, brigade of Hussars and horse battery. It's more than we need to make them pay dearly.[7]

The problem was that once Menshikov had received the letter from the czar, all power of thought seems to have deserted him as regards a strategy for defeating the Allies other than what the czar had advised. There never was much attention given to preventing the Allies from making a landing, which was certainly one of the better options open to him. Indeed, if the Allies could be caught in the act of landing the consequences for them would undoubtedly be disastrous. But, given the possibility that the Allies might lure his troops away from Sevastopol only to sail rapidly south again and attack a relatively undefended town, he chose not to oppose the landings. The czar's letter only served to reinforce this course of action. In his mind, Nicholas had 'ordered' him to allow the Allies to come before Sevastopol where they would greet them with their batteries. Thus, his course was set.

Chapter 5

The Landings

At half-past eight on the morning of 14 September, a boat from the *Ville de Paris*, carrying General Canrobert and Rear-Admiral Bouet-Willaumez, hit the beach, the sailors having rowed furiously in their efforts to be the first to reach the shore. In the event, the men of the French 2nd Regiment of Zouaves claimed the honour of doing so. Jean Joseph Gustave Cler was one of their officers:

> The first to touch the beach at Old Fort, were four companies of Zouaves, – who were not a little astonished, at beholding no signs of an enemy. The beach here, was low, destitute of trees or vegetation, and with, here and there, a shallow pool of brackish water. In a short time, the whole regiment was assembled, and marched in company with the other troops belonging to the 3d division, to occupy a point, about half a league in advance of the landing-place. The 3d division, which was commanded by Prince Napoleon, here took its place on the left of the French line, and not far from the English right; – and, in almost the twinkling of an eye, the Zouaves had formed their bivouac, and thrown out their guards.[1]

Canrobert was close behind them, and no sooner had his boat hit the shore than he leapt onto the sand to unfurl the tricolour. It was, as one French historian proudly remarked, 'Forty-two years before, day for day, – on the 14th of September, 1812, – the Grand Army commanded by the Emperor Napoleon, entered Moscow.' Soon afterwards scores of other French boats reached the beaches to land their human cargoes, all of this under the supervision of the commandant of the landing beaches, Captain Anne-Duportal. A British officer, George Bell, described the race to the beaches:

> It was now a race of boats between England and France who should first plant their standard on hostile ground. The French had the inside of the course, and had the advantage, and even if they had not the first landing, they would have claimed it. The landing was accomplished most admirably and with great success, thanks to the great Russian

army who declined to be inhospitable to England's first visit to their soil. Had they marched down in hostility, there must have been a frightful smashing of our boats coming ashore, from their guns and mortars, however well we may have been covered by our own ships of war. But so it is in war, the invading or attacking army have the advantage of selecting their own time and place for action, and here we took the enemy by surprise. The sea was calm, the sandy beach favoured approach, and every boat landed its cargo in safety. The different divisions quickly formed and marched onward a mile or two to bivouac. It was dusk when I got all my regiment ashore and ready to move off. The men left their knapsacks on board by order, taking three days' cooked provisions in their haversacks; a blanket, greatcoat, shirt, pair of shoes and socks, all strapped up in the greatcoat. The officers had nothing but what they carried on their backs, little or much, as they pleased. We were all in full dress uniform![2]

Captain Octave Cullet was an infantry officer with the 20th Ligne. His regiment had sailed to the Crimea in the *Euphrates*. His account of the war was published fifty years afterwards:

> The marshal disembarked and all the army paraded in front of him whilst marching from the beach to occupy its position. All the men saluted him with cries of 'Vive l'Empereur!' Everyone also knew of the poor state of his health. The disembarkation continued after dark with the unloading of artillery and horses. Our men carried their knapsacks containing eight days' rations of rice, sugar, coffee, bacon and biscuit. In front of our brigade, the 1st battalion of the 20th sent out a company a thousand metres further on to act as outposts. In the evening our pack mules arrived and our tents. A fine rain had already begun to soak us; wrapped in our overcoats, we slept after a fashion on the wet ground. On the 15th, Forey's division arrived. It disembarked in the evening in a rather rough sea and was placed in the centre of the position, close to the general headquarters.[3]

Thirty minutes after the French began landing, the first British boats reached the shore, the men jumping into the surf before taking the final few strides to the beach itself. The men of Sir George Brown's Light Division were first ashore, their large flat-bottomed boats having been towed by brawny sailors who heaved at the oars to get them from ship to shore. Octave Cullet was on shore when he was approached by a British officer, little knowing that it was Sir George Brown. He could not help noting how old he looked:

> Behind our tents and a little to the left, camped the English division of General Brown; it occupied a village that we saw far off in the plain; our men explored it soon afterwards; they returned loaded with poultry and ducks, their cans filled with a white light local wine which we enjoyed with pleasure. The wells in the village were the only ones we found in this immense plain; sutlers came to find the water needed by the army. We looked in vain to the horizon for signs of the enemy, but nowhere could we see any trace of them. The officers expressed great surprise at the inactivity of the Russians. Two English officers came and joined our conversation. One of them was an old man; their dress was simple. They wore neither epaulettes nor decorations, only black staff frock coats. These two men spoke to us in a very fatherly manner before they left us. An English officer whom we know came and told us we had been speaking with generals Brown and Codrington.[4]

The graphic descriptions of William Russell, the correspondent from *The Times*, were to gain for him great fame as one of the first war correspondents. His description of the landings at Kalamita Bay is typical of his vivid but informative style:

> A gig or cutter, pulled by eight or twelve sailors, with a paddle-box boat, flat or Turkish pinnace in tow (the latter purchased for the service), would come alongside a steamer or transport in which troops were ready for disembarkation. The officers of each company first descended, each man in full dress. Over his shoulder was slung his haversack, containing what had been, ere it underwent the process of cooking, four pounds and a half of salt meat, and a bulky mass of biscuit of the same weight. This was his ration for three days. Besides this, each officer carried his greatcoat, rolled up and fastened in a hoop round his body, a wooden canteen to hold water, a small ration of spirits, whatever change of underclothing he could manage to stow away, his forage-cap, and, in most instances, a revolver. Each private carried his blanket and greatcoat strapped up into a kind of knapsack, inside of which was a pair of boots, a pair of socks, a shirt, and, at the

request of the men themselves, a forage-cap; he also carried his water canteen, and the same rations as the officer, a portion of the mess cooking apparatus, firelock and bayonet of course, cartouche box and fifty rounds of ball-cartridge for Minié, sixty rounds for the smooth-bore arms.[5]

Major Daniel Lysons, of the 23rd Royal Welsh Fusiliers, was one of the first ashore:

We arrived off our landing-place by daylight the day before yesterday at about 7 o'clock. Boats from Admiral Dundas's flagship, *The Britannia*, came alongside our ship, and I was ordered to get our men into them as quick as I could. I did so, and went off with about 60 men into men of war boats, one towing the other.

When we started no other boat was moving from the fleet. After we had got about half way towards land we saw a gig shoot out from our headquarters ship, the *Emperor*. The naval officer in charge of our boats, Lieutenant Vesey, shouted to his men to 'give way,' and they did so with a will. The soldiers sitting on the thwarts between them also gave their weight to the oars. Our heavy boats boiled through the water, the gig flew after us, it was a close race. At length we shot up onto the beach, and the big barge which we were towing, crashed up alongside of us. I jumped along the thwarts and was the first soldier to land, my men followed me. Sir George Brown was a minute or two after me, then the men from the barge and Drewe. No one opposed us, so we formed up. The rest of our men and the 7th came next.[6]

By midday on the 14th, the beaches at Kalamita Bay were swarming with British, French and Turkish soldiers. There was, naturally, much confusion, despite the elaborate arrangements that had been made. Horses ran loose, men wandered around, lost and looking for their commanding officers, whilst sergeants bellowed loudly, calling men to their mustering positions. Given the state of affairs on the landing beaches it seems remarkable that Menshikov did not attempt to interfere in any way. Even a relatively small force of Russian troops would surely have made the landings incredibly difficult, and the consequences catastrophic for the entire expedition. But, other than a few Cossacks and Russian officers, who sat somewhat inquisitively making notes, no other Russian troops appeared on the scene to make a nuisance of themselves. The only 'enemy' presence came in the form of the local Tartars who, quick to see an opportunity to make some money, were on the scene with sheep, cattle and vegetables, which the Allies were only too happy to purchase. They also proved very useful in supplying the Allies with much-needed intelligence of the whereabouts of the Russian troops in and around Sevastopol. One French soldier wrote:

> The Allied troops disembarked and camped between the Old Fort and the beach. The inhabitants had not been informed of our coming, and with news of the appearance of a large army many took refuge in Sebastopol. Some of our scouts found a hundred oxen in a meadow and seized some of them, but, much to the amazement of the Tartar who owned them, the troops paid him for all of them. The news encouraged other Tartars to come forward in order to do business with the Allied army.[7]

Jean Joseph Gustave Cler, of the 2nd Zouaves, took a patrol inland to explore an abandoned house. The occupants had evidently left in a hurry:

> The disorder, in which every thing seemed to be, showed plainly, how precipitate had been the flight of the master. Just opposite to a glass door, which opened out upon one of the terraces, a handsome piano stood open, its top strewed over with pieces of French and German music; – upon a stand in the middle of the parlour, lay scattered a confused heap of those innumerable little trifles, with which women of elegant tastes so love to surround themselves; – portraits of the colonel and his lady hung suspended from the walls; while, upon a work-table, in a corner of the room, lay an open volume of Lamartine's poetry, – showing that the fair mistress of the house was busy with thoughts of France, even at the very moment when a French army was disembarking within but a few hundred paces of her lordly residence.[8]

At two o'clock in the afternoon Marshal Saint-Arnaud himself reached the shore and, mounting his horse, proceeded to ride down the lines of his cheering troops. By the evening of 14 September the French had landed the bulk of their force, although they would not complete their operation for a day or two. All five divisions of British infantry – the 1st, 2nd, 3rd, 4th and Light – had also got themselves ashore, although the cavalry and artillery had to wait until the following day to complete their own respective disembarkations. Sir

Edward Colebrooke was a non-combatant who had travelled to the Crimea with, amongst others, Alexander Kinglake, the future chronicler of the war. Colebrooke, whose passage had been secured largely through his friendship with Admiral Boxer, later described the beaches:

> The beach on which we landed was a strip of land, scarcely a hundred yards in breadth and about a mile in length; a salt water lake extending about a mile inwards, protected the landing. The Guards and Highlanders were forming as we got ashore, and soon marched off to the right. After walking about on the beach for awhile, amused with the exciting scene, and greeting our friends, much disguised with beards, we walked up the hill to the right, which was already occupied by the Light and 3rd Division not far from the landing place. Here we found ourselves on a wide undulating plain, covered with corn, cut but not carried. There were but few traces of dwellings. We went as far as our outposts, which consisted of Rifles. Not a sign of an enemy. The appearance of three persons in plain clothes walking in from the plain caused some surprise, and an officer asked us where on earth we came from. The day now became dull and threatening, and everything betokened a wet afternoon and night; the rain in fact began to fall before we got again on board. The soldiers looked bronzed and healthy for the most part, and their beards and the absence of a stock gave them a rough and ready look, but many of the 79th Highlanders, who marched past us, were weak and sickly.[9]

In the meantime, the troops that had come ashore were given a taste of what they could expect later in the campaign, when the 'black and lowering' skies opened up, soaking all of the British troops – for no tents had been landed – and those of the French who could not get under cover, the majority of the French having landed with their small campaign tents. Even the senior British officers, including Sir George Brown and the Duke of Cambridge, had no shelter, the former trying to sleep under a cart, and the latter simply lying down in his waterproof coat. Only De Lacy Evans appears to have had a tent. An officer with the 4th Division, Lieutenant George Peard, described their situation on the beach:

> We were left on the narrow strip of beach which separates the Salt Lake from the sea, where we had landed. It was a very low, unhealthy

spot, and our men suffered much from cholera, which generally carried them off after three or four hours' illness. We now took up our position for the night, just before dusk, and piled our arms. At dusk our men lay down under them, for the first night's campaign in the Crimea. Before our first hour's sleep however had passed over, we were aroused by a drenching rain, and before long were wet to the skin; so there was nothing left for us but to congregate around the huge bonfires the men had made out of the broken barrels and planks they had picked up upon the beach.

Of all the miserable nights I ever spent in my life, this was the most wretched: its discomforts it would be impossible to describe. It gave us a little foretaste of the comforts we were likely to enjoy in the Crimean campaign.[10]

William McMillan, a 29-year-old Scot, had landed with the Coldstream Guards. Soon to be promoted corporal and then sergeant, McMillan woke stiff and cold on the morning of the 15th after a miserable night spent lying on some weeds. He entered his experiences into a small diary which he kept throughout the campaign. Although McMillan could read and write his grammar left something to be desired:

It was dark when we halted last night and the rain came down in torrents. We got a few dead weeds to lay on and we lay all night exposed to the pelting storm with nothing to protect us or cover us from the rain. We kept our belts on all the time and our firelocks piled near us. When I got up this morning I was that stiff I scarce could stand, the men got together some of the weed we had to lay on and made fires. I managed to boil about half a pint of water after a great deal of trouble in getting nearly blinded with smoke and made some tea. Went to a small village about two miles off to get some water. They had plenty of corn in small stacks and put in long rows like walls. Indeed their yards was walled around with it. There was a lot of Frenchmen there and they were taken away everything they could lay their hands on, fowls of every description, calves, sheep, lambs, water of which there was plenty. They even took the bell out of a church, built of wood, sticks and mud, indeed nothing seemed to come amiss to them, some things they paid for but I am afraid they took most of these things for nothing. Outlying pickets of the rifles were there. I got some water out of a well it was very brackish.[11]

It was indeed a miserable first night, although it was mild compared to what lay ahead during the coming winter. Another British soldier wrote:

> The first night in the Crimea there was anything but pleasant. The enemy's country gave us a very inhospitable reception. The few inhabitants had fled, leaving nothing behind them, and even water was scarce and had to be fetched from a distance. Fuel was also scanty, so that we could not light those roaring watchfires which make a bivouac tolerable under almost any circumstances; and a hard biscuit, with a slice of still harder 'salt junk,' was not a meal to put an Englishman in particularly good humour. And to add to our discomfort, the rain began to fall; first a drizzle, and then in larger and faster drops, so we were all pretty well wet through. We were somewhat inclined to envy our allies and their little '*tentes-abris*', or 'shelter tents,' which they carry on their knapsacks, and which turn a good deal of rain.[12]

But if things were bad on shore, it was worse for those who were still offshore, attempting to land. Tossed about by the ever increasing swell, men such as Edward Bruce Hamley would have gladly settled for being on terra firma, despite the lack of shelter:

> At night, the rain came down in torrents, and the troops on the beach were drenched. Bad as their situation was, I envied it. At eight in the evening I had left the transport with another officer in a man-of-war's boat, which, assisted by two others, towed astern a large raft, formed of two clumsy boats boarded over, on which were two guns, with their detachments of artillerymen, and some horses – two of my own among them. The swell from the sea was now considerable, and made the towing of the raft a work of great labour. As we approached the shore, a horse swam past, snorting, and surrounded by phosphorescent light as he splashed rapidly by. He had gone overboard from a raft which had upset in attempting to land. The surf was dashing very heavily on the sand, though it was too dark to see. Fires made of broken boats and rafts were lit along the beach, and a voice hailed us authoritatively to put back and not attempt to land, or we should go to pieces.

Unwillingly the weary oarsman turned from the shore. The swell was increasing every moment, and the raft getting more and more unmanageable. Sometimes it seemed to pull us back, sometimes it made a plunge forward, and even struck our stern, while the rain poured down with extraordinary violence. It was a long time before we reached the nearest ships, which were tossing on the swell, and not easily to be approached. The first we hailed had already a horse-boat alongside, with Lord Raglan's horses, and needed assistance, and two or three others which we passed were unable to help us. By this time the raft was fast filling with water, and the men on it were much alarmed; and our progress was so slow that we took at least ten minutes to pull from the stern to the stem of the *Agamemnon*. At length a rope was thrown us from a transport near, whose bows were rising on the swell like a rearing horse; and, getting the artillerymen who were on board her out of bed, we hoisted in our horses and guns; – but the gun carriages, too heavy for our small number of hands, were lashed down to the raft, which was allowed to tow astern of the ship, and which presently sank till the water was up to the axles, when the *Agamemnon* sent a party and hoisted them on board, and the raft shortly after went to pieces. A horse, which had been swimming about for two hours, was also got safely on board.[13]

The landings continued throughout the following day, with the cavalry and artillery coming ashore, the operation being supervised by Captain Dacres of the *Sanspareil*. But it was a slow process. Indeed, Saint-Arnaud, sick and beginning to suffer the effects of cholera, wanted to get off the beach and begin the advance south on 17 September. However, the ever ponderous Raglan was unable to do so, citing a lack of transport. Meanwhile, Canrobert, with generals Thiery and Bizot, took themselves off on board the *Primauguet* to carry out a reconnaissance of the shoreline between the Alma and Kacha rivers to try to discover whether there had been any movement by the Russians.

In the meantime, the cavalry began coming ashore, which was not an easy business. Lieutenant Colonel George Paget, of the 4th Light Dragoons, described the difficulties:

Sept 16. We are at last landing now horses. Lucan and staff just landed. Surge rather increasing. Herds of cattle being driven in by those picturesque-looking fellows, the 'Spahis,' with their white flowing robes and veils. It is distressing to see the poor horses, as there are upset out of the boats, swimming about in all directions among the ships. They swim so peacefully, but look rather unhappy with their heads in the air and the surf driving into their poor mouths. Only one has been drowned as yet, to our knowledge. We get on but slowly with our disembarkation. The French have secured for themselves the right flank, that protected by the ships, and nearest the provisions, which gives the English the post of honour, and of hard work.[14]

Another British cavalryman, Albert Mitchell, of the 13th Light Dragoons, thought the low strip of land on which the British were coming ashore resembled the Kentish coast at Romney Marsh. Mitchell, destined to be one of Tennyson's 'Six Hundred' at Balaklava, was mightily glad to get ashore with his horse after being cooped up for the past few days aboard the *Jason*, one of the large transport ships:

The sand was not above a hundred yards wide, and beyond that there was a good sized salt lake. Into the sand we drove our pickets pegs, and picketed our horses for the night. It was very difficult to get the pegs to hold in the sand. As I was not for any duty that night, and I found a capital bed among some hay nets which had been sent on shore all filled with hay, and laid in a heap, I slept here very soundly until morning.

At an early hour a party of us were turned out to escort a number of Arabas loaded with sacks of flour. These had been stopped and taken possession of on their way to Sebastopol, I believe, by some of the men who landed here first night, but am not certain. They were taken and piled in a large heap. I never heard what became of the flour. It was there when we marched away.

After we returned to our landing place, our horses were taken to water with the rest, and we were told to get our breakfast. But that was much easier said than done, for there was no signs of wood or water so far as we could see. However, we took a camp kettle and went along the shore watching the waves as they rolled in, hoping to get a fragment of wood that washed in. This was our only chance for firewood. By dint of much patience we managed to get enough to make a fire, and after we had gone about a mile we saw a crowd of soldiers, both English and French, gathered together at one spot. On arrival there we found a small well about a dozen feet deep. The only way to get the water was for one to descend into the well and dip the water up in a tin pannikin, and so fill the kettle. We got a kettle nearly full, but were obliged to let it stand and settle and, then pour it off into another kettle. In this way we manage to get a little drinkable water and, having brought a little tea ashore, we soon had quite a nice breakfast. Soon after this the troops returned from water. They had succeeded in finding a little water, but not sufficient to give the horses their fill.[15]

Lieutenant Strange Jocelyn, of the Scots Fusilier Guards, wrote to his family from his bivouac on the evening of 16 September:

I have only this scrap of paper to write you on. But we landed with nothing but what we can carry on our backs; no tents or baggage. The first night it rained tremendously and we bivouacked on a ploughed field. It was my first experience of real hardship and it was not pleasant. I luckily had a waterproof sheet which I placed under me. Yesterday and last night were fine, and to date I hope we shall get our tents up. We have landed 25 miles from Sevastopol, near a salt lake, and expect to have to fight two battles before reaching Sevastopol. Our outposts are a little harassed by Cossacks at nights, but our Minié rifles keep them off pretty well, though there are clouds of them all around; but from all accounts there are not so many men in the Crimea as was thought. There are two rivers which we have to cross between this and Sevastopol, at each of which we expect a general action; but there is no knowing; as we are very strong they may have retreated before we come up. The French have already pillaged very much, but our soldiers I am happy to say behave very well and pay for everything, as of old in the Peninsula. Altogether it is an odd thing to be in an enemy's country, without any opposition, but I suppose we are too strong for them, though I have no doubt at Sevastopol we shall have hot work. I have not washed or had my clothes off for three days, as we have only just water enough for drinking. They have just come for my letter. Excuse this scrawl, but it is written on the ground on a ploughed field.[16]

Two days later Jocelyn wrote again, this time to report some improvements in conditions:

We had two more nights' bivouacking, but now I am happy to say have got a few tents, that is, we have one between 6 officers, but even that is luxury compared to sleeping in a wet ploughed field. I do not think I told you that on landing Gen. Browne, who advanced with his A.D.C. to reconnoitre, was nearly being taken prisoner by some Cossacks, but the Rifles, who were not far behind him, sent a few bullets in amongst them, that soon put them to flight. The army is now nearly all ready, and I believe we advance today, or tomorrow.[17]

There were further delays on 18 September, again caused by the British and their enormous quantity of impedimenta – at least according to the French – but by the evening of 18 September the entire Allied force, of 61,400 infantry, 1,200 cavalry and 137 guns, was ashore, and so Saint-Arnaud resolved to march the following day, whether the British were ready or not. Captain Octave Cullet expressed his frustration at the delays:

The 16th, 17th and 18th of September were passed in a state of inactivity. It was not difficult for us to see that the English were the cause of the delay. This might be disastrous as it allowed Prince Mentschikoff time to strengthen his position which sits on the road to Sebastopol.[18]

Cullet was also somewhat concerned to learn of the prospects that awaited the Allies a few miles to the south:

The few Tartars who appeared in the camp, whom we made prisoners, gave us a good account of the position and size of the Russian army. A rumour began to spread through our ranks that fifty thousand men, with many guns and cavalry, were waiting for us to the south, on heights with very difficult access. They said no army in the world would dare to climb the heights under such a heavy fire from a resolute and well-led enemy.[19]

On 19 September the Allies finally began their march south towards Sevastopol. The French Army marched with its right flank resting on the coast, having the protection of the Allied fleet. Its formation took the shape of an 'immense lozenge' with the 1st Division and artillery leading the way, covered on their right by the 2nd Division and the 3rd Division on its left. The 4th Division of the French Army, along with the Turkish contingent, formed the rearguard. The baggage marched in the centre. By contrast, the British moved in two great columns. The left column consisted of the Light Division, leading, behind which came the 1st and 4th Divisions. The right-hand column consisted of the 2nd and 3rd Divisions. The baggage followed behind. The British cavalry, meanwhile, covered the British column from the front and flank. Lord Cardigan rode in front at the head of two regiments of his light cavalry, the 11th Hussars and 13th Light Dragoons, whilst the 8th Hussars and 17th Lancers covered the left flank of the column. Lord George Paget and the 4th Light Dragoons brought up the rear. Octave Cullet again described the march:

> On our left was the English army, but as always a few hours late. The weather was superb; there was no obstacle anywhere in these vast steppes to embarrass the march of our columns. Frightened hares, surrounded by our columns, leapt about everywhere beneath our soldiers' feet.[20]

Despite the discomfort experienced during the march – at least by the British troops – the Allies' march towards Sevastopol on that hot, sunny day presented a wonderful sight. The British infantry in their predominantly red coats, the French, and Cardigan's light cavalry, resplendent in a mixture of blue, crimson, red and gold, made for a spectacular sight. The bands played, colours danced in the breeze, bits jingled and harness creaked, and all the time the sun shone brightly overhead, creating a perfect autumn day. But it was the sun that quickly proved to be the undoing of the men. Indeed, the uplifting beat of the regimental bands soon gave way to the wearied, muffled groans of men falling out, suffering from cholera, which now returned with a vengeance. Things had been bad enough at Varna, but there had been signs that the plague had given way. It was a false hope, however, to which scores of ashen-faced bodies, crumpled up in agony and strewn across the plain, now testified. Fortunately, cholera would not rip through the Allied camps before Sevastopol as it had done at Varna, although death through sickness and disease would prove the major killer amongst the Allies in the Crimea. Not all victims died, however, as Albert Mitchell recalled:

> As we marched away we left two poor fellows on the sand. They appeared to be in the last stage of cholera. The assistant-surgeon stayed with them, but had no hope of their recovery; but, contrary to his

expectations, they both rallied, and were sent on board ship. They both recovered, and rejoined us in a month quite well. They both said the doctor had nothing with him but rum, which he gave them to drink freely of, so they believed the rum cured them.

After leaving the seashore we ascended the rising ground, and on arriving at the top found a nearly level plateau. We followed the road leading inland. As the day wore on it became very hot, so much so that we suffered much from thirst. Our water barrels were long since empty. We saw French infantry soldiers and some of our Guardsmen fetching water, but they had to go a long way for it, so could not afford to give us a drink. One Guardsman had a full kettle, and passing by me I offered him a shilling for a drink, but he declined the offer. I certainly had the pleasure of seeing the water, that was all. Soon after this we arrived at a village, where we landed and bivouacked for the night. As soon as possible after picketing our horses, we started to procure water. There was a good large well, and a great number of men around it. We managed to quench our thirst and fill our barrels.[21]

Despite the ravages of cholera, the Allied advance upon Sevastopol continued with just the odd burning farmhouse here and there. Otherwise the landscape was bare and devoid of any buildings, with little to interrupt the view across the vast, grassy plain. However, every now and then a lone horseman was spotted, giving the Allies some indication of the presence of the Russians, although there was still no sign of any large bodies of Russian troops. On the afternoon of the 18th, however, Cardigan's cavalry came into contact with groups of Cossacks who sat keeping a wary eye on the invaders. Albert Mitchell was amongst those sent forward to confront the Cossacks, and he left some interesting comments about the effectiveness of British cavalry carbines:

Part of our troop, which was the right troop, was thrown out in skirmishing order, and advanced nearly to the top of the rising ground before there was any move made by the enemy. However, they did not keep us waiting long. There appeared to be two regiments of cavalry. They were comfortably dismounted, resting themselves. Probably they were the same party we had been in search of two days before. They very soon got mounted, and threw out eighty-five skirmishers, nearly as many as our party altogether, for we were not much more than one hundred strong that day. The number of our skirmishers was twenty-five, so it was anything but an equal match.

They soon commenced firing as we retired at a walk, but as their shots did not come anywhere near us, the officer in charge of our skirmishers told us not to waste ammunition, and not to return their fire, unless they came closer. It must be borne in mind that at that time we were armed with the old smooth-bore carbine, with which you will be lucky, indeed, if you hit a man at a hundred yards. They did not come nearer, but allowed us to return to our camp without any attempt on their part at cutting off our retreat, which they might have tried to do, considering their great superiority in numbers. We continued to walk the whole way back, and about two miles before we reached camp the enemy called in his skirmishers and retired.[22]

The Allied advance continued, and by the afternoon of the 19th they had reached the Bulganak river, the first of four rivers that lay in their path towards Sevastopol. The Bulganak was, in fact, little more than a small stream and was certainly no barrier. What was rather inconvenient, however, was the sudden appearance of a Russian force, estimated to be in the region of around 2,000 and mainly Cossacks, which was positioned on the brow of a hill on the south bank of the Bulganak. Cullet again:

> After four hours' march, we arrived at a range of relatively low hills which bordered a wide and gentle valley; we could not see far in front of us because of a line of raised slopes running perpendicular to the sea. In front of us lay a gullied plain. In front of us there were some parties of Cossacks and, ahead, on the heights, there were more bodies of cavalry. Far away on the plateau which crowned the chain of heights there were tents and long lines which seemed to be moving. It was the Russian army.[23]

Cardigan immediately sent forward a patrol which discovered that, in addition to the Cossacks, there were also two hussar regiments and a brigade of infantry, the whole force being commanded by Lieutenant General V Kir'yakov. Both the 11th Hussars and the 13th Light Dragoons pushed forward, with Cardigan and Lord Lucan in attendance. Skirmishers were then sent out in front at intervals of 10 to 12 yards as the Cossacks moved forward. The British cavalry had barely wheeled into line, ready for action, when Raglan and Airey saw in the valley beyond the glint of bayonets, whilst dark masses of cavalry were spotted also. Raglan immediately ordered the cavalry to halt and retire, whilst at the same time ordering forward the 2nd and Light Divisions, as well as the 8th Hussars and the 17th Lancers. Cardigan's men had just begun to fall back when some Russian guns appeared and opened fire, causing light casualties. The Russians' fire was quickly returned, however, by the 6-pounder guns attached to the cavalry, C Troop and I Troop, and by the divisional 9-pounder guns of the 2nd Division. The fire from these guns, commanded by Captains Brandling, Maude and Henry, settled the business, for the shot from their guns sent the obviously reluctant Russians hurrying to limber up and move off, their infantry and cavalry following likewise. Regimental Sergeant Major Loy Smith was with the 11th Hussars as they advanced against the Russians:

> After marching across beautiful undulating country for some 10 miles, we came to the River Bulganak. It was but a small stream, not more than knee deep. We rode through it and ascended the hill in front; the 11th and 13th being now some distance in advance of the main body of the Army, the Cossack skirmishers retiring before us. On gaining the crest of the hill, we came in sight of the main body of Cossacks, spread out in skirmishing order in a beautiful valley about a mile across and two miles in length. The scenery was magnificent. The 13th skirmishers were still in front. As we descended the hill, the two regiments being in line, we lost sight of our Army. When about half way across the valley, we halted; the Cossack skirmishers were twice as many as ours.
>
> It was now that the first shot of the campaign was fired. A Cossack directly in front of the 11th raised his carbine and fired. It was instantly taken up by the whole line. Our trumpets now sounded the 'Fire,' so that we beheld for the first time skirmishing in reality, for we could now hear the bullets. This continued for some little time, when the crest of the hill in front suddenly became lit up with the glitter of swords and lances. Lord Cardigan now gave the order, 'Draw Swords – skirmishers In – Trot.' The ground in front of us was uphill. As we moved off we began to throw off our haynets. Most reluctantly I threw off mine. By doing so both my horse and myself lost part of our suppers. We had not proceeded far, when an aide-de-camp galloped up with an order from Lord Raglan that we were to retire. His Lordship had seen from the hill behind us that the enemy were in force just below the brow of the hill in front of us. The Cossacks now called in their skirmishers and were

galloping rapidly across our left, ready to take us in flank should we charge their regular cavalry, or they us. It was a clever move. The Horse Artillery gave them a shot or two which made them keep a respectful distance.

At this point, the 1st and 3rd squadrons of the 11th Hussars went about and retired a hundred yards, leaving the 2nd and 4th squadrons halted facing this body of cavalry.

> No other troops were visible to us at this time. The 1st and 3rd squadrons now halted and fronted; we then went about to retire through their intervals. We had not proceeded far, when I heard the rattle of wheels behind us. On looking round I saw a Russian battery coming at a gallop down the hill behind us. They then halted and unlimbered; we could distinctly hear the trails come to the ground. In another moment a loud report, and a cannon ball passed through us, followed quickly by a round from every gun in the battery. A body of infantry had followed them and formed square. Our 'I' and 'C' Troops RHA had come up and were behind us at this time, unlimbered for action. The 11th now inclined to their left and the 13th to their right. The moment we had cleared the front, they opened fire and soon compelled not only the artillery and infantry to retire, but the cavalry also. The 8th and 17th had now come up to our support. In this affair Private Henry of the 11th had his foot shot off – from the effects of which he died on the 6th of the following month. A sergeant of the 13th lost his right hand, also two men were wounded and five horses killed.[24]

Albert Mitchell was with the 13th Light Dragoons as they faced up to the Russian cavalry on the Bulganak river:

> We did not cross by the bridge, but forded the stream lower down. We were ordered to fill our barrels, if possible, so we dismounted for that purpose. The 11th were called in, and we being again remounted, were sent on at a trot to take their place. Lord Cardigan went with us. After trotting about two miles in column of troops up a gently rising ground, we came in sight of a line of the enemy's skirmishers in our front. Half the right troop (to which I belonged) was sent out to oppose them.

They allowed us to get within two hundred yards of them, when they retired. We followed until they arrived at the top of a steeper rising ground.

Here they made a stand and we still advanced until we were within about a hundred yards of them. As before, their skirmishers were more numerous than ours, and they soon opened fire, which we promptly returned. They were better situated than we were, for as they were on top of the hill, they could easily rein back out of our sight and then come forward and fire, and then back again. We only being halfway up the hill, had no cover. I was the third file from the right to the line, and opposite to me I saw a man, whom I supposed was an officer or non-commissioned officer. He appeared to be directing the left of their skirmishers, as he was continually shouting words of command. I fired several shots at him, and believe he was hit by the last shot, for he reined back out of sight, and the next moment a riderless horse was galloping along the crest of the hill. At any rate, he did not show himself any more. I expect we had been nearly half an hour skirmishing. They hit none of us; a few of theirs got hit, which proved that bad as our carbines were, theirs were still worse. The trumpets now sounded 'Rally to the left.' This gave us who were on the right a good long trot, so strapping our carbines as we went, we quickly drew swords. The adjutant, who was in command of a party gave the word, 'Threes right, leading threes right wheel,' and led the route towards the regiment. Just at this time, the enemy brought a couple of guns about half way down the hill, and before we reached the regiment, let fly a couple of round shot at us. They both passed over our heads, making a most unpleasant noise. In another minute we were formed in our place in line on the right of the regiment. They still kept on firing as fast as they could, each time with greater precision, for we were not moved, but had to sit still, not quite so motionless as statues, but quite unable to do more just at that time. By this time the 11th had come up and formed on our right. Several shells burst close to us, and some fell in the ranks; one struck the Troop horse a few files on my left. It struck him in the side, and bursting inside the horse, cleaned him out as though a butcher had done it. His rider and the next man were both wounded and taken to the rear, and afterwards sent home to England.

Our Horse Artillery now galloped up, and quickly came into action just as the enemy was moving a column of infantry round the spur of the hill opposite our right. Captain Maude was in command, and his first discharge disabled one of the guns that had been practising on us. We saw the splinters fly in the air quite plain. The next round (a shell) landed in the centre of the column of infantry. They did not wait for a second, but scampered off the same way they had come as fast as they were able. Some batteries of Field Artillery had by this time arrived on the scene, and came into action on our left, firing several rounds at them.[25]

In his book *Un régiment de ligne*, Captain Octave Cullet relates that the French were involved in the fight also, something which is often overlooked in most British accounts of the Crimean War. Indeed, he claims it was the French who were attacked first of all:

Two companies were detached to act as a forward guard twelve hundred meters in front of our battle line. Colonel Labadie came himself and selected the two companies of the 20th Ligne, from Thomas's brigade. The first company was placed on a small rise, the second slightly to the rear on the slope of a ravine. A piquet of thirty men from the same company was thrown out, four or five hundred metres beyond. In the middle of the ravine, amidst some burning farms, some parties of Cossacks were hiding; facing us, on the opposite slope, there was a body of cavalry whose weapons glinted in the sun. Hardly had the officer returned to our camp than a regiment of uhlans descended into the ravine, passed to the left of the burning farms and made straight for our outpost.

The situation was critical; our men took their weapons and prepared to defend themselves against the cavalry. The enemy were not more than three hundred meters when suddenly the scene changed. From behind a small rise on our left which covered the English outposts, a group of twenty-five English hussars suddenly emerged at the gallop. They discharged their carbines at the enemy and withdrew. The Russians were astonished by their audacity. At the same time an English battery, which had followed these riders, opened fire on the Russian cavalry. On our right, some pieces of artillery from Canrobert's division arrived at the gallop, and sent some balls into the middle of the uhlans who stopped and, turning abruptly, galloped off to the foot of the heights.[26]

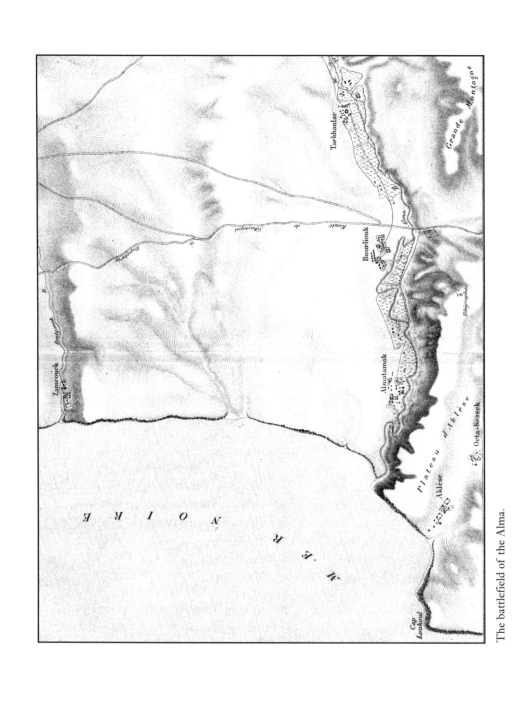

The battlefield of the Alma.

Cullet also relates an unfortunate incident that occurred just beforehand:

> A few moments before this skirmish, a staff officer rode in front of us, driving his horse towards the plain; we recognised him as Colonel Lagondie, who had travelled with us on the *Euphrates*. Owing to his poor eyesight, he rode straight into the middle of a party of enemy soldiers who he thought were English. He was surrounded and taken prisoner before he could turn.[27]

The Russians duly retired after this first skirmish and drew off to the south towards the river Alma. Cardigan's men likewise retired and returned to join the main British force. In all, it was a satisfying end to the Allies' first encounter with the Russian Army in the Crimea, with casualties – all British – of two men wounded and five horses killed. It was also the first example of Raglan's reluctance to use the British cavalry, probably as a result of his being present during several high-profile misadventures of the British cavalry during the Peninsular War and Waterloo campaign, where he saw at first hand what British cavalry could do when given their head. Indeed, as with many aspects of the campaign in the Crimea, Raglan allowed events from the distant past – the only experience of war that he had ever had – to influence him far too much.

But it was a good start to the campaign in the Crimea, and on that same evening the British and French armies bivouacked on the banks of the Bulganak stream. Rations of rum and meat were served out, after which the casks were broken up and the staves used to make fires for cooking, helped by nettles and long grass. Lieutenant Peard, of the 20th Regiment, was looking forward to a well-earned rest after a long day's march, but was dismayed to find himself ordered out on piquet duty:

> Our men commenced to gather the scorched weeds and thistles, to make fires to cook their rations, and all seemed delighted that this long, fatiguing day's march was over. I had scarcely washed myself in the stream, and swallowed some cold pork, when I was informed that I was to go, with two other officers and several men, on outlying picket, which was not a particularly pleasant duty after so hard a march in the broiling sun. The enemy were very near us, and we rather expected an attack. The night was very dark, and the fires in our camp shone bright and clear when I left it, as our picket post was at some little distance, and our sentries were thrown out all around the Division, to ensure its

safety and to guard against being surprised during the night. I went down for orders to Lord Raglan's quarters (the Imperial Post-house), and a very good house it was. Nearly everything had been taken out of it by the Russians, except a few bundles of herbs which hung in the kitchen, and a solitary pea-fowl, which was found at the door, and which I have no doubt afforded his Lordship a sumptuous supper.

I shall not easily forget my vain endeavours to find the bridge over the river in the dark, and walking up to my knees in the water. This little casualty did not, it may be imagined, tend to make me more comfortable for the night. Sleep was out of the question, for the sentries had to be visited every hour; and when the morning dawned, it found us wet through with the dew, which was heavier than I had ever before experienced.

Fortunately nothing occurred to prevent our men having a good night's rest; and at daybreak we drew in our sentries, and returned to the camp, where we found they had all finished their breakfasts, and were ready for a start. Many had died during the night. I was buckling my cloak on my pony, and had given up all idea of breakfast, when I espied a pot of coffee boiling on a fire, and found on approaching it that it belonged to the Quartermaster Sergeant, who immediately offered me a portion of it. I believe it saved my life, and I am sure he will say I was grateful for it.[28]

The French likewise threw out their piquets, making sure to keep a wary eye open lest the Russians try a surprise attack at night:

The night arrived; it was wet and cold. Commandant Leblanc, of the 22nd, came to visit our outposts. The companies had dug a ditch around them, whose epaulement would shelter them during the night. 'Men,' said the commandant, 'you are well advanced. It will be difficult to send help to you if you are attacked; be ready and hold steady.' Our work was finished by midnight; our knapsacks, the pack-mules and our canteens were placed by the entrance of our small redoubt; we could repulse several squadrons. The Cossacks came to reoccupy the farms in the ravine. All along the French line the guards were doubled.[29]

The first barrier on the road to Sevastopol had been passed with little effort, although the real test would come the following day on the banks of the second barrier, the river Alma.

Chapter 6

The Russians

We read much about the British and, to a lesser extent, the French armies in the Crimea. But what of the men whom Menshikov would send against the Allies? There were two very different sides to the Russian Army of the Crimean War. On one hand, the czar possessed an army which, like the British Army, suffered in the aftermath of the defeat of Napoleon, for even as endless parades were being held to mark the defeat of the French, the czar's army was slipping slowly into a state of some decay which, whilst not being on the same scale as that which plagued the British, was nevertheless damaging. On the other hand, the Russian Army was, in some ways, comparable to the French – which had seen action in Algeria – on account of the campaigning it had seen in the Caucasus and on the Danube, and in various trouble spots in the Russian Empire that had required military intervention. In this way, both officers and privates in the Russian Army gained much useful training and fighting experience.

According to the report of the minister of war, dated 1 January 1853, Russia possessed about 1,400,000 regular and irregular troops, including 31,400 generals and other officers. There were 1,151,408 regular troops, including 938,731 men on active service and 212,677 on indefinite and one-year leave. Irregular troops numbered 245,850, including 89,168 who were on active service. The infantry formed two-thirds of the total number. Regular troops were organized into six army corps: I to IV Corps were front-line troops, deployed in the west; V Corps was situated to the south of Podolye and Novorossiya, and VI Corps was based in the central regions. Both V and VI Corps, together with the reserve cavalry, were under the control of the minister of war and made up the strategic reserve of the front-line forces. The Guards and Grenadier corps were located in the outskirts of St Petersburg. Some regiments – the Kavkazsky, Orenburgsky, Sibirsky – and the troops located in Finland had their own staff and structure and were under the Caucasian governor-general.[1] The majority of the troops who took part in the Alma battle were the troops of the VI Infantry Corps which was sent to the Crimea in December 1853 at the request of Prince Menshikov, who was concerned at the relatively low number of troops at his disposal. By April 1854 two more divisions, 17 and 18, arrived in the Crimea.

In each of the six infantry corps there were three divisions with four regiments in each. After 1840 each regiment consisted of four battalions with one administrative company and two reserve battalions (5th and 6th), which in peacetime were amalgamated into a single reserve battalion. In each corps the reserve battalions formed the reserve divisions, the numbers of which corresponded to the number of the corps. Two regiments formed a brigade, which was not the tactical unit but an administrative unit to manage the divisional troops. Like the British and French armies, the main tactical unit of the Russian Army was the battalion. Each corps in turn had a cavalry division which consisted of two brigades with two cavalry regiments in each.

Despite the deterioration of the inter-war years the Russian infantry of the mid-nineteenth century was still a formidable and well-trained fighting force, but it was the deterioration that was the problem, for although the infantry remained steady and numerous, few advances had been made in terms of tactics and training and the principles of war generally. Essentially, the Russian Army of 1854 had developed little since the heady days of 1812. This is explained by the overall backwardness of the Russian Empire itself, which reached its zenith during the reign of Nicholas I. The only achievements during the inter-war years were a far more effective and quicker system of mobilization and the creation of a distinct structure of the army reserves.

When a man from the western part of the empire was conscripted into the Russian Army his period of service was 20 years, as opposed to the 25-year term to which all those living in the east were subjected. In the Guards regiments they served for 22 years, whilst recruits from the military settlements served for 20 years. Criminals, tramps and other 'good-for-nothing' men were often sentenced to serve in the army, whilst noblemen had the right to send a serf to the army if he was a disagreeable fellow. Indeed, this is how the famous Russian sailor Pyotr Koshka, who distinguished himself during the siege of Sevastopol, found himself in the service of his czar.

In peacetime, a steady system of recruitment kept the army up to strength. According to the regulations of 1854, 'ordinary' recruiting took recruits no younger than 22 years of age. 'Urgent' recruiting made it possible for the army to recruit anything from seven to ten men out of every thousand, their age being of no importance, whilst in time of war or crisis 'extreme' recruiting permitted the army to take more than ten men from each thousand. During the Crimean War the army units were formed mainly from regular units from garrisons and from reserve battalions.[2]

According to the recruiting regulations of 1831, recruitment took place during the last two months of each year. Since 1851, in order to save money and to improve the lot of the soldiers from the lower ranks, a system of 'indefinite leave' was introduced, whereby it was possible to transfer soldiers to the reserve after fifteen years' service (twenty years from 1854). In the case of an emergency or in time of war these soldiers were drafted again and formed a ready-trained army reserve. The Russian Empire had the potential to mobilize huge numbers of men and, indeed, by the end of the Crimean War would mobilize almost 2 million men.

In addition to regular recruitment, there was one other means of obtaining manpower for the Russian Army. This was the so-called military cantonists, the children of soldiers who had been trained in military settlement schools. The more intelligent amongst them were taken for the elite corps, or to training regiments where they became non-commissioned officers. In 1854, owing to the Crimean War and in order to strengthen the officers' staff, the length of time a corporal had to serve before being promoted to an NCO was reduced twice, from six years to one year, depending upon the man himself.[3]

The army constitution in 1844 forbad the employment of foreigners who had served in the army previously but had since retired, largely because there were too many adventurers amongst them. However, in 1853, and with war looming, it was decided to change the policy and allow the army to take volunteers from neutral countries. Many served in the Russian Army in the Crimea, particularly as officers, although most appear to have been given the rank 'zauryad' (mediocre).[4]

The conditions of service were very poor and demanded improvement, for despite the poor conditions in the British Army they were nowhere near as bad as those in Russia. Indeed, compared with conditions in other European armies, the state of the Russian soldier was by far the worst, and despite the army's reasonably high level of medical services diseases brought about by lack of decent food were widespread. One contemporary writer was moved to remark that the soldiers may well have been the decoration of the empire but they were not its strength. Indeed, long before the Crimean War the Marquis de Cuistin had noted in his memoirs:

> The Army, which is outstanding in terms of its discipline and good military bearing when on parade, consists, except for a few selected corps, of soldiers who are neatly dressed on the parade-ground but untidily in the barracks. Their unhealthy, grey complexion speaks of

hunger and destitution, and all this because the commissaries rob the poor men shamelessly.[5]

Captain Hodasevich, a Polish officer serving in the Russian Army, left a very detailed insight into conditions:

He receives ninety kopecks for four months' service (about 3s.), of which, however, he never gets more than sixty kopecks, nor even that if his Colonel has thought his diet required improvement. The rest of the money goes for various stoppages; there is $1^{1}/2$ kopecks for the barber of the company; about three kopecks for an image of some saint belonging to the regiment, before which a lamp is supposed to be continually burning; then the men have to find their own caps, and they are charged a percentage for changing the money, which is usually paid in twenty-five or fifty rouble notes. Besides this he gets ninety kopecks a year to supply himself with the necessary things to clean his arms and accoutrements. A corporal receives one rouble fifteen kopecks (about 3s. 10d.) every four months, and a sergeant-major three roubles (about 10s.), of course subject to the same stoppages as the soldier. Besides their pay, each soldier receives the leather for two pairs of boots a year, but he must make them himself or pay for the making; a suit of uniform every two years, and a grey great-coat every three years; coarse linen for three shirts every year, and for the lining of their uniform; this linen of the worst possible quality. All the articles of clothing provided by the Government must be worn the full time, and, to enable the men to keep their things in order, a certain sum is allowed every year to the men for repairs; but during the four years I served in the Russian army, I never saw or heard of a soldier receiving this money. What then becomes of it? is the natural question. It goes into the Colonel's pocket. If a man in charge of the company should ever dare ask about all these things, he will soon find himself struck off the list of captains, and turned adrift.[6]

The Russian cavalry set themselves apart from the rest of the army, still bathing in the glory of the 1812 campaign. They continued to consider themselves an elite, but the glorious cavalry era was fading fast. Nicholas I instigated several changes to the organization of his cavalry at various times during his reign. No other branch of the army was reformed more times than the cavalry. The regulations alone were changed three times.

Not including reserve units, the Russian cavalry in September 1854 consisted of 59 regiments, 454 squadrons, 93,368 men and 61,759 horses. Irregular cavalry consisted of the Cossack regiments, divisions, hundreds and batteries, numbering more than 80,000 men in the European seat of the Crimean War. Cuirassiers were armed with sword and pistol, with those in the first line having a lance also. Lancers had sabre, lance and pistol, whilst hussars were armed with sabre, two pistols and a carbine. In each squadron, 16 men had rifled carbines to operate whilst skirmishing.

An unusual feature of the Russian cavalry was that the horses were selected according to the colours for the regiments and sometimes for the squadrons. In 1833 regulations stated that the 1st regiments of cuirassiers were to be mounted on bay horses, the 2nd regiments on dark bay, the 3rd regiments on sorrel and the 4th on black. The 1st regiments of the dragoons and light cavalry in the 1st regiments had bay horses, the 2nd regiments grey, and the 3rd and 4th black. All trumpeters were mounted on grey horses. Cavalry tactics had not changed greatly since the Napoleonic wars. The line was used during the charge, whilst all other manoeuvres on the battlefield were done in column. The troopers who skirmished on the flanks formed a line ahead.

Under Czar Nicholas I, military parades and shows virtually became the basis of the army system, for instead of normal military training involving field manoeuvres, musketry drill and so on, the Russian Army was turned into a sort of military machine which went through various evolutions on the parade ground which, although pleasing to the eye, were of little use on the battlefield. It was clear to everybody, including the foreigners. For example, Colonel F Gagern was amongst the retinue of the Dutch prince Alexander Oransky during a review of the Russian Army at St Petersburg. He was shocked to see just how pedantic and fussy the emperor was in demanding strict adherence to dress regulations and to drill:

> Even in the field he wanted to maintain this pedantic correctness and fastidiousness. For example, he forbad the practice which those soldiers marching with long coats used to adopt, of tucking up the flaps of their coats in order to make marching more comfortable.[7]

A visiting Prussian general was equally dismissive of the Russians, and in particular the officers, whom he saw training at Peterghof:

The material of this formidable army, as everybody knows, is perfect.
But fortunately for us, all of the commanding officers, without
exception, are absolutely useless, while the majority of the higher
ranking officers are no better. Only a small number of generals think
about their real vocation; the others, on the other hand, think that they
have achieved everything once they have managed to lead their
regiment in a march-past in front of the Czar. Nobody thinks about the
correct training for the officers or of the appropriate exercises for the
troops.[8]

Denis Davidov, one of the heroes of the 1812 campaign against Napoleon, best
summed up the new trends within the army that characterized the officer corps
in Nicholas' reign. Gone were the long days of drilling and training in the field
for future combat. What was now important was:

the in-depth inspection of small straps, the rules regarding toe
stretching, the dressing of ranks, and ensuring the correct position of
guns. These are demonstrated by all our leading generals and officers
who take the regulations as a mark of perfection and give them the
greatest of pleasure and delight. This is why the army is being
gradually taken over by the rude ignoramuses who take great pleasure
in devoting their lives to the study of the trifles of the military
regulations.[9]

Much of this was due to Nicholas I himself, who published *Regulations on the
Service in Garrison*, which had great influence over his officers. These exceeded
even the rigorous regulations laid down by Pavel I. It also led to more criticism
from Davidov, who added, 'the system of the Russian Army has prevented the
talented officers from getting on, whilst at the same time allowing the many
dullards not only to gain a foothold in the army but to expel the gifted ones
everywhere'.[10]

Captain Hodasevich was another who was critical of the Russian system of
drill and of the generals in particular:

The General of Division frequently inspected us, and drilled the men
in marching without ever taking the trouble to ascertain whether the
men knew how to load or fire their pieces, or anything about
skirmishing, which are absolutely necessary for every man to know, in

order to be of use in war-time. But the Russian generals, or at least a large portion of them, seem to think that if their men can march well, with their toes pointed and their bodies inflexible, the main object is gained. But it has been of late repeatedly proved by experience that this is not enough.[11]

Even the much-vaunted Russian bayonet drill suffered as a result of this shift in emphasis from fighting skills to parade-ground perfection. Training with the bayonet in the Russian Army only really existed in the eighteenth and at the beginning of the nineteenth century; by the middle of the 1850s it was put into practice only occasionally and with no real system. Training in close-quarter fighting was largely given by the experienced older soldiers rather than by way of official training. Only after the end of the Crimean War in 1856 did a special commission revise the programmes of infantry training, including bayonet fighting. In the late 1850s bayonet fighting was included in training, and in 1857 the 'rules of bayonet and butt fighting' were issued.

Even without an effective system of bayonet drill the Russians were masters of its use. Indeed, Marshal Suvorov famously described what he perceived as the best way of fighting, and set it down in a discourse which was issued to every regiment in the Russian Army. Part of it ran:

> Keep your ball three days – it may happen, for a whole campaign, when lead cannot be had.
> Fire seldom – but fire sure!
> Push hard with the bayonet! The ball will lose its way – the bayonet, never! The ball is a fool – the bayonet, a hero!
> Stab once! And off with the Turk from the bayonet! Even when he's dead you may get a scratch from his sabre.
> If the sabre be near your neck, dodge back one step, and push on again.
> Stab the second! – stab the third! A hero will stab half-a-dozen!
> Be sure your ball is in your gun!!
> If three attack you, stab the first, fire on the second, and bayonet the third! – this seldom happens!![12]

This fearsome advice was used to great effect by the Russians at Inkerman in November 1854. As we shall see, however, the Russians would not get close enough to use the bayonet effectively at the Alma.

One of the other consequences of the Russian officers' obsessive attention to trifling details was that it prevented both officers and men from thinking individually or from acting on their own initiative. After years of strict adherence to a system whereby men acted in blind obedience to verbal orders, they could not make important decisions under battle conditions. One observer commented:

> Automatism, which is the inseparable companion of close formation drill, left its heavy and harmful mark on the training of the commanders of all levels. Thus, it was not possible to develop the most essential battle qualities of the commanders nor could their qualities be passed on to the troops.[13]

Even minor departures from the drill regulations were not allowed: 'We trained according to the adopted system of the field training till the very Crimean campaign. Drill training was the main occupation of our troops.'[14] Thus, the fighting in the Crimea 'resulted in the terrible and unexpected disasters and heavy waste of life'.[15]

Discipline within the army was enforced with extremely cruelty, with corporal punishment surpassing all the other punishments in terms of harshness. The infamous 'rods' had already been introduced into army discipline practice by Peter the Great, who considered this form of corporal punishment acceptable because it allowed the soldier to maintain his martial honour, in contrast to the usually fatal knout punishment. The knout was a vicious, heavy whip, usually multi-pronged, and sentences of 100 lashes or more usually proved fatal. Indeed, even 20 lashes were known to have finished off the hapless recipient. Many laws were passed to limit the usage of corporal punishment, but most were never actually implemented, and so the harsh practices continued.

Coupled with the flawed system of drill, the harsh discipline naturally left its mark on the private soldier, living in continual fear of the knout or the *pleti*; there was seen to be little honour in soldiering and even less incentive to do well. For the majority of the officers the opportunity to beat the soldiers served only to illustrate the gulf between the officer class and the private soldiers. By constantly beating their men the officers were simply demonstrating their superiority, and cultivating the notion that all private soldiers were mere serfs.[16] It is little surprise, therefore, that Hodasevich, the Polish officer, considered the Russian soldier to be perhaps the unhappiest in the world:

When the Emperor inspected our regiment at St. Petersburg in 1853, he remarked that the men kept their eyes fixed on the ground, and did not appear in good spirits. The captains of companies were blamed for this, though I was burning to explain to the colonel why the men looked dejected. However, I remembered Siberia, and held my peace. Captain Gorieff flogged one of his men to make him laugh! He happened to be a man who seldom or never have laughed – one of those morose-looking fellows that one meets sometimes. It is hardly to be credited, but after receiving one hundred lashes the man managed to get up a laugh, though I must say it bore a great affinity to the sobs that followed this effort. This is Russian justice! The outward appearance is all that is necessary for the chiefs. If a man has eaten nothing for two days he is still expected to laugh![17]

As well as defects in the infantry arm, the support services of the Russian Army were also far from perfect. Embezzlement of public funds was the worse cause, although this was considered to be just the tip of a very large iceberg, for in reality, the whole of the Russian Army was defective. The future reformer of the Russian Army, D Milyutin, said at the beginning of the Crimean War:

According to the papers we are quite ready, but from the very first days we will discover a terrible lack of everything ... . Saltpetre will be worth its weight in gold because at the moment we are not buying any, and when the war begins its shipping from abroad will be impossible. The medical service is also in a sad state; there are not enough instruments for operations and those we have are bad, so the doctors will have to amputate the wounded with blunt knives. The commissariat is in such a sorry state that even in peacetime it is useless, while in wartime it will leave the troops without boots, coats and dried bread. Everything is fine for the parades but grubby for the war ... . More soldiers will die in the war of disease because of the absence of sanitary arrangements, which it is necessary for the authorities to provide.[18]

Another Englishman, Captain William Jesse, visited Sevastopol immediately prior to the outbreak of war. Both Russian soldiers and sailors may well have been very numerous but they were, in his opinion, of poor quality when compared with those in the service of Queen Victoria:

One cannot help smiling when contrasting the seamen of other nations with theirs [the Russians]. Look at a blue jacket in our own service! He is all ease and freedom, agile and muscular; his countenance is open, his bearing independent; and though he shows implicit obedience under discipline, his demeanour is manly as well as respectful, and he is clean. A Russian sailor has no pretensions to be called one; his head is nearly shaved, and his jacket of green cloth, made like a dragoon's, fits quite tight; this is buttoned all the way up the front, and padded out as an army tailor would make one for a young cornet. His lower extremities are cased in Wellington's! and on his head is a worsted forage cap, all on one side. If a mate, his pipe is stuck between the buttons of his jacket, like an eye-glass; and last, though certainly not least, when addressed by his officer, he uncaps, and bringing his feet together, stands, oh ye tars! At what? – 'at ease?' oh, no! at 'attention!' with his 'little fingers down the seams, and thumbs pointing outwards.'[19]

Jesse was slightly more complimentary about the soldiers, but thought their conditions of service to be very poor. Their seven roubles a year did not go very far, particularly when a portion of this went on 'blacking, and candle to grease his mustacios'. It is little wonder that many men worked on public works or roads in order to supplement their income. Their food 'was of the coarsest and cheapest kind; usually peas, salt cucumbers, water melons, buck wheat, rape oil, and black bread.' This was served in an immense bowl, 'round which they would sit or kneel, and dipping in their wooden spoons, continue the operation till the porridge or borsch is eaten.' He was more complimentary about their uniforms but still thought them inferior to British ones:

The clothing, that is the uniform and accoutrements, are excellent; the cloth, though not quite so good as English, is close; the belts, of a white patent leather, are much more easily cleaned than our common buff, and the sling of the firelock is of red leather; were it not, therefore, for the bright barrel of his musket, the Russian soldier would have scarcely anything to occupy him in barracks. His knapsack, however, is all but empty; socks, even amongst officers, are not always worn, by the soldiers never; a few of them tie or swathe a dirty piece of calico round the leg and foot.[20]

Jesse went on to comment further on the men's clothing and on their living conditions in camp:

> In country quarters, and on the march, the men are dressed in a slouching grey great coat and forage cap, with a pair of dirty cotton drawers stuffed into their Wellington boots ... . I went to see the camp at Sarsko Selo [this whilst Jesse was in St Petersburg], and as it had rained for several days the troops appeared to be in a most forlorn state; the interior of their tents was full of mud mixed up with straw, and upon this the men were lying, in dirty cotton drawers and shirts, without either coats, trousers, or shoes, – very different from Chobham ... I saw a picked man from each company of a battalion of the Preobrajensky regiment. They were remarkably tall, but being very much padded out at the breast, and drawn in tight at the waist, they had, in their great coats, a very lank appearance; many regiments of the line that I saw in Moscow, and in the South, would have worked them off their legs in a campaign of any duration. Their coats were well brushed, and they were, no doubt, made to look their best. Brushing is continually going on.[21]

What disturbed Jesse more than anything was the manner in which discipline was enforced. Military punishment in the British Army was bad enough. Indeed, the lash – and fear of the lash – had helped preserve order in many a British unit over the years, but the rigorously harsh system employed in the Russian Army surprised even Jesse:

> Discipline is kept up with the men by extreme measures, and the cane is used at pleasure; but a soldier who has received the ribbon of St George, is, by the regulations of the service, exempt from this species of punishment. The officers not infrequently give way to violence of temper; I once saw a captain inspecting his guard near the quarantine at Odessa, strike one of his men a blow on the face with his fist, and, seizing him by both ears, shake him until he pulled him out of the ranks; the man's cap then fell off, and the officer, ordering a corporal to pick it up, jammed it down on his head with another blow; the whole system is carried on in the same tyrannical and overbearing manner; and the Russian soldier rarely meets with any kindness or consideration to soften the misery of being imperatively driven into the service.[22]

But though his pay was poor and the conditions of service harsh, the Russian soldier, along with his brother in the navy, remained steadfast in his duty to Russia, to God and to the czar. There was also one other important factor from which each Russian soldier could take some crumb of comfort: there were almost a million more like him, for the czar possessed an immense army, far more numerous than the Allies could muster. The problem was that his equally vast empire demanded garrisons which would tie down thousands of men, many of whom might otherwise have been brought to bear against the Allies. Thus, Menshikov could send barely 40,000 men north to face the Allies. In the meantime, reinforcements would have to be hurried to the Crimea as fast as possible, marching hundreds of miles to join their comrades in the south. These would have to make their way on foot as the Russians, for all of their mighty empire, possessed barely 400 miles of railway, a line which ran between St Petersburg and Moscow. Compared to the 8,000-odd miles of railway in Britain this was a reflection of the technological backwardness of Russia, an agrarian state ruled by the czar and a rich aristocracy, who held sway over millions of people, a large percentage of whom were simple peasants.

How this poorly equipped but dedicated army would fare would soon be seen for, even as Menshikov sent the last of his battalions north from Sevastopol, the Allied ships were beating fast towards the Crimean coast and the landing beaches south of Eupatoria at Kalamita Bay.

Chapter 7

Preparations for Battle

The first skirmish with the Russians on the Bulganak had ended in success for the Allies, although it was only a very minor one. The Allies knew full well that much tougher tests lay before them. However, the success did at least give them cause for optimism. After all, there had been no Russian opposition to the landings and now, having brushed aside the first Russian troops that dared to oppose them, the Allies began to think it might all turn out to be an anticlimax. Furthermore, reports suggested the defences of Sevastopol still barely existed. It was true that various works had been thrown up round the town but there appeared to be nothing that the powerful Allied artillery would not be able to deal with. Perhaps the destruction of the great Russian naval base in the Black Sea would prove to be nothing more than a formality. Time was to prove otherwise, of course, but for now hopes were high for a quick end to the campaign.

Russian opposition to the Allies' advance had certainly been virtually non-existent but the Russians were, nevertheless, well aware of the arrival of the Allied fleet off the Crimean coast, for the smoking funnels of the British and French steamers had been spotted as early as 13 September, not that Menshikov had done much by way of opposing the landings. Indeed, the Russian commander is frequently criticized for not opposing the landings. But his lack of aggression towards the Allies was because of his fears for the safety of Sevastopol, fears that were born of the advantages the Allies enjoyed with their fast moving steamships. Menshikov might well have moved his troops north to Eupatoria to oppose the landings, but suppose they were only a feint, designed to lure the Russian troops out of Sevastopol? With the Russians on the march north the Allied ships would have little difficulty in steaming to the south, catching Sevastopol without an effective garrison.

With such an antiquated transport system in Russia, it is little wonder that Menshikov was very cautious about marching away from Sevastopol. The lack of good communications is reflected in some of the huge marches undertaken by Russian troops to get to the Crimea. For example, the Tarutinsky Regiment left its base at Nizhnii-Novgorod on 2 December 1853, intending to fight the Turks, only to be rerouted to the Crimea following the declaration of war by the Allies in March 1854. The regiment finally arrived in the Crimea in April. This was typical of a country where railway systems had yet to be developed.

Instead of sending large numbers of troops to oppose the landings the Russian commander contented himself with sending riders and Cossack patrols to keep an eye on the Allies and report back on their strengths and movements. These reconnoitring forces varied in strength, and it was one such patrol, commanded by Kir'yakov, that had first encountered the Allies on the Bulganak river on 19 September. Meanwhile, Menshikov himself set about preparing his troops to meet the Allies in what would be the first major engagement in the Crimea.

Whilst the Allies were coming ashore at Kalamita Bay the Russian Army was beginning to take up positions on the southern bank of the Alma river, and by the evening of 14 September almost 20,000 Russian troops had arrived there, including the 1st Brigade of the 16th Infantry Division and the 1st and the 2nd batteries of the 16th Artillery Brigade, which had arrived previously. They had been joined on the evening of 13 September by the 4th battalion of the 2nd Brigade of the 17th Infantry Division and the Minsky Regiment with the 4th light battery of the 4th Artillery Brigade, which came from Sevastopol. On 15 September from Sevastopol came the last battalions of the regiments of the 2nd Brigade of the 17th Infantry Division with the light No. 4 and No. 5 batteries of the 17th Artillery Brigade, the Volynsky Regiment with the light No. 3 battery of the 14th Artillery Brigade, and the 5th and the 6th reserve battalions of the Belostoksky and Brestsky regiments. On 14 September itself two regiments came from Simferopol, the regiment of Grand Prince Mikhail Nikolaevich with six guns of the light No. 2 battery of the 16th Artillery Brigade and the Hussar Regiment of the Grand Duke of Saxe-Weimar. On 15 September the Hussar Regiment of Prince Nikolai Maximilianovich, along with the light cavalry No. 12 battery, came up from the Kacha river. On 18 September one of the newly formed naval battalions was sent from Sevastopol. From Perekop in the north came the Uglitsky Chasseur Regiment with six guns of the light No. 2 battery of the 16th Artillery Brigade and Cossack Regiment No. 60. By the evening of 19 September the 1st echelon of the Moskovsky Regiment came from the detachment of General Khomutov. On the morning of the battle came the 2nd echelon of the same regiment, with the Don horse-battery No. 3 and the Cossack *sotnyas* (hundreds) of the 57th

Regiment. On these last two days two companies of the 6th Field Engineer Battalion arrived piecemeal from Sevastopol. Amongst the Russian troops were two battalions of sailors from Sevastopol:

> It was very amusing to see the advance of the sailors: their four guns were taken out of the condemned ordnance stores at Sevastopol, with carriages tied together in many places with ropes. These guns were each drawn by two miserable horses assisted by eight men, and frequently, where the road was heavy or up hill, the whole battalion had to assist in hauling their guns. This was no doubt an idea of the Prince, for, being a naval man, he always showed a greater partiality for sailors than for the regular army; and I have no doubt, had we been successful, these amphibious warriors would have gained all the credit and reaped all the reward.[1]

By the evening of 19 September, Menshikov's force numbered 33,600 troops, consisting of 42 infantry battalions, 16 squadrons of cavalry, 1,100 Cossacks, 8 troops of horse artillery and 16 batteries of other artillery, totalling 84 guns. In Sevastopol, meanwhile, the commander-in-chief left behind as a garrison the sailors and four reserve battalions.

When Menshikov claimed he could hold the Alma position for weeks, it was no idle boast. Or at least it wouldn't have been if he had been even a half-decent military commander, for the position which blocked the Allies' march towards Sevastopol was a strong one. Nearly 6 miles in length from west to east, it blocked the only road to Sevastopol, the old post road, and covered the wooden bridge over which the road ran across the Alma river, close to the Tatar village of Burliuk. The river itself was deep but fordable along most of its length, but its southern banks were steep in many places, particularly to the east of the Sevastopol road. The northern approaches were planted with vineyards, making it difficult for the attacking troops to maintain their formation, whilst low stone walls likewise hindered progress. At the mouth of the river, on the Russian left, there were steep, cliff-like hills, rising to a height of around 150 feet, dominating both the river itself and the northern approaches to it. Although the cliffs themselves were inaccessible there were at least five tracks or paths which wound their way through them. These tracks were found, from west to east, close to the coast, at the village of Almatamack, and opposite a place known as the White Homestead, with two others issuing from the village of Burliuk or thereabouts. Apart from these

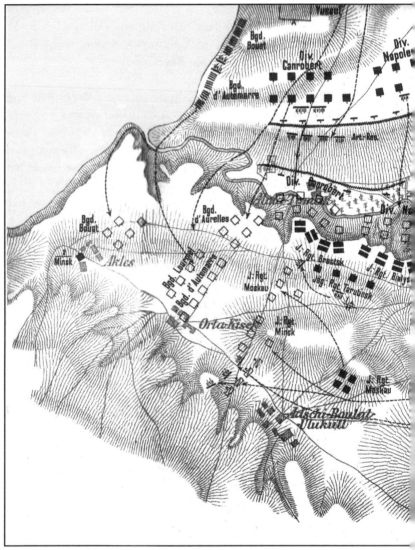

Allied and Russian dispositions.

last two tracks, none of them were guarded by Russian troops, nor had they been broken up. Thus, any enterprising Allied troops would find it possible to gain the heights on the Russian left without too much difficulty.

The plateau itself, extending east from the coast and bordered by the heights, ran inland as far as Telegraph Hill, which lay just over 1,000 yards to the south of the Alma river, opposite Burliuk. From here, the plateau dropped away to the Sevastopol road, before rising again on the east of the road,

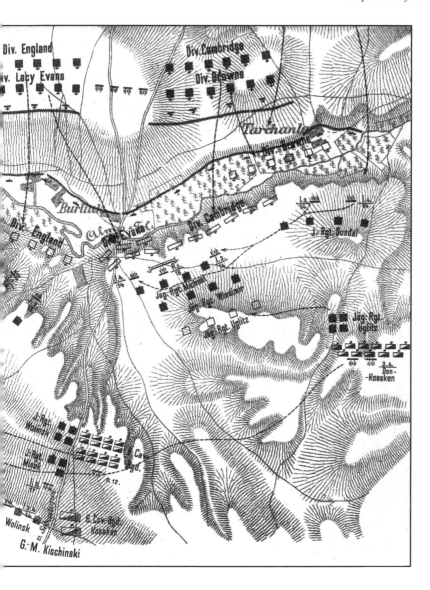

culminating in a commanding height called the Kourgane Hill, the summit of which was about 1,500 yards south of the river. From here the land rolled away to the east and to the south. Apart from Almatamack and Burliuk, there were three other villages, all of which lay on the southern bank of the Alma at around 1,500 to 2,000 yards' distance from the river. These were Orta-Kisek, Aklez (or Akles) and Adzgi-Bulat (or Ulukul).

But despite the natural strength of the Russian position, it had one major

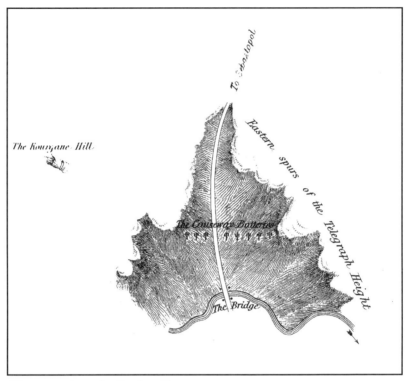

The post road crossing the river Alma.

disadvantage in that it was vulnerable to attack from the west, along the coast, for although the steep cliffs gave the Russian left flank immense strength, the terrain alone would not be enough to prevent the Allies from turning the flank. The two tracks that cut through the hills allowed Allied troops to gain the plateau, something which should have been easy to prevent with just a few battalions of infantry and artillery. However, any Russian troops positioned close to the coast would immediately come under fire from the Allied ships situated offshore. This was a great problem for Menshikov. The position was also too great in length for the number of troops available to the Russian commander, although this problem was solved – somewhat ironically – by the presence of the Allied ships. For although the 6-mile-long position was too long to defend in any great depth, Menshikov decided that, rather than expose his men on the left flank to the deadly fire from the Allied ships, he would trust instead to the lie of the land, and to the steep cliffs in particular, to thwart the Allies. This allowed him to concentrate the overwhelming bulk of his force to the east and west of the Sevastopol road. The plan was fatally flawed.

One of Menshikov's greatest errors at the Alma was that he placed far too much faith in the topography of the battlefield, and in the cliff-like face of the hills at the mouth of the Alma river itself. If he had taken a close look at the ground, or at least sent his staff to take a look, he would have seen that any half-decent troops would find it relatively easy to ascend the cliffs and establish themselves on the south bank of the river. Sadly, the Russian commander, wary of the expected fire from the Allied fleet, and trusting in the lie of the land, chose to keep his men well away from the coast and thus exposed his left flank to a direct threat from the Allies. Furthermore, not a single spade of earth was turned to dig entrenchments along the Russian position, save for the crude earthworks thrown up around the Great Redoubt on the forward slope of the Kourgane Hill, which mounted twelve guns, and the Lesser Redoubt, away to the east. Given the amount of time the Russian troops had been in position on the Alma the oversight is all the more puzzling. Not only would earthworks have afforded the Russian troops on their left flank some degree of protection from the guns of the Allied fleet, but they would have allowed the defenders to dispute the possession of the heights there far more effectively than they were to do. Good, sound field works occupied by both infantry and artillery, and sited behind the river obstacle, would have made the task of fording the river extremely difficult for the Allies. In the event it was difficult enough, but the task would have been immense had Menshikov put his men to work turning over the soil. Instead, he simply placed skirmishers along the south bank, near the village of Burliuk and in the vineyards to the north. Captain Hodasevich certainly felt there were flaws in the Russian dispositions:

> In conversation with my brother officers I found that it was the general opinion that we should be able to hold this position for at least a week, and the only danger that threatened us was, that the enemy might outflank us on the right of our position.
>
> If I might venture an opinion which I conceived at that time, but did not express, I should think that our left flank ought not to have been left entirely without artillery, while the ravine that led up to it was quite undefended, and the stone bridge across the river remained undestroyed. If, as was expected, our right flank had been turned, we could easily have changed our front and so held on our own. At least

it appears to me even now, but with good generalship we might have held the position till night, and then retreated without disgrace.[2]

Occupying the heights to the west of the post road were the Brestsky, Belostoksky and Borodinsky regiments, with the Tarutinsky Regiment behind them. To the east of the road, on and to the west of the Kourgane Hill, were placed the Kazansky, Vladimirsky and Suzdalsky regiments. The Volynsky, Minsky and Moskovsky infantry regiments, along with two light foot batteries, were placed in reserve in the centre of position, whilst the Uglitsky Regiment was positioned behind the right wing. One battalion of the Minsky Regiment was then detached from the reserve to occupy the village of Ulukul, whilst hordes of Cossacks covered the Russian right flank. Commanding the Russian left flank was Lieutenant-General V Kir'yakov, commander of the 17th Division, said to be a man of no great intelligence, and lacking any real military abilities. He is reputed to have been rarely sober. Despite this – or rather because of it – Kir'yakov declared before the battle that he would emerge victorious by sheer numbers alone. Commanding the right flank was General P D Gorchakov, brother of the commander-in-chief of the Russian Army on the Danube. Undeniably brave, Gorchakov was not exactly tactically astute, although his men were to give the attacking British troops a real test. Elsewhere, however, some Russian officers thought the dispositions to be flawed. Despite his less-than-impressive reputation General Kir'yakov, commander of 17th Division, was concerned by the positions given him by General Vunsh:

> Except for two battalions of the Moskovsky foot regiment, the army of Prince Menshikov was already at the Alma when the enemy landed at eight o'clock on the morning of 14 September. The two battalions arrived only two hours before the battle.
>
> The regiments were ordered up on to the upper slopes of the left bank of the river by Colonel Vunsh but not in any particular order. Despite being in camp between 14 and 20 September no works were begun nor preparations made in our camp for battle. On 18 September we were given our dispositions for the coming battle. The front line was placed on the slopes of the left bank of the river Alma, the troops taking up their positions on that same day. I was absolutely certain that my dispositions on the ledges of the left bank would be disadvantageous and told Colonel Zalessky in the presence of Prince

Gorchakov's aide-de-camp, Colonel Durnovo, and other officers. I said, 'If we must fight in the position we now occupy, you, as an officer from headquarters, must use all the means in your power to ensure the troops are not positioned down the hill but up on the upper slopes of the bank.' I learned the next day that Colonel Zalessky did not share the same opinion.

On 19 September the enemy advanced to within a short distance of our positions. There was no cover in the area we occupied. Thus, the enemy could see our dispositions, the locations of the batteries and battalions, and the strength of our army. The commander-in-chief ordered me to make a reconnaissance in order to discover the enemy's intentions and, if possible, to force him back. The movement of my detachment duly forced him to move away.

In my explanation of the troops' disposition I limit myself to the part of the army that was placed to the left of the high road, or the left flank, that was under my command. To the left of the high road the Borodinsky Chasseurs of His Imperial Majesty's regiment stood in two lines; to the left of it in the first line there were four reserve battalions of the Brestsky and Belostoksky regiments; behind them in the second line there was the Tarutinsky Chasseurs regiment. There was no artillery amongst the twelve battalions of front line troops on the left flank; both front lines were moved down from the heights to the ledge and were formed in columns to charge. No epaulements were raised anywhere along the whole of the left flank.

Owing to a lack of space on the slopes and at the bottom of the bank of the Alma river we were compelled to place our first line within 150 paces of the second line, and extend our skirmish line not more than 500 paces in front of the battalions. Two companies of the 6th rifle battalion, sent out in front of the Borodinsky Chasseurs regiment, were moved forward just ten paces. The concentration of troops, with the rocky bank of the Alma behind them, proved very disadvantageous to us and gave the enemy an easy target. This is why our troops began to climb out of it once the fighting had started. It was very difficult for the men to stand in the face of such a concentrated fire from the enemy, as we were in the open and subjected to fire from the enemy's batteries and their skirmishers. That is the reason why the battle of 20 September began with the Allies' flanking movement on our left flank.[3]

By the standards of the day, infantry regulations in the Russian Army were not too bad. The infantry regulations of 1848 retained the practices of the Napoleonic Wars. These regulations may appear to have been outdated, but little had happened in the inter-war years to bring about much change, nor did anyone feel the need to do so. After all, neither had there been too much change in the British and French armies. The infantry battalion was the main tactical unit, divided in turn into companies. It was considered that small, flexible company columns could adjust themselves to the area much better and were not such an obvious target as a battalion. The company was divided into two platoons, the platoon into two semi-platoons. Forty-eight picked marksmen in each company were trained to be the skirmishers to act in pairs, 200 paces or so in front of the main column. Considerable changes in infantry tactics, particularly in the 1840s, followed the introduction of the rifle with its improved range and accuracy. Wherever possible, at least half of the skirmishers were given rifles, although this was not always the case.

In general, the battle order of the infantry consisted of two lines and a reserve. The battalions of the first line formed in columns with intervals from 100 to 300 yards in extended line. The battalions of the second line also stood in columns. In the third or reserve line the battalions stood in the semi-platoon columns. The second line was placed 100 to 300 yards from the first, and the reserve line 400 to 500 yards from the second line. Up to half of the troops were detached to form a reserve. Various methods of manoeuvring the lines were devised, but these were often too complex for the troops to carry out, with the result that, during battle, lines often advanced piecemeal.

The majority of the Russian infantry at the Alma were armed with smoothbore percussion muskets, some of which were actually converted flintlocks. In fact, reserve units were armed with flintlocks even in the Crimea. The better shots in each regiment were, however, armed with a rifled percussion musket, although this was still far less effective than the Miniés carried by the Allies. It is ironic that so many historians claim the Crimean War as the first of the modern wars when the rate of fire of Russian percussion muskets, one per minute, was slower than that of a trained British infantryman of the Napoleonic Wars, who could fire his flintlock musket three times per minute. In fact, the rate of fire for a British infantryman in the Crimea was only two shots per minute. Thus, a British infantry battalion under Wellington could deliver one third more shots each minute than one of

Raglan's battalions in the Crimea. Of course, this was compensated for by the marked increase in the range of the Minié over the old Brown Besses. Even so, the range of the Russian muskets in the Crimea was no better than those the Russians had used against Napoleon, just 150 to 200 yards. This put the Russian infantrymen at a tremendous disadvantage against the Allies, particularly at the Alma, where they had to stand and take the hail of bullets coming at them without being able to offer any effective reply until the Allies got within range. Given the poor condition of the muskets and rifles, many of which were made in Poland, it is little wonder that the Russians preferred to use the bayonet.

In September 1854 the Russian infantryman was still relatively well equipped, his uniform was not worn out and on the whole his appearance was fairly good. This would, of course, change dramatically after only a few months in the trenches at Sevastopol. Indeed, it would not take long for the uniforms to become very threadbare; according to some sources, the Russians resorted to taking coats from the bodies of dead Allied troops. The Turkish coats were very popular for they were very similar to Russian ones in terms of colour and style. They also had a hood that gave protection from the wind and rain.

Several changes to uniforms were made during Nicholas I's reign, including the change from a double-breasted to a single-breasted coat. Greatcoats were also issued to hussars to replace their cloaks. Cossacks were issued with a new uniform, whilst there was also the introduction of iron stars on the epaulettes to designate ranks for officers, with stripes on the shoulder straps denoting other ranks. But the most unpopular change, made in 1844, was the introduction of a helmet to replace the old shako. The helmet was made of black patent leather, had two peaks (front and back), and had a metal frame inside formed from a metal tube topped with a flaming grenade. For full dress a black horsehair mane was put into the tube. The helmet, like the shako, had decorative scales and a coat of arms, with the regimental number being fixed to the front. It was so uncomfortable to wear and maintain that during the march soldiers were often ordered to hand them in to be stored in depots or wagons.[4] Indeed, Pyotr Alabin, a thirty-year-old Russian officer, wrote:

In Nikolaev, we [11 Infantry Division] were met by the aide-de-camp, Count Levashov, with the order to leave our helmets in the special warehouses. The men are sincerely grateful for the order to leave the helmets. The helmets gave the soldiers no advantage but, on the contrary, did them more harm than good. The helmets warped and contracted so much because of the rains and the terrible heat that they were held on the soldiers' heads only with great difficulty, often causing headaches. A light wind and the helmets were blown off. And as to looking after them, it took so much time and efforts.[5]

The forage cap was certainly adopted by most of the Russian soldiers throughout the 349-day defence of Sevastopol, despite the obvious advantages a helmet would have had during the bombardment. But, during the Battle of the Alma, some regiments were still wearing the helmet, despite its being uncomfortable. According to the memoirs of A Rogozin, who fought at the Alma with the Vladimirsky Regiment, he and his comrades wore the helmet, and although he noted the advantages which it gave him during the fighting, he was still very glad to get his forage cap on afterwards:

> Soon, to the great delight of all the ranks, the metal helmets were handed in to the warehouse. Although they brought some advantage in the Alma battle, and sometimes protected you from bullets, but taking into account their heavy weight, especially during the forced marches in the southern heat, that advantage cost too much.[6]

In 1851 regulations were issued regarding the items to be carried in a soldier's knapsack during the march. These included two pairs of foot-wraps, boots, two undershirts or vests, ear-flaps, mittens, a forage hat, a tin for the percussion caps, several feathers with cut-out points, a greased rag, a dry rag, screwdriver, a stick for the wads, a pointed wooden scraper, small cleaning stick for the buttons, clothes-brush, shoe-brush, lime brush, chalk, glue, soap, scissors, dye and comb for the moustaches, a pair of soles and a tin with shoe polish or fat, not fewer than three needles, thimble, awl, sewing thread, waxed thread, penknife and a comb. Besides this, a soldier should have some dry bread and salt for four days.[7]

As with all armies, the Russian infantry colours provided both a rallying point and a morale factor on the battlefield. Traditionally, the colours were a great source of inspiration to the Russian soldier, although they were rarely used in the Crimea, at least not after the Battle of the Alma. The possible reason was that, during the battle, the Russians saw that the French and British made a point of attempting to capture their colours. Indeed, during the battle British troops mistook the red camp marker-flags of the Vladimirsky Regiment for the battalion colours and tried furiously to capture them, whilst at the same time the cased regimental colours attracted little attention. In subsequent actions, the colours were usually left in camp under guard.[8]

The Russian artillery would certainly prove formidable during the defence of Sevastopol. In the field, however, it had far less effect. Russian artillery officers – and also engineers – were, on the whole, far better than their counterparts in the infantry and cavalry, largely because of the higher level of education required for these two sciences. In the Crimean War, the Russian artillery system was effectively a much improved version of the 1805 system which had been developed by A A Arakcheev, the inspector of artillery during the reign of Alexander I. In fact, Arakcheev had been present with the czar at the Battle of Austerlitz. The new system brought about improvements to the staff structure as well as to the arms and munitions. The system was used successfully in the battles of the 1812 campaign and existed, with a few modifications, right up until the end of the nineteenth century. The guns themselves were barely any different from those used at Borodino: 6- and 9-pounder guns were used in the horse artillery and light batteries, whilst 12- and 18-pounders were used in the field. At the Alma, some eighty-four guns were brought into the field by the Russians, firing round shot, common shell and grape or canister, the farthest range being around 1,500 yards. Between them, these guns were responsible for about seventy per cent of all Allied casualties.

A battery was the main tactical unit in the artillery, usually consisting of eight guns. Artillery brigades were attached to infantry divisions and consisted of one battery and two light batteries. The horse artillery batteries belonged to the reserve artillery brigades and were attached to the cavalry divisions to support them with fire and to create a mobile cavalry reserve. In 1834 all officers of the foot artillery became mounted and in 1845 new types of gun-carriages and ammunition wagons with flat covers were introduced, allowing extra men to be 'mounted' on them when moving from position to position. Thus, by the beginning of the Crimean War the difference between foot and horse artillery was largely insignificant.[9]

If the Russian plan for the defence of the Alma river was lacking in any sort of imagination, the Allies' own plan can hardly have laid claim to be anything other than ordinary or predictable. Lord Raglan and the increasingly ill-looking Saint-Arnaud, accompanied by Colonel Trochu, had met on the night of 19 September in the small house on the Bulganak which Raglan used for his headquarters. Remarkably, no reconnaissance of the Russian position appears to have been carried out, save for a distant view from the French fleet. Thus, the Allied commanders discussed the coming battle on little more than a rough map. As one historian put it, 'no enterprising young officers on lean, well-bred horses had been sent over those few miles of grass down, to dodge the Cossacks as they would have dodged the French forty years before.'[10]

Despite his illness Saint-Arnaud was able to give full vent to his optimism for the coming fight. He informed Raglan of how the battle would be fought, with the French attacking the heights on the Russian left whilst the British went straight for the centre and right. His plans were delivered with typical Gallic gusto and animation, and with typical British nonchalance Raglan nodded politely, appearing to agree with everything his French comrade suggested, and yet agreed to nothing, save that an advance and attack would be made upon the Russian position the next day. Raglan's approach to his dealings with the French was understandable, if a little harmful to the Allied cause. His active military career in the Peninsular and Waterloo campaigns had been spent fighting the French. Indeed, they had cost him an arm at the latter battle. Schooled firmly in the cautious views of the late Duke of Wellington, Raglan was reluctant to relinquish any control of his army, nor was he going to allow his former enemies to dictate to him. Nevertheless, he fully appreciated the delicate balance to be struck with his French allies, and his grasp of the situation allowed him enough tolerance of them to be able to maintain a good if sometimes shaky working relationship. And so, whilst Saint-Arnaud rode off into the night with his staff, satisfied that his British allies apparently understood and agreed to 'his' plan, Raglan went to bed, happy that the French commander had been kept outside the narrow limits of his own thinking.

Preparations for battle could not have been more different amongst the men who were destined to fight the Battle of the Alma. September 20 was an Orthodox religious holiday in Russia, marking the birth of the Blessed Virgin, and prayers were said amongst the Russian regiments. And so, whilst British and French troops cooked their breakfasts and drank their coffee, priests went amongst the Russian troops holding aloft the sign of the cross and casting consecrated water, praying to God to deliver them victory against the Allies.

Captain Hodasevich's regiment had gathered for the Holy Mass at seven o'clock. Two hours later, he and some of his fellow officers noticed a large white box, drawn by six horses, bearing the words *pour nous asphyxier*, being brought forward by the French towards the village off Almatamack. A rumour quickly spread through the Russian ranks that the French had brought up a box filled with gas. The rumour reached the colonel of the regiment, whereupon Lieutenant Katansky, who commanded the riflemen of the regiment, suggested his men fire rockets at the mysterious box to try to set it on fire. Finally, Hodasevich himself asked leave to go forward and find out exactly what the box was.

> Every one of the officers tried to dissuade me, saying that I should be shot from the steamers, or that the box might be connected by galvanic wires. Still, every one of them was burning with impatience to know what it could be. Without listening to their objections I started to examine this supposed new engine in warfare, and I found it to be a large cubical stone! During this walk I remarked how extremely exposed our left flank was to an attack, and on my return informed General Kiriakoff of my observation, when he sent the 2nd Battalion of the Moskovsky Regiment into the ravine, with orders to hold the bridge and to detach sharpshooters into the gardens on the right bank of the river.
> The commander of the left flank had occupied this ground during four days, but had never once taken the trouble to examine the position, to enable him to dispose of the force under his orders to the best advantage.
> I expressed my opinion to the Major that I thought the stone I had seen was a forerunner of an attack upon our left, where it would be easier to succeed than on the right or centre. Nobody, however, would believe my reasoning, opposing the steepness of the heights on that side, but forgetting the undefended ravine and the absence of artillery. The transporting of this stone I can only account for by supposing that the French, wishing to ascertain whether there were any troops in the village of Almatamack and to reconnoitre the banks of the river, adopted this ruse as being less likely to expose them than a reconnaissance.[11]

The Allies themselves were present in overwhelming strength. Saint-Arnaud could call upon some 30,000 French infantry, supported by sixty-eight guns. There were also around 7,000 Turkish troops attached to the French Army. The British contingent under Lord Raglan numbered 25,000 infantry and

1,000 cavalry, and like the French had sixty-eight guns. In other words, the Allies enjoyed an advantage of two to one in personnel, and had nearly forty more guns than the Russians. How they would make this advantage count was soon to be seen.

In the meantime, the British and French made final preparations for what would be their first battle on European soil since Waterloo. Jean Joseph Gustave Cler was with his regiment, the 2nd Zouaves. The regiment formed part of Monet's brigade in Prince Napoleon's division which had formed up to the right of De Lacy Evans' 2nd British Division:

> As the centre of the army was not to stir, until two hours after the departure of the wings, their *reveille* was not sounded so early; but, long before it did sound, the Zouaves were already up, and busy, – some in getting their coffee ready; others in cleaning and reloading their arms. The colonel then called round him his officers and non-commissioned officers, – and, whilst the soldiers, all ears, as is usual under such circumstances, drew round, and as near as possible, – he gave them his instructions for the coming battle; – then, turning to the men, he addressed them as follows: 'Your place in the fight will be between the 1st Zouaves, your peers in glory, and between the English, – the hereditary foes of France, but now her allies. Let every man among us then, make it a point of honour to let no other get ahead of him. – Remember, that, as sons of that heroic generation, whose valour and conquests shed such an imperishable lustre over the early part of this century, you are called upon to illustrate the second Empire, by new and equally splendid victories.' Pointing with his finger to the Russian army, ranged along the heights of the Alma, he added: 'You shall be placed in the first line; – before reaching the enemy, you will have to cross a river, force your way through dense thickets, and up yonder heights – but recollect, that, when once the battle is fairly begun, it must be fought out a l'Africaine: as soon, therefore, as you shall have achieved a first success, charge the Russians with that same invincible impetuosity, which has so often enabled you to dislodge the Kabyles from their formidable positions.'[12]

Captain Octave Cullet, on the other hand, perhaps echoed many a French officer's frustrations at the lack of activity in the British camp:

On the morning of 20 September, the army was impatient and excited. The plateau was covered by the Russian army, with the enemy formed in dense columns; its artillery was moved forward and placed in the battery on the slope; at the foot of the slope the Alma was lined with riflemen; cavalry covered the right flank; the left was covered by cliffs whose peaks seem to us like ramparts.

From six to ten o'clock, we waited for the order to move; we knew only later that, in order to give the English time to put themselves in motion, the marshal had to delay the hour of march by four hours.[13]

Away to the French left, the Duke of Cambridge's 1st Division waited patiently for the order to advance against the Russians. John Astley, of the Scots Guards, was amongst them, and appears not to have realized he was on the verge of going into battle for the first time:

When the dawn broke on that event for morning (about 5am), we shook ourselves up a bit, and after a snack of salt pork and a bitter biscuit, with a drop of hot coffee, we paraded; but were told we should not march before seven o'clock. The majority then lay down again; but as I felt wonderful well and extra keen to have a peep at the ground in front of us, I took my haversack with my writing things in it and my telescope, and made my way a little beyond our outposts. As I was going I met Colonel Gordon, of the Grenadiers, who was on the staff, and asked if there was any chance of getting our letters, as they were three or four days overdue. He was in a great hurry, and as he rode off he said: 'Oh no! We shall be in a general action in an hour or so.' This fairly woke me up, and I got on a bit of a hillock, pulled a good arm-full of dry weeds, and, lying on them, took a good spy towards the Alma. As the sun rose and dispelled the mist, I could discover a few Cossacks prowling about in our front, and examining the ground where we had killed a few of them and their horses the evening before. Beyond these Cossacks were some regiments of Russian cavalry. About a mile off and straight to our front, extending some five or six miles, was a long undulating range of hills, steepest just next to the sea-cliffs on our right front. As the sun rose I could detect large bodies of infantry on the hillsides. I could see their campfires and the glitter of the sun's rays on their piled arms.[14]

Elsewhere on the battlefield men stretched, drank coffee and looked to their equipment, whilst staff officers flew back and forth, a plethora of cocked hats and feathers. In all, around 70,000 men stood to their arms, gazing out across the battlefield, the Russians peering out from their positions on the heights to the south of the river Alma, whilst the Allies, numerous and confident, scanned the hills, picking out the various Russian units, whose bayonets and swords glinted in the morning sun. All were waiting for the first moves to be made of what would be the first major battle on European soil since the Battle of Waterloo in 1815.

Chapter 8

The French Move First

The Allied troops were up well before daylight on the morning of 20 September 1854. The men of Sir George Cathcart's 4th Division shivered their way into the gloom to parade before their commanding officer. Lieutenant Peard, of the 20th Regiment, later recalled the morning:

> Before daylight on the morning of the 20th of September we paraded in perfect silence, except the hum of five thousand voices, as there was not a drum or bugle to be heard in the camp. The troops remained under arms for about an hour, during which time the Generals were employed in informing the Brigadiers and commanding officers of the different regiments of the order of march. Our pioneers were employed by Sir George Cathcart in levelling the banks of the river Bulganak, to give a passage to the troops and artillery; and as soon as this was completed, we moved off. The French were on our extreme right, on the high road near the sea, and the Turks acted as their reserve. It was known that the enemy had been busy in fortifying the heights beyond the river Alma, about four miles distant from the Bulganak, and that, as we had to cross that valley, they had resolved to resist our advance there, and try their strength with the Allied Armies.[1]

Gradually, dawn gave way to a fine, sunny morning. For Saint-Arnaud and the French Army it was as if the years were rolling back. Almost four decades had passed since the end of the Napoleonic Wars, when the great Emperor Napoleon led his armies to countless great victories. True, they were now fighting alongside their old, traditional and most dogged opponents, but the spirits of countless old warriors were with them, and the sight of row upon row of dark blue coats and fluttering tricolours was enough to make the breast of every Frenchman swell with pride. With so many memories and traditions thus evoked, Saint-Arnaud's men needed little else to inspire them. There was also the bitter memory of 1812 and the ill-fated Moscow campaign.

At half-past five in the morning the French troops began to quit their camps.

The Battle of the Alma: the opening phase.

There was no great blaring of bugles or beat of drums, but a silent, grim determination to succeed. By six-thirty in the morning they began forming to the north of the Alma river. It all bode well. But as they began to deploy for their forward movement in concert with their British allies, they realized that the latter

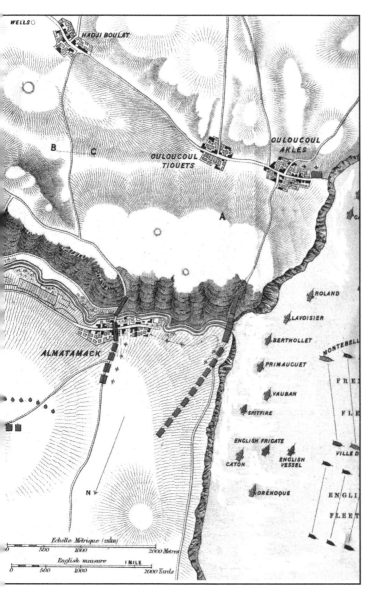

had yet to stir from their camps. This British inactivity so astonished the French that both General Canrobert and Prince Napoleon, commanding the French divisions closest to the British right, rode quickly over to try to discover the reason. They found Sir De Lacy Evans, whose 2nd Division was to attack on the left flank of Canrobert, still in his tent. 'I have received no orders,' the British general replied to his bewildered French colleagues. Evidently, Raglan had kept not only Saint-Arnaud from knowing his plans, but also his own commanders.

The point was, of course, that General Bosquet, who had been assigned the task of scaling the heights close to the mouth of the river Alma, had already begun his forward movement, at which the rest of the Allies would move forward. Bosquet's division, unsupported, and some way from the Russian position, nevertheless risked being destroyed unless it was halted. The order was duly dispatched and Bosquet thankfully halted, much to his annoyance, as his aide-de-camp, Captain Fay, later recalled:

> At around six o'clock, having eaten soup, the right wing got under way, whilst the remainder of the French Army, under arms, prepared to leave their bivouacs, when the marshal was informed that the English had not left at the hour agreed the day before, and were not yet able to do it. He immediately sent an order to General Bosquet to suspend his march; it was eight o'clock, and we had already covered half of the distance which separated us from Alma. The General, stopped in his tracks, expressed his displeasure at the slowness of our allies, who caused us to lose the most valuable hours of the day. However, he ordered the halt and rode on ahead to reconnoitre the passages of the river. Around ten o'clock, the waiting continuing, the soldiers ran towards the sea, where some of them had found fresh water, and they made their coffee.
>
> The general rejoined the column and dismounted. There arrived a lieutenant who had come into the bar in a boat from the *Roland*; he had recognised that it would be useful to our men; without doubt, this was a good suggestion, but our attention was distracted, for we looked while laughing at the two sailors who accompanied it. These were blundering about arguing and hitting each other with fistfuls of fresh bread. When the argument was finished we grabbed the precious cargo and distributed it in pieces amongst us. It was a real gift, because we had not eaten any biscuit since the disembarkation. It also provided us with a moment of diversion caused by our lack of activity.[2]

Colonel Trochu rode over to see Raglan and ask why his men had yet to break camp. It was seven o'clock when Trochu reached Raglan's headquarters, by which time the British commander was in the saddle. The exchange between the two was duly recorded in the French history of the war:

'My Lord,' said the latter [Trochu], 'the Marshal thought, after what you did me the honour of saying, last night, that your troops forming the left wing of the line of battle, were to have marched forward at six o'clock.'

'I am now giving my orders,' replied Lord Raglan. 'We are preparing and are about to march; a part of my troops did not reach the camp until very late in the night.'

'For Heaven's sake, my Lord,' asked the Colonel, 'be speedy; every minute of delay takes from us a chance of success.'

'Go and say to the Marshal,' answered Lord Raglan, 'that at this moment orders are despatched along the whole line.'[3]

The delays had been caused by faulty staff work and by wheeling two divisions which had been posted to cover the open British flank into line. There were further delays whilst the British brought up the ammunition wagons, and the other divisions wheeled into line, ready for the advance. Meanwhile, the French settled down and waited, drinking coffee amidst fields of reaped corn with some using it to light fires, whilst others used it to lie on. By half-past ten Raglan's men were finally and belatedly ready to advance, by which time the sun was well and truly up and beginning to beat down on the battlefield. At around half-past eleven the left flank of the French Army and the right flank of the British finally came into touch with each other, and soon afterwards they topped a low rise, beyond which, at a distance of about two miles, rose the heights on the south bank of the Alma river. It was a spectacular sight for the Allied troops, the heights presenting a mass of sparkling and flashing along the entire length of the position as thousands of swords and bayonets caught the sunlight. Once within a mile and a half of the river the Allies halted.

The halt in front of the river afforded Lord Raglan his first opportunity of studying the Russian position. It was soon clear to him that although the Russian right flank appeared to be open, with no significant topographical feature on which to anchor it, it would be dangerous to try to attempt an outflanking move, particularly as Menshikov had almost three times the number of cavalry possessed by Raglan. There was nothing for it but to allow Saint-Arnaud to attack the Russian left, after which Raglan would launch his British divisions against the Russian right and right centre. It would be a hard fight but there was little other option. The French, too, expected a hard fight, but at least they would be covered by the guns of the Allied fleet hovering out at sea against the Russian left flank.

During the lull, an eerie silence descended over the battlefield, broken only by the cheers of the British as they greeted Saint-Arnaud, who rode over to see Raglan. Then, as if to bring the men to their senses, the order to load ball cartridge was barked out along the line. After so many years of inactivity, save for far-off colonial scrapes and training camps in England, the men suddenly realized this was the real thing, and the effect of the order is said to have turned many men white. Finally, at some time after noon, Bosquet's division, supported by the Turks, began its move along the shore towards the Russian left. Once on the move, the rest of the Allies lumbered into motion and followed suit.

Prince Menshikov and his Russian Army watched the initial Allied movements – or rather the lack of them – with an uninterested air. Russian outposts noticed a movement to the north by the Allies at around seven o'clock, after which they began to take a greater interest in proceedings and prepare for battle. Menshikov himself had no actual headquarters, although Telegraph Hill seems to have been his main position during the day. More alarming, however, was the apparent absence of a plan. Menshikov appears to have had no actual battle plan, other than to stop the Allies. His generals had no idea of his strategy or of his intentions. Instead, they relied only on themselves, on the memories of 1812 and on God's will. General Vasiliy Kir'yakov, commanding the 17th Division, was a little more apprehensive than his commander:

> At eight o'clock in the morning the enemy came into sight of our position. Colonel Rakovich, a brilliant officer, who was in the observation post with the 2nd Battalion of the Minsky regiment close to the sea, was the first to exchange fire with the troops of Canrobert's division. Having heard it, I took from the reserve two battalions of the Moskovsky regiment along with No. 4 light battery of the 17th brigade and positioned them to the left of the telegraph, with their front towards the sea within $2^1/_2$ versts from the shore, out of range of the fire from the enemy's ships. The 3rd battalion of the same regiment under Colonel Solovyov was sent to the left to the end of the left flank on the heights of the Alma river. The 4th battalion was left in reserve. At 10.30 the French were still approaching and climbing the steep left bank. It is wrong to think that Canrobert was going along a narrow path and that it was difficult for him to debouch from the river valley. The coast road is as good and comfortable as the other Crimean roads: the Tatars often used it to transport hay, water-melons and other bulky products of agriculture to Sevastopol. Having climbed the hill Canrobert, under cover of the ships' fire, could easily form and extend the troops, which is what he did.

At about eleven o'clock His Serenity Prince Alexander Sergeevich Menshikov arrived on the left flank. His Serenity told me that the enemy were turning our left and went in the direction to the sea. Soon he ordered up the Moskovsky and then the Minsky regiments with No. 4 and 5 light batteries of the 17th artillery brigade. The regiments advanced towards the French but the French showered them with shrapnel, case-shot and other shells from the ships, and soon the regiments were in disorder. Seeing this, and in order to contain the enemy's attack on our left flank I ordered forward some batteries from the reserve: the No. 12 battery of horse artillery and the Donskaya No. 3 reserve battery and positioned them near the place where the Moskovsky regiment stood in reserve. These batteries opened the fire over the heads of the Tarutinsky regiment and the reserve battalions of the 13th Division against Canrobert's division and against the troops of Prince Napoleon to the right across the Alma. They prevented the French field artillery from moving their limbers.

At about half an hour after midday, Prince Alexander Sergeevich returned to the Tarutinsky regiment, where I had been up until that time, and ordered me to ride to the Moskovsky and Minsky regiments to take command of them. My horse had been just killed under me; I took another one and galloped to the regiments, put them in order and committed them to the attack. Canrobert's division could not stand our advance; they withdrew their batteries and retired down the steep bank. At that moment, the first enemy success was stopped on the left flank. But on the right flank and in the centre the state of the battle was becoming more and more disadvantageous for us. I do not know the full details for I was busy with my own command and did not see what was happening to the right of me. Nevertheless, it was impossible not to notice that the enemy had already gained a foothold on the left bank of the Alma.[4]

Meanwhile things were beginning to hot up on the French right. Bosquet had taken advantage of Saint-Arnaud's earlier order to halt and had ridden forward with his staff and with the heads of the artillery and engineers, under cover of some sharpshooters, to reconnoitre the cliffs. Two passes were clearly marked, one close to the sea and the other just over half a mile farther inland, close to the burned village of Almatamack. Both were accessible to infantry, if a little difficult, but what concerned Bosquet was the difficult accessibility for his artillery. Nevertheless, Bosquet assumed command of D'Autemarre's brigade and sent it forward to the pass close to the village of Almatamack, whilst Bouat's brigade and the Turks headed for the pass close to the sea. Captain Fay later recalled the moment the advance began. He also thought Menshikov had been completely deceived by the direction of the French attack:

> Around half past eleven o'clock, the men sent their knapsacks to the rear; drums, bugles and music were heard all along the line, and we finally marched on the enemy. The second division advanced in two columns: Bouat's brigade towards the bar, the brigade of Autemarre towards Almatamack. Each one of these columns was accompanied by its own battery; but the first ford being found impracticable for the wagons, the battery which followed the first brigade also came through the village, which brought it quicker to the crest.
>
> The Russians, placed on the heights on the left of the river Alma as on the steps of an amphitheatre, had been able to watch since dawn, all our movements. A captive Russian officer taken prisoner told us he believed the move was only a diversion to weaken them in the centre; but we always thought that the main part of the army would pass close to the village of Burliuk.
>
> Also, Prince Menshikov did not think it necessary to have to send reinforcements to his left wing, which he did not consider seriously threatened; he had restricted himself to placing everything on the bank of the Alma, for riflemen were spread out in the vineyards from Almatamack until Tarkhandar, whilst an abattis had been placed behind the bridge of Burliuk, at the end of the valley through which passes the road to Sevastopol; as the Russian right was held in great strength we suppose the Prince had rejected the idea that we were to turn the Russian flank on the coast; he held back reserves around and behind Telegraph, which became the most important point on the battlefield.[5]

Bosquet's column had little difficulty in passing the village of Almatamack, and his Zouaves quickly threw themselves into the river, heading for the south bank:

> They were speedily seen, spreading to right and left, on the side of the cliffs, clinging with their hands to anything protruding from the ground, and assisting each other up the ascent. Often, these fragile supports would suddenly give way, and the soldiers roll from top to bottom of the slope.[6]

Captain Octave Cullet, of the 20th Ligne, went into action with his regiment shortly after ten o'clock in the morning:

> At ten o'clock everything stirred in front of us; the Zouaves and the marines crossed the plain at a fast pace; the Prince was in the centre. The soldiers were in cloaks, the officers in parade dress; our march lasted one hour and a half; it was not yet midday, we were not more than a few hundred metres of the river. A violent firing from skirmishers struck our first brigade; the white smoke of the cannonade covered the heights. Around us the balls started to fly in the sun.
>
> Over on our extreme right, General Bosquet skirted the sea; his brigade seemed to bury itself in the cracks of the cliff; its artillery followed the columns. On our side, Canrobert's division went straight ahead to the river, and, like ours, the head of its column was hit by fire from riflemen posted in the vines and in the undergrowth which bordered the course of the Alma. On our left, the English army advanced slowly in an imposing manner. Soon, on our extreme right, the guns of General Bosquet thundered on the top of the plateau, and we saw the Russians, amazed at this sudden attack, fall back in disorder towards one centre of the position.
>
> There was firing right along the line. In front of us the Zouaves and the marines pushed the enemy riflemen back, crossed the Alma on the right of the burning village of Burliuk, and boldly began to climb the heights. A hail of projectiles passed over the first brigade and ploughed the ground around us but we were too advanced to suffer from it; the balls were buried behind us after whistling over our heads.
>
> Our battalions marched on en masse, our weapons on our shoulders, straight towards the river; the Prince was in the middle of us, calm like Napoleon; his aide, Leblanc, who was at his side, had his leg shattered by a shell and was carried from the battlefield.
>
> The Alma was quickly crossed; Commandant Bertrand opened up a route for the artillery on the opposite bank, and we all went up together behind the Zouaves who were already at the top of the heights. On our right, Canrobert's division went up on the hill; each gun had ten or twelve horses each; the soldiers pushed the wheels; they went forward with admirable élan. Until now the projectiles had passed over our heads; now, General Thomas fell from his horse, struck in the groin when climbing the first slopes. We arrived on the plateau where the

prospect of a fierce combat awaited us. On the extreme right, General Bosquet showered the left flank of the Russian army with grapeshot and musketry from a peak which dominated the enemy's position.

In the centre a dense mass of Russian infantry and artillery began to waver under the pressure from Canrobert's division. The 2nd Zouaves and marines threw themselves at these same masses, and supported by the furious advance of the 1st brigade of Forey's division, they pushed back the enemy who slowly retired keeping up a terrible fire on these intrepid regiments.[7]

But despite the difficulties it took just five minutes or so before the first troops were standing on the summit of the cliffs, from where they opened fire upon a body of Cossacks, who retired without offering too much resistance. At this, Bosquet himself rode forward, accompanied by his staff, and he too was quickly on the summit with his men. Here, Commandant Barral told him it was possible to get his artillery across and up, and so orders were dispatched for this to be done. Some fifteen minutes or so later Captain Fiévet's battery was splashing its way across the Alma, after which it ploughed its way to the top of the cliffs, the guns being helped on their way by dozens of infantrymen who had left their packs and equipment at the foot of the hills. Once on the summit, Fiévet had his guns moved forward a hundred yards and immediately they opened fire. 'It was the French artillery who fired the first cannon-shot upon that memorable day.'[8] Captain Fay, Bosquet's aide-de-camp, was one of the first up on the plateau:

Bosquet's Division, having reached the Alma around midday, the 1st battalion of Zouaves passed the ford at once; it climbed the hill on the opposite slope and reached the crest, and opened fire to clear away some cavalry close to the coast, as well as a weak detachment of Russian infantry sent from the left. Our general followed the battalion, while the remainder of the brigade, still climbing unprotected, benefited from the enemy's hesitation and established themselves on the perpendicular height.

Two battalions of the 50th Ligne were behind us, half having deployed and half in column, ready to form the square; with us also were the Algerian riflemen and a battalion of the 3rd Zouaves, which had been the first to scale the heights. The other battalion of this last regiment sheltered behind an undulation and covered the brigade with its riflemen. One of our batteries had joined the infantry, but not without much effort, and had had the honour to fire the first shot of the battle; finally, Bouat's brigade, formed en echelon more than two kilometres behind, and also the Turkish division, and advanced at great speed towards the right of Autemarre's brigade. By this bold, and yet very simple manoeuvre, we threatened the left flank and rear of the enemy; what results it might have produced if it had been possible to support with cavalry!

Prince Menshikov, sitting on his horse close to the Telegraph, watched the movement of the French army with great attention, always assuming that our main effort would be against the right of his line, for he had rejected the notion of an attack along the coast, when a Russian officer came galloping up, and informed him that Bosquet's division had gained the heights, not only with his infantry, but with his artillery.

It is said that with this news, which he did not want to believe, the Prince shouted at the officer; but upon hearing our guns he was obliged to go there. He sent four battalions of the 17th Division to the left and two batteries that had been with him at the Telegraph; it then took from the reserve as support, three light batteries, with four battalions and eight squadrons of hussars. These accordingly placed themselves opposite our troops, who, in the face of such a terrible fire, hesitated for a moment; the Algerians, in particular, who were facing the discharges of artillery for the first time, watched with amazement as whole files were cut down by the enemy's fire, and I watched the expression of the old soldiers who could not help themselves saluting the balls. However, as the enemy appeared to want to limit himself to a cannonade, General Bosquet, in order not to expose his men unnecessarily, left only two battalions in front to protect our batteries, and made the remainder of the brigade retire, by sheltering it behind the crest at the head of the ravines; at the same time he gave an order to Bouat's brigade to quicken its march.

During the fight, which lasted more than one hour and a half, our pieces of artillery, 12-pounders, commanded by Commandant Barral, successfully fought the forty pieces of ordnance which were used against them, but which were of a lower calibre. Their infantry had remained motionless; their cavalry tried to turn us by the ravine of Ulukul; some shells fired by the *Megere*, le *Cacique* and the *Canada*, opposite Ulukul, and some shots, fired at a thousand metres by our chasseurs à pied, obliged them to turn and disengage our right flank.[9]

Farther to the west, the river was full of French and Turkish infantry under Bouat who plunged waist-deep into the water, making for the south bank with a little difficulty. Once across, the troops began ascending the steep and difficult cliffs, but before long they too were on the summit, whilst a second battery of artillery, under Captain Marcy, also came up using the path at Almatamack. The Russians watched and waited in silence, much to the surprise of Bosquet, who is said to have remarked, 'Obviously these gentlemen don't want to fight.' The silence did not last long, however. Sir Edward Colebrooke, a non-combatant, had gone aboard the *Agamemnon*, having learned that a battle was imminent. He watched the opening moves from the deck of the ship:

> We found the poop crowded with officers, and every glass in use to follow the advance which had already commenced. A line of troops was passing along the shore, while darker masses traversed the plain at greater distance, their skirmishers thrown in advance and approaching the wood on the banks of the river occupied by the enemy. The village opposite the centre of the Russian position was already in flames, and a few Russian soldiers could be seen setting fire to the hay or corn in the fields, almost within gunshot of the French. The column on the shore halted for a time, when presently a line of troops diverged from the main body, and advanced to the river about half a mile from the coast, and commenced ascending the cliff by a steep winding road. Still not a shot was fired by the enemy, and to our surprise we saw the leading battalion, apparently Zouaves, establish themselves without resistance, and form in line on the summit. A knot of French officers gathered on one of the tumuli so common in the country, evidently watching the enemy. The artillery next followed, but two of their guns had scarcely reached the top when one of the carriages broke down, and the whole line came to a stand still, just as the Russians opened their fire. The French were evidently hard pressed, and one of their battalions fell back under shelter of the hill. Our suspense was not of long duration, the road became clear, the guns moved up rapidly, and swarms of skirmishers pressed up in all directions. The French advanced beyond the crest and had apparently established themselves in force on the summit.[10]

The news that the French were deploying upon the heights which were considered to be unassailable took Menshikov by surprise. He immediately dispatched forward three batteries, each of eight guns, to try to dislodge

d Raglan, 1788–1855, commander-in-chief
he British Army in the Crimea.
hors' collection)

General François Antoine Certain Canrobert,
1809–1895. Commanded the French 1st
Division at the Alma. (*Authors' collection*)

shal Leroy de Saint-Arnaud, 1801–1854,
mander-in-chief of the French Army.
hors' collection)

Sir George Brown, 1790–1865, commander of
the British 2nd Division. (*Authors' collection*)

Prince Alexander Sergeevich Menshikov, 1787–1869. Commander-in-chief of the Russian Army at the Alma. (*Authors' collection*)

The Duke of Cambridge, 1819–1904. Commanded the British 1st Division at the Alma. (*Authors' collection*)

THE UNITED SERVICE.

'The United Service.' *Punch* magazine's view of the new spirit of cooperation between the old enemies. (*Authors' collection*)

VICTORY OF THE ALMA.

Another cartoon from *Punch*, this time following the Allied victory at the Alma. (*Authors' collection*)

Brigade of Guards attacking the Great Redoubt during the Battle of the Alma, as seen by the [corr]espondent of *The Illustrated London News*. (*Authors' collection*)

Battle of the Alma, after a print by Dupray. The Duke of Cambridge and his staff watch as the [D]ivision begins its attack. (*Authors' collection*)

The battlefield shortly after the end of the fighting. The Great Redoubt can be seen on the right. A somewhat exaggerated depiction of the heights, as drawn by Major E. B. Hamley from his *The Position on the Alma*. (*Authors' collection*)

The defile at Almatamack through which Bosquet's troops passed to begin the battle. This is the Russian view looking north. (*Authors' photo*)

ther section of the drawing by Hamley, showing the ground to the west of the Sevastopol road.
hors' collection)

defile at Almatamack. This is the view which Bosquet's troops would have had as they began
ing up to attack the Russian left. (*Authors' photo*)

The battlefield of the Alma today. A view looking east from a position just south-east of Almatamack. The river Alma is in the trees, Burliuk lies to the left, and the site of the Great Redo is to the top extreme right. Canrobert and Prince Napoleon attacked over this ground from left to right. (*Authors' photo*)

The river Alma today, just to the east of Almatamack. (*Authors' photo*)

The river Alma today, looking east, at a spot where the 2nd Division crossed. The shelf on the southern bank can easily be defined here. The river was, of course, rather wider in 1854. (Authors' photo)

A British infantryman's view of the Great Redoubt as seen from a position just to the south of the river Alma. The ground here was strewn with British dead and wounded. (Authors' photo)

The obelisk and battlefield memorial inside the Great Redoubt today. To the right, the large white slab marks the location of one of the mass graves containing Russian dead. (*Authors' photo*)

The memorial to the Vladimirsky Regiment, inside the Great Redoubt. The Lesser Redoubt lies on the heights in the distance beyond the obelisk. (*Authors' photo*)

Bosquet, following these shortly afterwards with a further two batteries. Some forty Russian guns were now turned against the French and a fierce exchange of shot ensued. The unequal contest between the twelve French guns and the forty Russian guns continued for almost ninety minutes, Bosquet growing increasingly anxious about his isolation, whilst Saint-Arnaud also worried. There were no other French troops on the plateau, save for Bouat's brigade almost a mile away to the west. Their British allies still sat – or in most cases lay – motionless in the fields and vineyards to the north of the Alma.

Meanwhile, the struggle on the cliffs continued, with Menshikov sending some hussars to join the artillery opposing Bosquet. He also sent forward four battalions of the Moskovsky and three of the Minsky regiments, but these too failed to make any impression on the French. One of the rarer accounts of the fighting in this sector and, in fact, of the Battle of the Alma, comes from a Russian private, Pavel Tatorsky, who served in the 1st Grenadier Company of the Moskovsky Regiment. He was wounded during the battle, receiving two bullet wounds in his left hand which smashed the bone. He was taken prisoner during the battle by the French and sent to Constantinople, where his arm was amputated just below the shoulder. He was afterwards sent to Toulon in France, where he remained for many months. On his return to Russia he dictated his story to Nikolay Sokalsky, who worked for the newspaper *Odessky vestnik*. Sokalsky gathered many stories from wounded soldiers recovering in hospital in Odessa. Tatorsky's story was then sent to St Petersburg to Nikolay Nekrasov, the Russian poet and the editor of the magazine *Sovremennik*, who published it at the end of the war. Here, Tatorsky describes the march to the battlefield and his part in the action:

> We marched merrily to the Alma, singing songs. We left Tavria [Simferopol] at about five o'clock in the evening, came to the Alma at eleven in the morning, and were in action at one o'clock ... Our position was on the left flank on the hill in front of the lighthouse. There, the Moskovsky and Minsky regiments stood. About twenty of our men positioned themselves in the lighthouse. We were attacked three times by the French lezguavs [Zouaves] but three times they were driven away by our bayonets until their artillery came up in our rear. We were very comfortable on the hill because it made it difficult for the French to send their balls and grape-shot amongst us. It was easy for us, on the other hand. Each time ten or twenty men came forward from behind the hill we waited for them to get close before we took aim and fired before rushing back again. We just had to load and wait. We often

argued; 'Let me shoot him,' one would say. 'No, let me,' came the reply ... Their artillery, having got into our rear, began to fire on us with case-shot. At that moment I was wounded, at the same time as our captain, with two case-shots in the hand and I fell down motionless ... Below us, near the village on the Alma, the meadow was covered with a red colour, like velvet; covered with English and French dead.[11]

Tatorsky also recalled how a sutler, presumably French, gave him a drink: 'A woman in red trousers, black skirt and a sailor's hat, gave me some red wine and a cup of coffee.'

It was on the Russian right that the effects of the French ships began to be felt, with the Moskovsky and Minsky regiments suffering in particular. It was for this reason that Kir'yakov decided to pull them back and get them out of the line of the ships' fire:

I began to take the Moskovsky and the Minsky regiments out of the fire from the enemy's ships. The French did not pursue us, possibly because they did not want to compromise the operations of their ships or because they saw two divisions of our hussars under the command of Colonel Voinilovich. It is difficult to know. But our retreat was made in perfect order; the battalions retreated in good step, stopped and turned about to the left. The No. 4 and 5 light batteries that acted with these regiments removed their guns and ammunition boxes. The enemy spoke favourably of our retreat, and not without reason; it was absolutely cool-headed and it would be unforgivable for me not to bear witness to this fact and not to give honour to the regiments and batteries that kept their strength, presence of mind and cheerfulness.

Having taken the Moskovsky and the Minsky regiments out of range of the ships' fire, I positioned them behind the left flank of the Alma position, almost on the very place where initially I put the Moskovsky regiment. Meanwhile the French again began to advance up the steep bank and opened artillery fire against our reserve battalions and the Tarutinsky regiment both from there and from behind the Alma.[12]

In the meantime, Bosquet's men continued to fight hard to maintain possession of the heights, but despite the efforts of the Russians to dislodge the enemy at bayonet point, the French held on and began to consolidate their position. And it was not only the fighting men that were there on top of the plateau, for following close behind them came a man of the cloth, no lesser person than the head chaplain of the French Army:

> General Canrobert was accompanied by Father P. Parabère, the head chaplain of the Army of the East. At the beginning of the action, the horse which carried this ecclesiastic was mortally wounded after being struck by a ball. Canrobert told the father there was nothing he could do and that, as he could not get another mount for him at that time, he bade him goodbye for the time being. However, Father Parabère did not leave; he believed it was his duty to remain during battle. But how was he to get to the top of the escarpment? While he was looking for a way forward, a piece of artillery passed by him, affording him a solution to his problem. Without hesitation, Parabère jumped onto the gun and bade the gunners continue on their way to the top. It was on this gun that he climbed the mountainsides and arrived, in spite of the balls, the shells and the bumpy ride, at the plateau where, alas, he was going to undertake many spiritual consolations. He followed the columns, step by step, blessing the men who fell whilst under fire, giving the last rites to those who were mortally wounded, and lavishing his care on the other wounded. The Army of Africa had long since known of Father Parabère's devotion, and it was for this reason that Marshal Saint-Arnaud appointed him as head of the body chaplains of the Army of the East.[13]

The disadvantages under which the Russians fought soon became obvious as the power and accuracy of the French rifles proved far superior to the old Russian smoothbore muskets. Indeed, Menshikov's men trusted far too much to the power of the bayonet over the bullet, but in the event were unable even to close with their enemies. It is true that some Russian troops were armed with rifles, but this may have been as few as 2,000. The vast majority of the Allied troops, on the other hand, were armed with modern Minié rifles. These, with a range of around 1,200 yards, easily outranged the Russian muskets, limited to just 300 yards' range. The problem was noted in the memoirs of one of the Russian soldiers, V Beytner, who wrote:

> The reserve battalions of the Brestsky Regiment had nothing to do on the ledges they occupied. They were armed with old firelocks, which couldn't fire more than 250 paces. The Brests suffered many casualties without causing any damage to the enemy at all.[14]

The same problem was noted in the memoirs of another Russian officer, positioned on the left flank of the Russian position at the very moment when General Bosquet arrived on the plateau:

> On 20 September the enemy, with its terrible fleet and huge army, began to approach us. Our hearts wavered when we saw the well-shaped, endless mass of troops moving towards us. But our artillery managed to occupy a favourable position and prepared to meet the enemy. But it began to fire too early so that the balls fell short of the enemy and the charges were wasted ... Ours set a garden near the sea and the village of Burliuk on fire. Smoke – straight in our direction, a bad omen ... It had to be done beforehand, as the experienced people say, in order not to give the enemy the opportunity of seeking shelter behind the buildings and of firing at us without suffering any losses. The enemy was approaching closer and closer to us, so that our bullets were now reaching them and claiming victims. As soon as they got within cannon-shot our artillery began to annihilate them but they continued approaching as if they didn't see their comrades being killed. At last they came within range of us but soon they began to use their deadly rifles, whilst a shower of cannon balls began to fall from the direction of the sea and in a few minutes almost destroyed the Minsk Regiment, which was placed near the sea under the guns of the enemy. God knows for what. I say 'the deadly rifled guns' because each bullet hit its mark. Many officers and staff officers were wounded, especially the generals, and all those who were on horseback. But that was not all. Our artillery was smashing the enemy, its ranks thinned out, but there was a lack of shells! Two ammunition-wagons for each gun were put out of range, that is, two versts from them. They were afraid of the explosions, and our artillery fire, which began so brilliantly, had to be stopped at the very beginning! We went in with bayonets but the enemy case shot killed our soldiers by the rank. In spite of this, it was not only Russian bayonets that worked hard but also Russian butts. However, the Russians had to cede their position to the enemy, not having any real command, not getting help from anywhere else and being afraid to be outflanked by the enemy and cut off from the others.[15]

With the situation worsening away to the left, Menshikov sent his chief of staff, Colonel V Vunsh, to the left flank to try to rally the men of the Minsky Regiment, many of whom had begun to fall back towards the village of Orta-

Kisek, almost a mile south of the Alma. Soon afterwards, Menshikov himself arrived on the left to see what needed to be done. He was greeted with a brisk fire from French skirmishers, one of the bullets apparently hitting the hoof of Menshikov's horse. The 2nd battalion of the Minsky Regiment, under the command of Lieutenant Colonel A Rakovich, together with the battery under the command of Lieutenant Colonel Kondratiev, were brought forward to stem the French tide. Rakovich's battalion was fighting against a whole brigade, but despite their inferior numbers the French had difficulty in halting the Russian assault, which was carried out with the bayonet. A furious fight ensued with the colours of the Minsky battalion changing hands many times. Indeed, on one occasion Rakovich saved them himself, bayoneting the Zouave who tried to capture them. But in spite of their gallant efforts to halt the French they were unsuccessful, suffered great losses and were forced to retreat.[16]

The fighting on the western flank of the battlefield had been in progress for almost ninety minutes, and still there was little sign of much activity from either the British or, indeed, from Canrobert and Prince Napoleon. Finally, an understandably anxious Saint-Arnaud ordered his two divisions forward to cross the Alma in support of Bosquet, who himself must have wondered where on earth the rest of the Allied army had got to. Captain Fay later wrote of Bosquet's increasingly tenuous position:

However, it was time the main army began its advance; it is true we had succeeded, by our demonstration, in weakening the Russian centre by drawing towards us many troops and, in particular, the fire of the five batteries which the first and the third divisions had found in front of them in their advance; but General Bosquet had to inform the marshal that our artillery was lacking ammunition, that many horses had been killed, and that it could not send ammunition to the reserve still engaged in the river. The marshal then sent the brigade of Lourmel, Forey division, to support the right, towards Almatamack, to go in line close to General Bosquet, and, although the English were late again, it gave the signal for the general attack.

Like all the army, the marshal had followed with interest the advance of the Zouaves; then, when they had disappeared behind the peak, he had listened with anxiety to the firing of our riflemen; finally, hearing the guns, there was a discussion and everyone wanted to know whether it was ours or those of the enemy, and if our troops had been able to gain the plateau. 'I tell you,' exclaimed the marshal joyously, 'those are Bosquet's guns! He has taken the heights; I see the red trousers! Ah, I recognise my old Bosquet of Africa!'[17]

It was indeed Bosquet, and help was not long in coming. Fay again:

> Our general galloped from one battery to another with his small group of officers and staff, encouraging everyone while waiting impatiently for the arrival of the remainder of the army. Suddenly, opposite us, French riflemen appeared on the crest in front of the Telegraph: those of the first division in the White House, those of the third on the right of the village of Burliuk, had resolutely approached the enemy outposts; a battery from the cavalry division, from the division of Prince Napoleon and two of the reserve, were posted on the right bank, to protect this movement.[18]

General Canrobert's division crossed the Alma at the White Homestead, the 1st and 9th Chasseurs leading the way with the 7th Ligne. Behind them were the 7th Zouaves. The men went up with typical French élan, crying 'Vive l'Empereur!' Despite opposition from the Moskovsky Regiment the French made good progress, although they found it impossible to get their guns across, forcing them to turn to the west and cross at Almatamack, using the same path by which Bosquet had got his guns across.

At the same time Prince Napoleon's 3rd Division advanced on the left of Canrobert. As they approached the village of Burliuk, which lay to their left, they noticed hordes of Cossacks darting in between the houses, setting them on fire, and soon clouds of thick smoke hung over the battlefield. The smoke afforded a measure of cover to the advancing French, the Russian gunners on the heights being unable to see them. Two companies of skirmishers from the 2nd Zouaves, under Captains Sage and Du Lude, led the way. Jean Joseph Gustave Cler, commanding officer of the 2nd Zouaves, later described the attack, unusually in the third person:

> At half-past twelve, the skirmishers began to make their way through the right of the village of Burliuk, and the gardens which extended along the right bank of the Alma. Just at this moment, the enemy, whose light troops, armed with long-range rifles, had commenced the engagement, opened fire with his guns. A few round shot came

pitching among the troops of the first line, whereupon the colonel instantly deployed his two battalions, and reinforced his skirmishers with Captain Fernier's 2d company of the 2d battalion. On arriving near the gardens, the men, upon an order given them to that effect, deposited their knapsacks, by which means, they were both greatly lightened, and acquired more freedom in their movements.

The 1st battalion of the regiment, under Major Malafosse, promptly took up a position in the muddy bed of the river, near the ford whence ascends the road leading over the lofty and precipitous heights of the opposite bank. The 2d battalion, under Major Adam, was held back a little to the left and rear, near the gardens. But it was impossible for the regiment to remain long in this first position; for, soon, the companies of skirmishers, already hotly engaged amid the tangled cover which lined the other side, would be seriously jeopardized; and it was therefore necessary to come to some positive determination.

There were three Russian battalions posted in advance of their line, upon a detached hill adjoining the plateau, which crowned the heights on that side of the river. This hill, a sort of buttress to the opposite bank, jutted obliquely out into the river and whilst the slopes on its right and left were easily swept by the fire of the enemy, the dip of its summit, on the contrary, was so abrupt, as to make their fire in that direction very uncertain. At the same time, the 1st division was on the point of assaulting the left face of this hill, together with the high bluffs extending out towards the sea.

The colonel of the 2d Zouaves [Cler himself], seeing, at this juncture, the necessity of making a sudden dash at the enemy, asked and obtained permission from his brigade commander, to assail and carry, with his 1st battalion, the projecting face of the cliff. At the same moment, one of Prince Napoleon's aides-de-camp, Captain Ferripisani, who had been reconnoitring the bed of the river, brought orders to General de Monet, to take his brigade across the ford, before alluded to, and endeavour to get out of the river bottom, towards his left. The colonel of the 2d Zouaves repaired at once to his 1st battalion, posted, as before said, in the stream, itself. The fire of the enemy's artillery was raking the whole lower part of the valley and the outlet of the ford. The branches of the great trees, which lined the bank, were torn away by the round shot, and came crashing down in every direction, – shells burst over the bank, and a very hail of shrapnel and canister was poured down every slope.[19]

Having passed the burning village, the 1st Brigade, under General de Monet, had crossed the river, with Colonel Cler leading at the head of his Zouaves, with the marines, under Colonel Duchateau, close behind. But as soon as they began to debouch on the south bank and on the heights above, they came under intense fire from Russian artillery, as did Canrobert's men. A severe fight now broke out along the heights where the French frantically deployed to meet the oncoming Russian counter-attacks, all the time being showered with shot from Russian artillery. Fortunately for him, Canrobert received timely assistance from Commandant Barral, who sent forward Fiévet's battery of artillery, which had an immediate effect on the Russian columns, particularly at such close range. Captain Fay recalled the scene:

> Our troops, after flushing out the Russian riflemen from the vineyards, followed them on the left bank, and the Zouaves, having put their knapsacks on the ground, continued with the attack, followed by the first line of battle. At this sight, the general brought forward the brigade of Autemarre to join us, at right angles, with the remainder of the army; on the right of this brigade, there followed the Turkish division; finally, the brigade of Lourmel in turn came onto the plateau. At their side, the battalions of the first division were formed on the crest. Three of the batteries which were opposed to us, as well as two others, having withdrawn, we continued our turning manoeuvre without any obstacle.
>
> At this time, the main fight concentrated around the Telegraph, the principal point of the Russians' resistance; we looked attentively at this small height, covered with the enemy, resolute and ready to receive the attack of our soldiers. At the same time and on the same side, a large mass of Russian infantry appeared to want to fall on Canrobert's division which, only having just arrived, was not formed yet, and did not have its artillery yet. At the request of the general commanding the first division, one of our batteries ran on this point and opened fire with grapeshot, a violent one and at so short distance which soon put disorder in the rows of the enemy column, in spite of the bravery of their officers. One of them put himself in extreme danger, calling out to the men, and directing them with his hand. 'The brave officer!' our general said, when told of this episode. 'If he were before me I would embrace him!'[20]

The fighting around the Telegraph intensified with the French Zouaves playing a key part. Colonel Cler, of the 2nd Zouaves, later described the attack:

> The Zouaves ... prepared to climb the opposite bank; the colonel had the 'charge' sounded, and putting his horse into a gallop, was followed by the whole of his 1st battalion. The advance began but, unable to keep to the road, which was too completely enfiladed by the enemy's fire, the soldiers inclined to the right, crossed a bend which the river here took, under a perfect hurricane of iron and lead, and, swinging themselves up the bank, were re-formed at the foot of the hill occupied by the Russian battalions, and where they were in a measure protected by the very steepness of the overhanging ridge.
>
> Making, however, but a brief pause here, the battalion quickly scaled the face of the cliff, and hurled itself upon the Russians, just at the very moment that the latter were taken in flank by the gallant 1st regiment of Zouaves; and, after a short, sharp struggle, the enemy was compelled to abandon his formidable position, leaving behind him his wounded, his knapsacks, – and even a quantity of arms.
>
> The 2d battalion of the 2d Zouaves, had followed and supported this movement on the left; the marine regiment had pushed on immediately after it; and, thus, the whole of General de Monet's brigade was, in a short time, warmly engaged with the Russians.
>
> Masters of the first slopes leading up to the plateaus, the 1st battalion of the regiment, in spite of a murderous fire, formed itself into a column at half distance in front of a long line of Russian columns by battalion.
>
> Near it, on its right, were the 1st Zouaves, and the 1st and 9th battalions of Chasseurs à pied. The 2d battalion of the regiment, which, to effect its movement, had had a much greater distance to pass over, and over very rough ground and under a heavy fire of grape, formed painfully and slowly on the left of the 1st, which was thrown back *en potence*, so as to form an angle with and protect the left flank of the 1st division, now deploying into line. Forming at length into column of divisions, at platoon distance, the 2d battalion was in readiness to deploy instantly, if necessary, into line of battle, four deep, to resist a threatened charge of cavalry, which as it was apparently aimed at the left flank of the line, looked imminent.
>
> The position taken was, in every way, full of danger; for, under the concentrated fire of several batteries and numerous battalions of the enemy, the regiment was beginning to suffer sorely, and the men were

falling thick and fast, under the storm of bullet, ball, and grape shot, rained upon them. On the other hand, to attempt a deployment into line within striking distance of an enemy so strong in numbers and in a strong position seemed, at best, but a hazardous manoeuvre.[21]

Prince Napoleon's situation could have been made worse save for the conduct of General Kir'yakov who, with his 2nd Brigade of the 17th Division and the reserve battalions of the 13th Division, left his position to the west of the Sevastopol road and the heights above that road without any fighting. At this very moment the French placed their artillery on Kir'yakov's former position and began to smash the Russian left wing from there. Kir'yakov's conduct continues to be the cause of some debate even today. He defended himself, claiming he withdrew only when the battle was as good as lost. However, many believe him to have retreated far too early, and without orders from Menshikov. Whatever the reason, it left a gap for the French to take advantage of, which was duly done. Saint-Arnaud watched as his troops fought their way up the cliffs and established themselves on the plateau. 'Oh! My brave soldiers,' he said, 'worthy sons of Austerlitz and Friedland!'[22]

There remains a great deal of confusion about the progress of the French attack at this point, and it concerns eight battalions of Russian infantry which Menshikov had handed over to Kir'yakov earlier in the afternoon. According to Kir'yakov himself, he took the eight battalions and threw back Canrobert before the latter's artillery had come up. This is a version accepted by Kinglake in his history of the war.[23] According to Kinglake, Kir'yakov massed the great column of eight battalions with a frontage of two battalions and a depth of four after which he moved against Canrobert. According to Kir'yakov's own version the French were completely driven back. 'Canrobert's division,' he wrote, 'could not resist our charge. Hastily taking off their batteries they began to descend the hilly bank.'[24] The French, however, make no mention of this reverse whatsoever. Even allowing for national pride, it is unlikely that they would have failed to mention it in some way. Kinglake was almost certainly correct when he said that the truth probably lay between the two versions. Namely, that Canrobert, without artillery, was unwilling to attack such a strong Russian force and so simply fell back until his guns came up, remembering that they had been forced to turn west in order to get up on to the plateau.

Battle was now well and truly joined. The French were on the plateau in good numbers and beginning to cause the Russians problems. The question now was: where had the British got to?

Chapter 9

The British Enter the Battle

Whilst Saint-Arnaud's troops fought their way onto the plateau, Raglan's British infantry remained frustrated and motionless, watching their allies stealing the glory in front of them. Raglan's plan was based on whether or not the French would be able to make headway against the cliffs away to the west. At around 1 pm his men had advanced to within a short distance of the village of Burliuk, close enough for them to feel the heat and smoke of the burning houses. But there they were ordered to lie down and wait once more whilst Raglan watched the progress of the French in front of him. Then, when he was satisfied, he would order his men into the attack on the left of their French allies.

The long wait for the red-coated British infantry was not only frustrating but a trial also. As they lay down in the fields and vineyards they had to endure a galling fire from the Russian guns placed in the Great Redoubt. They looked on inquisitively as, every now and then, small black dots emerged from the grey smoke, flying towards them. Bouncing across the fields, these solid iron balls dealt death to anyone unlucky enough to be in the way, tearing off limbs, and ploughing men into the ground. It was a real ordeal. The 95th (Derbyshire) Regiment was one of many that lay waiting for the order to advance, suffering casualties as they did so. Captain Dowdall was the first of many of their officers to be struck down at the Alma, when a round of grapeshot tore off his arm and shattered his chest, mortally wounding him. Other shells fell amongst the men, killing many, including Private Avery, soldier servant to Captain Eddington, who commanded the grenadier company. No. 1 Company also suffered when a shell burst in the middle of it. The 95th was just one of many battalions suffering whilst waiting for the order to advance.

Finally, Raglan, seeing that the French were establishing themselves on the plateau, turned to his staff and gave orders for the men to advance, orders which had an immediate and transforming effect on those around him. 'Every man, whether he had heard the words or not, saw in the gladness of his neighbour's face that the moment long-awaited had come.'[1]

The word flew back and forth along the long red lines waiting in the fields to the north of the river Alma. They were to attack immediately. Staff officers

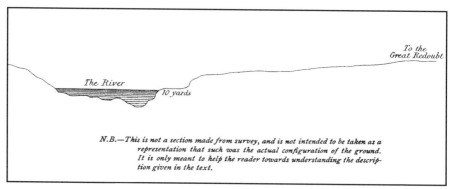

The ground beneath the Great Redoubt.

galloped back and forth whilst regimental officers looked to their men and ordered them to their feet. De Lacy Evans' 2nd Division would advance against the bridge over the Alma, attacking the centre of the Russian position, whilst the Light Division advanced on their left. Behind the 2nd Division came Sir Richard England's 3rd Division, and on their left, following the Light Division, came the Duke of Cambridge with the 1st Division of the army, including the Brigade of Guards. The order from Raglan was delivered to De Lacy Evans by an excitable young cavalry officer, a certain Captain Louis Nolan. Evans, a veteran of the Peninsular and Carlist Wars, got his men into line in the traditional manner, and with Sir George Brown's Light Division on its left, the entire two-deep British line presented a front of almost 2 miles. Cathcart's 4th Division was incomplete on the day, owing to the fact that it had been on outpost duty the night before covering the flank of the army. Nevertheless, three of his battalions were up in time to form a reserve to the left rear of the 1st Division. And then, with the men of the Rifle Brigade out in front, and with colours flying and bugles blaring, the line moved forward towards the river Alma and the waiting Russians beyond it. Not since the days of the Peninsular War forty years before had such long red lines been seen on a European battlefield, and the sight of them must have stirred vivid and cherished memories in the minds of men such as Raglan, who had seen them at their greatest. How his old chief would have been proud of them. Lieutenant George Peard later described what they were up against:

> At about one p.m. the English Light Division came in sight of the village of Burliuk, and the French Light Division that of Almatamack, both being situated on the right bank of the river Alma, a small

winding stream with high banks, in most places about knee-deep, though very frequently with pools and eddies which are unfordable. There were many trees and small hamlets on the right bank, with gardens and vineyards attached to them; but they were all gutted and in flames when we arrived, and a number of the trees were thrown down by the Russians, to impede us in our course. Here and there could be seen bundles of straw, fastened on poles, at which no doubt their artillery had been practising and getting the range of their guns. On the north or right side of the river the country is very level, sloping down within three hundred yards of the water, and at a quarter of a mile distant the stream is not visible, but its situation must be guessed at by the trees and shrubs, which only grow in the valley at the water's edge. On the south side of the river, which the enemy occupied, it is very different; ravines, formed by the winter's torrents and commanded by the shelving heights above, run in all directions. On the highest of these rested the strength of the Russian position, and their guns commanded the whole valley, far beyond the ridge on the opposite side, to a distance of fourteen or fifteen hundred yards. A curious ridge of mountain runs along the river's course, varying in height from five to eight hundred feet, and appearing like cliffs as you approach the sea. On the summit of these the Russians had erected earthwork batteries, containing 24 and 32-pounders, which were supported by field-pieces and howitzers; and lines of skirmishers were planted on the sides, armed with two-groove rifles, carrying a solid conical ball seven or eight hundred yards. It was these that did so much damage to the French, keeping up a brisk fire the whole time. In their first battery were thirteen 32-pounders, brass guns, of excellent quality, and in their other batteries about twenty-five guns in all.[2]

The British infantry had not gone far before they came under the increasing fire of the Russian guns. Initially they came under fire from round shot, but as the range decreased common shell was hurled amongst the men, the hot, jagged iron ripping holes through the ranks. Then, as the range reduced further, shrapnel shells began to explode above the men, followed by canister. Russian sharpshooters positioned on both banks of the river also took their toll. Despite this, the British lines rolled on, and when they came within range of the Russians they were able to hit back, as one Russian NCO recalled:

At about midday English rifle bullets, with their characteristic ricocheting 'ping', began to fly overhead – a sound not heard before by our troops who had never been under fire and knew little of rifles. It filled most of the men with alarm so that they kept asking each other in frightened tones what the sound was, though in reality they must have known. The first to be hit was a man named Cherenov, and the news of his fall went up and down the ranks. A Russian battery on our right, just below the Commander-in-Chief's tent, engaged the English and, as Burliuk was not yet aflame, we could see how its shots were falling short. Then the English guns opened up and straightaway caused havoc among our troops.[3]

The Russians who watched the ominous British advance from the west of the post road admitted that the firing of the village of Burliuk actually hampered the Russians rather than the British:

Our hearts pounded at the sight of the endless mass of troops marching steadily towards us, but when our artillery, which occupied good commanding positions, opened fire, the shells fell short as the enemy was still out of range. Our troops then set alight the village of Burliuk and we became blinded by the smoke which drifted back on us. It would have been wiser, as those with battle experience said at the time, not to have created a smoke screen for the enemy's benefit since this enabled him to fire on us without any loss on his side; but these mistakes were not the last. As the enemy got closer our shells began to blow great holes in his ranks; but the many gaps were immediately closed up and the enemy strode on, apparently indifferent to his losses. Soon afterwards we began to feel the terrible effects of his rifle fire.[4]

But despite the pessimism of these two Russian officers the British were indeed beginning to suffer. Their situation was not made any easier by the fact that Sir George Brown had not allowed himself enough space to deploy, and thus when the 2nd Division came forward, they discovered there was not enough room for them to pass to the left of the burning village of Burliuk, and so Evans detached General Adams to his right, taking the 41st and 49th Regiments with him, along with Turner's battery of artillery. It was all very cramped, and space tight. Nevertheless, they pressed on, coming under intensive fire as they pushed on towards the river.

Norcott's green-jacketed men of the Rifle Brigade drove the Russian skirmishers back across the river, leaving the way for the main British lines to come forward and cross. Also, they could draw some comfort from the fact that eighteen British guns were now in action, firing on the Russian position. But the trial was only just about to begin for Raglan's infantry, for as they approached the bridge over the river the ground was swept by grapeshot and canister from the Russian batteries. At last the British approached the river. Timothy Gowing was with the 7th (Royal) Fusiliers:

> We now advanced into the valley beneath, in line, sometimes taking ground to the right, then to the left, and presently we were ordered to lie down to avoid the hurricane of shot and shell that the enemy was pouring into us. A number of our poor fellows lay down to rise no more; the enemy had the range to a nicety. Our men's feelings were wrought up to such a state that it was not an easy matter to stop them. Up to the river we rushed and some, – in fact all I could see, – got ready for a swim pulling off their knapsacks and camp kettles.[5]

From the 47th Regiment, on the right of the main attacking line, right along to the regiments of Buller's brigade of the Light Division, out on the left, British infantry hurried through the vineyards and over walls, making for the river bank. Many of the men had discarded their knapsacks and even their shakos, mistakenly regarding them as superfluous items. Others snatched bunches of grapes from the vines and went into action with them hanging from their lips. With Adams' brigade having been split in two the task of anchoring the British line fell to Brigadier General John Pennefather's brigade, the 95th, 55th and 30th, but as they reached the last hundred yards or so before the river, Russian artillery fire brought the red lines lurching to a halt, sending the men running for cover behind walls and damaged buildings. The confusion was intense, caused by a combination of a lack of space and, of course, a heavy fire brought upon them by the Russian guns. Daniel Lysons, of the 23rd, was ordered to go and sort out the mess:

> My task was not an easy one, for the ground in that part of the field was enclosed, and the river appeared to wind, with high banks overhung in places by trees. At starting, I had to pass in front of Fitzmayer's two guns, which at the moment appeared to me a far more hazardous undertaking than advancing towards the enemy. However, I got safe

past them, and rode on to the right through the smoke from the village, till I came out on a ford across the river.

There I found the leading gun of Turner's battery trying to cross, but the horses would not face the water. I turned my old horse Bob at it, when to my surprise and annoyance he too refused. A cry of disapprobation burst from the drivers; I turned my horse at it again, put spurs to him, and in he went. I then rode down the stream in front of the battery horses, and they followed me.

I went on round the bend of the river to the left, passing on my way a single French soldier, sitting on a bank eating his dinner. I asked him what he was doing hanging back there? He replied, 'Ma foi, je suis blessé'; he seemed somewhat puzzled to say where! As I went on round the river I found I was ahead of our people, and a little farther on I saw the Russians still holding the left bank of the river; moreover, several bullets whistled past me, apparently from our own line, so we pulled up. I then attempted to recross the river in search of our men, but the banks were too steep and the river too deep. On returning up the bank my old horse started and fell, as I thought killed. I jumped up and examined him; when to my great joy I found him apparently not much hurt. He got up, shook himself, and seemed all right again.

A few minutes after I saw some of our men wading down the river looking for a place to get up the bank. They came on to the place where I had attempted to cross, and then came up. I sent them behind the spur of the hill close at hand. The men of Adams's brigade then came straggling on in numbers, but mixed together without any order. I got out markers for the three battalions, and, after some little delay, I got a good representation of the whole brigade in line of quarter-distance columns.[6]

Nevertheless, the British worked their way towards the river, advancing whenever a lull afforded them the opportunity to do so. It was simple fire and movement stuff. Pennefather's three regiments worked their way towards the partially destroyed bridge and towards the ground either side of it around the post road, drawing fire from the Russian batteries which began to take their toll. Grapeshot and canister were at their most destructive at such relatively short range. Indeed, Pennefather's brigade lost about a quarter of its strength at the Alma. With such a storm of shot and shell pouring down into them it was inevitable that Pennefather was brought to a halt, his regiments being forced to seek cover as best they could, whilst above them the intensity of the Russian artillery fire increased, as did that from the clouds of Russian skirmishers that covered the road.

But even as Evans' attack stalled, Sir George Brown's Light Division came storming forward on his left, making for the river and, beyond that, the Great Redoubt. This was no Light Division in the old sense of the word. Gone were the famous light infantry regiments that formed the famous Light Division in the Peninsula forty years earlier, save for the Rifle Brigade, who displayed the same fire and dash as their illustrious green-jacketed forebears. Indeed, two regiments of the Light Division from Codrington's brigade, the 23rd and 7th, had fought side by side at the Battle of Albuera in 1811, when they formed part of the famous Fusilier Brigade. Nevertheless, the Battle of the Alma was shaping into something resembling the bloodbath that their ancestors had come through over forty years before. 'Nothing could stop that astonishing infantry,' wrote the historian of the Peninsular War when referring to the conduct of these two great regiments at Albuera, and their descendants were determined to uphold their noble tradition. Timothy Gowing recalled the advance:

> Our men were falling now very fast; into the river we dashed, nearly up to our armpits, with ammunition and rifles on the top of our heads to keep them dry, scrambled out the best way we could, and commenced to ascend the hill. From east to west the enemy's batteries were served with rapidity, hence we were enveloped in smoke on what may be called the glacis. We were only about 600 yards from the mouths of the guns, the thunderbolts of war were, therefore, not far apart, and death loves a crowd. The havoc among the Fusiliers, both 7th and 23rd, was awful, still nothing but death could stop that renowned infantry. There were 14 guns of heavy calibre just in front of us, and others on our flanks, in all some 42 guns raining death and destruction upon us. A number of our poor fellows on reaching the top of the slippery bank were shot down and fell back dead, or were drowned in the Alma.[7]

Whilst Pennefather's men had to clear away the Russians from the vineyards and buildings themselves, Buller's brigade of the Light Division had the benefit of four companies of Colonel Norcott's riflemen, who did the job for them.[8] Codrington's men were without such protection, but once across the river Norcott had his men extend to their right to cover them. On the right of Codrington's brigade were the 7th Fusiliers under their firebrand colonel,

Lacy Yea, a hard-swearing, hard-fighting soldier, who brought his men storming past the 95th, which were halted on the south bank of the river under heavy fire from the Russian guns. The 95th, under Colonel Webber-Smith, were the left-hand battalion of Pennefather's brigade, and such was the shortage of space that the 7th actually passed through the ranks of the 95th to get to the river. As Lacy Yea's men hurried forward, the Derbyshire men looked on with dismay. They could not conceive of the idea of anyone fighting in their front, and in their anxiety to get forward many of them, including the Colour Party, simply abandoned the idea of remaining with Pennefather but instead set off after the 7th, with Major Champion calling out, 'Come, 95th, show them the way!' The colonel of the regiment, Webber-Smith, was wounded in the thigh here, whilst Captain Eddington, commanding the Grenadiers, was shot in the throat and killed. His younger brother was killed also, shot through the head, whilst Lieutenant Polhill was killed by grapeshot. It was murderous stuff.

Meanwhile, Codrington's brigade reached the Alma river. Codrington himself was one of the first to reach the river, spurring his horse down the bank and into the water, which was not a particularly difficult obstacle to pass. The men of the 7th followed close behind him, with his other two regiments, the 23rd and the 33rd, plunging into the water on their left. The three other regiments of the Light Division, from Buller's brigade, being the 19th, 88th and 77th, followed suit farther to the left, and before long both brigades of the division were scrambling onto the southern bank of the Alma. Brown's men were just sorting themselves out on the river bank when suddenly, behind them, came the 95th, one of their officers, Hume, splashing through the river proudly carrying one of the regiment's colours in his arms. Keen not to let the Light Division have all the fun, the men from Derbyshire had parted company with their own division and had followed Codrington across the river, coming up in the rear of the 23rd. Sir George Brown was with the 23rd as they advanced, as Daniel Lysons later recalled:

> I remember seeing distinctly a round shot coming straight towards us staff; it struck the ground and turned off. A little later a shell whistled amongst us and burst in the middle of our group, but touched no one. Someone then remarked, 'don't crowd so close round the General; you bring all the fire on him.' A short time after I heard someone else say, 'you're leaving the General all alone; will no one ride with him?' Our artillery passed through the line and came into action.[9]

The shortage of space naturally ensured that a great deal of confusion ensued in the ranks of the red-coated battalions now crowded together on the south bank of the Alma. Things were not improved either by the knots of Russian skirmishers that lined the top of the steep bank hanging above the heads of both Codrington's and Buller's men. There was no point in dallying too long on the river bank, otherwise both men risked losing their brigades. Codrington himself was 50 years old, and had joined the army at the age of 17, but had yet to savour the smell of powder in action. Nevertheless, he realized the folly of remaining where he was, and so spurred his small white Arab up the bank and onto the foot of the long, sloping glacis that led all the way to the Great Redoubt. As he emerged from the confines of the river bank he saw hordes of Russian skirmishers pulling back, which allowed the Russian guns to fire without fear of hitting their own men. Away to Codrington's right came the 7th Fusiliers, who also emerged from the shelter of the bank, with their commanding officer, Lacy Yea, driving them on relentlessly. Yea, 'a man of an onward, fiery, violent nature, not likely to suffer his cherished regiment to stand helpless under muzzles pointed down on him and his people by the skirmishers overhead',[10] didn't bother to wait for the order to advance. Nor did he wait for his men to deploy into smart, long lines. Instead, he sat upon his horse, roaring, 'Never mind forming! Come on, men! Come on, anyhow!' The order had the desired effect, not that his men needed any encouragement to scramble out from the confines of their sheltered position. Up they went, clambering out onto the glacis, crying, 'Forward! Forward!', sending the Russian skirmishers scattering in all directions, whilst on their left Codrington's other two regiments, the 33rd and 23rd, came forward with fixed bayonets, determined to get to grips with the Russians. Daniel Lysons later described the advance of the 23rd:

> Shot, shell, and bullets came whistling past us in every direction, and the din of our own artillery and musketry close to us, made it difficult to hear, or make oneself heard.
>
> Sir de Lacy gave the order to advance. As soon as the men appeared over the wall, a tremendous storm of bullets from the Russian batteries on the opposite bank of the river burst upon them, and they fell fast. Still onward went the line, though it became irregular – the 30th and 55th Regiments unbroken, but the 95th divided in consequence of their not having had room to deploy. The ground over which the 55th had to move was bare, and it had but little cover to protect it. The 30th

had to move over ground that was more enclosed, and the direction in which they advanced led them to a part of the river where the banks were higher and more precipitous than they were near the bridge. Part of the 95th were pressed towards the Light Division; the remainder were in rear of the 55th at this time.[11]

And they were not alone. We have already seen how the 95th had become detached from Pennefather's brigade in order to join the Light Division's attack. The four regiments were now joined by a fifth, the 19th, who left Buller's brigade and came forward also to join Codrington, Buller having halted his other two regiments, the 77th and 88th, away to the left, after having first formed the latter into square, believing the left flank of the British attack to be under threat from a large force of Russian cavalry that sat menacingly away to the east. Fortunately for the British, the Russian cavalry did just that for the remainder of the day. They sat there.

The British infantry at the foot of the glacis leading up to the Great Redoubt were now formed in a 'knotted chain', with the 19th on the left, continuing with the 23rd, 33rd and 95th, with the 7th slightly more detached farther to the right. The 77th and 88th, meanwhile, remained motionless away to the left or to the east. The expected storm of shot and shell failed to materialize, but if the British thought they were to be spared they were sadly mistaken, for instead coming down towards them at a good pace were two battalions of Russian infantry from the Kazansky Regiment. There were some 1,500 men in the eastern column, which made directly for the junction between the 19th and 23rd Regiments. It was immediately hit by a stiff fire from Norcott's riflemen who had been sent out earlier to skirmish in front of the Light Division. But this thin green line was unlikely to stop the mass of grey coming down the slope at speed. Instead it fell to the men of the 19th and 23rd whose brisk firing into the dense ranks of Russians first brought them to a halt, and then sent them retiring slowly back up the hill towards the Great Redoubt.

In the meantime, the second Russian column, away to the west, engaged Yea's Fusiliers, advancing from the cover of the river bank. But unlike their comrades retreating back towards the Great Redoubt, this second column of the Kazansky Regiment was not to be easily beaten. In fact, the fight between them and the 7th Fusiliers was destined to become one of the epic actions of the Battle of the Alma. As the Kazansky came down the slope towards them Yea, said to be 'the most detested commanding officer in the army',[12] struggled to get his men into line, trying to form some semblance of order from the

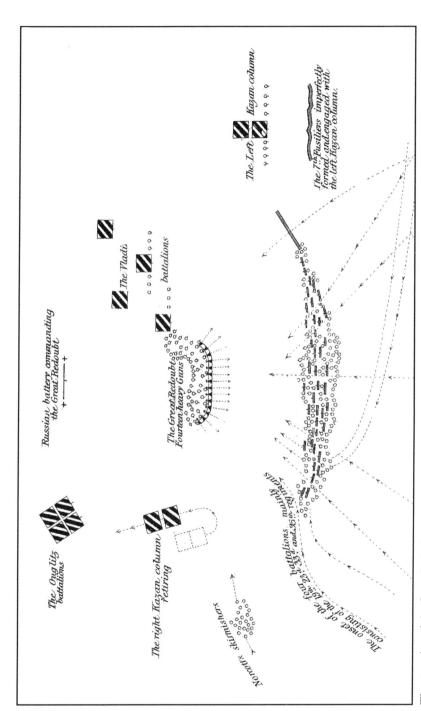

The storming of the Great Redoubt.

confused state the regiment was in after it emerged from the cover of the river bank. The Kazansky was too close, however, and for a while the 7th fought as best they could, pouring a withering fire into the dense Russian column, bringing it slowly but surely to a halt. But it was not easy. Yea himself was in the thick of the action, swearing and cursing, barking orders and cheering his men. At one point Yea called out to one of his subalterns lying on the ground, unable to move. 'Come on!' shouted Yea, 'why the hell don't you come on?' The subaltern replied, 'I am very sorry, Colonel, but I'm shot through the ankle and can't walk.' 'Why, damn your eyes!' replied Yea, 'I've got a bullet through my guts, and I'm going on!'[13] In fact, although Yea had indeed been struck by a spent bullet in the stomach, it had struck his belt buckle and had done no real damage.

Yea eventually got his men into line, the traditional British fighting formation, after which the Fusiliers turned back the clock, meeting the Russian column much in the same way that their predecessors had done at Albuera when they met the French columns. The effect was much the same. The British line overlapped the Russian column, allowing every fusilier to fire his rifle, whereas the Russians, hampered by their formation, could bring to bear only a fraction of their firepower, the vast majority of them being locked away inside their tightly packed column. But despite their formation the Russians could not be easily swept aside. A thick cloud of skirmishers was thrown out on either side of the Russian column, extending their formation right and left, compensating for their original lack of firepower, and drawing Yea's men into a deadly close-range duel that was to last for almost the remainder of the battle. At some point during the fight the range was as close as fifty yards, as both sides unloaded volley after volley into each other. It was as if the spirits of Albuera were with them as the Fusiliers traded volleys with their Russian adversaries, but despite the dreadful casualties neither side was willing to give an inch of ground. And so the killing continued.

Whilst Lacy Yea and his men were engaged in their struggle with the Kazansky, Codrington's men began the long advance up the glacis towards the Great Redoubt. With the first column of the Kazansky having been driven back, and with the Russian skirmishers now grouped around the redoubt, the way was clear for the twelve guns in the redoubt to open fire on the advancing British lines. The British formation presented a long mass of green-jacketed riflemen, along with the red-coated men of the 19th, 95th, 23rd and 33rd. With colours flying and with their officers mounted in front, the men from the shires of England and from the Welsh valleys began to move slowly forward, over the open ground towards the Great Redoubt. Ahead of them, up on the slopes of the Kourgane Hill, the Russian guns waited, primed for action. The barrels of the guns could clearly be seen in the crudely cut embrasures, but as yet not a single shot had been fired. But every man in the British host advancing up the slope knew that when the Russians did give fire it would be very unpleasant indeed. At such a relatively short range, grape and canister were at their deadliest.

Finally, when Codrington's men had got to within 300 yards of it, the Great Redoubt became a blaze of smoke and flame as the guns opened fire. 'Death loves a crowd,' wrote Kinglake, and how right he was. Russian round shot came first, the solid iron balls ploughing their way through the ranks of the British infantry, bowling men over like skittles, and smashing their bodies into a bloody pulp. Then, as the range shortened, grapeshot and canister burst from the barrels of the guns, sweeping away whole groups of men like grain before the wind. The men were seen to lean forward, as though walking into the teeth of a strong wind. They bunched together, as if there was safety in numbers, not realizing they were making it even easier for the Russian gunners, who sponged away furiously, loading and firing as fast as they possibly could.

Despite the storm of iron flying through their ranks, Codrington's men could not be stopped. They had crossed the Alma river under fire having driven the Russian skirmishers from the vineyards. They had then cleared the way of more Russian skirmishers lining the southern bank, and had seen off a column of the Kazansky Regiment. All of this had been achieved whilst advancing uphill, over ground devoid of any natural cover, and in the teeth of a devastating fire from the Great Redoubt. The men must have been exhausted, but they could not be stopped. Even the watching Russians could not help but admire the determined advance of their enemies. General O A Kvitsinsky, commanding 16th Infantry Division, wrote:

> The mass of English troops, notwithstanding our devastating fire of shot and shell that made bloody furrows through their ranks, closed up once more and, with new forces, protected by swarms of skirmishing riflemen and supported by a battery firing from behind the smoking ruins of Burliuk, crossed the river and drove back the brave Kazan, forcing our field battery to limber up and depart.[14]

As Codrington's men approached the final few yards before the Great Redoubt it seemed as though every Russian gun belched forth at the same time, tearing bloody lanes through them, but still the British advance continued:

General Codrington waved his hat then rode straight at one of the embrasures, and leapt his grey Arab into the breast work; others, breathless, were soon beside him. Up we went, step by step, but with a horrible carnage. When one get into such a 'hot corner' as this was, one has not much time to mind his neighbours. I could see that we were leading; the French were on our right, and the 23rd Fusiliers on our left. This was Albuera repeated – the two Fusilier regiments shoulder to shoulder – only the French were on our right as allies, whereas in the former battle they were in front as bitter foes.[15]

But as the smoke cleared, Codrington and his men looked on and saw not hordes of waiting Russian infantry, but instead the Russian gun teams desperately trying to limber up and draw off their guns. It was just the kind of morale lift Codrington's hard-pressed men needed to get them over the last few yards and into the redoubt itself. This unexpected turn of events brought hoots of derision from the oncoming British infantry. 'Stole away! Stole away!' they cried. 'He's carrying off his guns!'[16] It was true. As Codrington's men approached the parapet of the redoubt the Russian gun teams were seen retreating with their guns, although some were not quick enough. Indeed, it was impossible for the teams of horses to be moved at anything other than a slow pace, and not all of the guns could be got away.

Amongst the first to reach the parapet of the redoubt was 18-year-old Henry Anstruther, of the 23rd Royal Welsh Fusiliers. He was also one of the first to die, for as this brave, young officer stood and planted the bullet-ridden queen's colour of his regiment on the rampart, he was sent backwards by a Russian bullet that struck him in the heart. As Anstruther fell, so did the colour, but not for long, for it was picked up by one of his men, William Evans, who waved it proudly above his head amidst the cheers of his comrades who followed close behind him. Timothy Gowing and the 7th Fusiliers were not far behind either:

> The fighting was now of a desperate kind. My comrades said to me 'we shall have to shift those fellows with the bayonet, old boy,' pointing to the Russians. We still kept moving on, and at last General Sir G. Brown, Brigadier Codrington, under our noble old Colonel, called upon us for one more grand push, and a cheer and a charge brought us to the top of the hill. Into the battery we jumped, spiked the guns, and bayoneted or shot down the Gunners.[17]

By now scores of British infantry were pouring over the ramparts of the Great Redoubt. Codrington was amongst them, waving his hat in the air and cheering his men who brushed aside the few remaining Russian infantry. One Russian gun remained inside the redoubt, apparently a huge 24-pounder, and the sight of it sitting there unguarded was enough to spur Captain Heyland, of the 95th, on towards it, the exhausted British officer scratching the number of his regiment on the barrel. It was quite an achievement for Heyland, who had lost an arm during the advance. Not to be outdone, Captain Bell, of the 23rd Fusiliers, dashed after a Russian gun team as it was drawing its gun away from the rear of the redoubt. Despite being totally exhausted by the advance, Bell had enough puff left in him to chase after the gun team and, drawing his pistol and aiming it directly at the head of the driver, managed to stop the team and lay claim to the gun, which was quickly engraved with the number 23. Bell was later awarded the Victoria Cross for his action.

The men of the Light Division, and in particular Codrington's mixed bunch of the 19th, 23rd, 33rd and 95th, had performed heroics in taking the Great Redoubt. But as they gazed back over the open slopes towards the Alma river they saw the heavy price they had paid for their success. For along with the green-jacketed riflemen who had advanced under Norcott they saw hundreds of their dead and wounded comrades, stretched out on the grass. Limbs, torn off by Russian guns, were scattered here and there, as were the shattered remains of many a brave man. The Russians too lay thickly about, killed whilst they retired from the river to the redoubt, and scores lay in the redoubt itself. It was a tremendous achievement for the British, but their troubles were only just beginning.

As Codrington looked away to the western slopes of the Kourgane he could see Lacy Yea and his fusiliers, still locked in a fierce struggle with the left-hand column of the Kazansky Regiment. Beyond them Pennefather's brigade held its position around the damaged bridge and on the post road, whilst even farther to the west the French were heavily engaged on the plateau where they were supported by Turkish troops. But where, he wondered, were his own supports? When the Light Division advanced it did so supported by the 1st Division under the Duke of Cambridge. But now, at this critical moment, and with his men exhausted and running short of ammunition, Codrington realized he was alone in the Great Redoubt, with no supports other than the 77th and 88th of Buller's brigade, which had been halted and formed into squares away to the east. There was not even any indication of the whereabouts of the commander-in-chief, Lord Raglan.

Raglan himself had done what his old chief, Wellington, would never have done. He put himself in a position from where he could neither influence nor direct the battle. Wellington once said that he got greater effort from his men when he was on the spot, which is one of the reasons he could always be found at the hottest spots on any battlefield. He simply could not afford to be static during a fight. Raglan, on the other hand, had been extremely brave but very foolish in crossing the Alma river, some way to the west of the post road, and had galloped up with just a handful of his staff and some artillery, and had taken up position on a knoll with the French on his right and the Russians on his left. He was oblivious to the shot and shell flying around him, and in fact appeared to be enjoying himself enormously, tugging at the empty sleeve of his right arm and laughing whenever a shell flew close by. However, the knoll – some way inside the Russian lines – was not a good position for an army commander to be in, particularly if he wished to exercise full control over it.

Codrington, meanwhile, clung on to his prize, hoping for support from the 1st Division. And he needed it. Away to his right the two battalions of the Kazansky Regiment continued their fight with the 7th Fusiliers, whilst on his left were the two other battalions of the same regiment which had yet to be engaged. Along with these were four battalions of the Suzdalsky Regiment and, in a hollow directly in front of him, four battalions of the crack Vladimirsky Regiment, which in turn were supported by four battalions of the Uglitsky Regiment. Added to this there were 3,000 Russian cavalry hovering away to the east, a battery of artillery in the Lesser Redoubt, and two battalions of sailors for good measure. In all, the 2,000 or so British infantry found themselves relatively isolated in the presence of around 14,000 Russian troops. In a word, Codrington was in a perilous position and in dire need of help. Unfortunately, the 35-year-old Duke of Cambridge, devoid of any military experience, had halted his division some way short of the Alma river, leaving the Light Division isolated – save for the distant and somewhat hard-pressed 2nd Division – and exhausted on the south bank. The 1st Division of the British Army consisted of two brigades, being Sir Colin Campbell's Highland Brigade and the Brigade of Guards, and it was to these tall bearskinned gentlemen that all eyes on the battlefield now turned.

Chapter 10

Forward, the Guards!

The Duke of Cambridge's 1st Division was an elite in every sense of the word. During the Peninsular War, the 1st Division of the army was nicknamed 'The Gentlemen's Sons' because it consisted largely of the Foot Guards. The name derived from the very high percentage of titled officers and the sons of the landed gentry to be found within the ranks. Indeed, of all the titled officers in the British Army at the time of the Peninsular War, a third were to be found concentrated in the three regiments of Foot Guards.[1] The tradition was continued by the three regiments of Foot Guards now serving in the Crimea. The Guards were an elite body of men; they were the Household Troops, the royal bodyguards. They were truly the 'Soldiers of the Queen'.

Like the rest of the British Army, the Guards had watched as the French went forward to begin the attack on the Russian position on the south bank of the Alma. Then, at the word of command, they had advanced in rear of Brown's Light Division. The Guards were halted short of the enclosures on the northern bank of the Alma, where they came under sustained artillery fire for the first time since they had endured Bonaparte's 'unremitting shower of death' at Waterloo almost forty years before. Thus, when it was suggested that they be withdrawn lest they be destroyed by Russian artillery fire, Sir Colin Campbell retorted, 'It is better, sir, that every man of Her Majesty's Guards should lie dead upon the field than that they should now turn their backs upon the enemy!'[2] Frederick Stephenson was one of many officers of the Scots Fusilier Guards who endured the fire from the Russian guns:

Our Division now continued advancing for short distances and then lying down, all this under a very heavy fire of shot and shells, the men as cool and steady as anything you can conceive, as if they had been under fire all their lives. At length we reached a low wall parallel with the valley, about 700 or 800 yards from the enemy's position; we scrambled over this and entered some vineyards where the enemy had cut down all the trees to prevent them giving us cover, and also to break the steadiness of our advance from their forming a kind of abattis. The

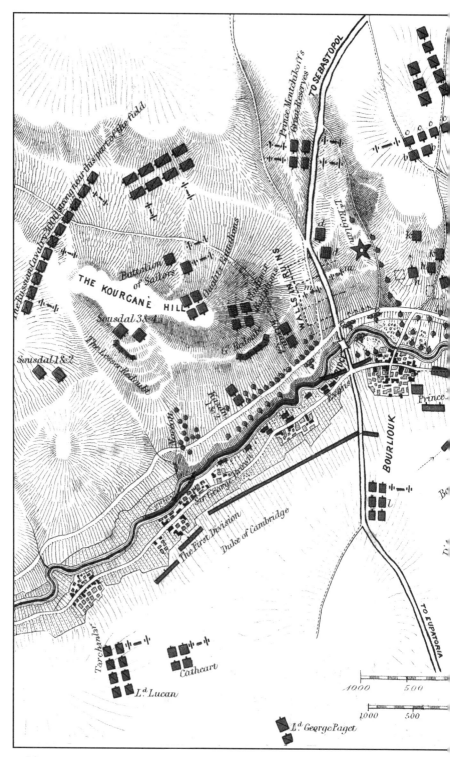

The Battle of the Alma: the second phase.

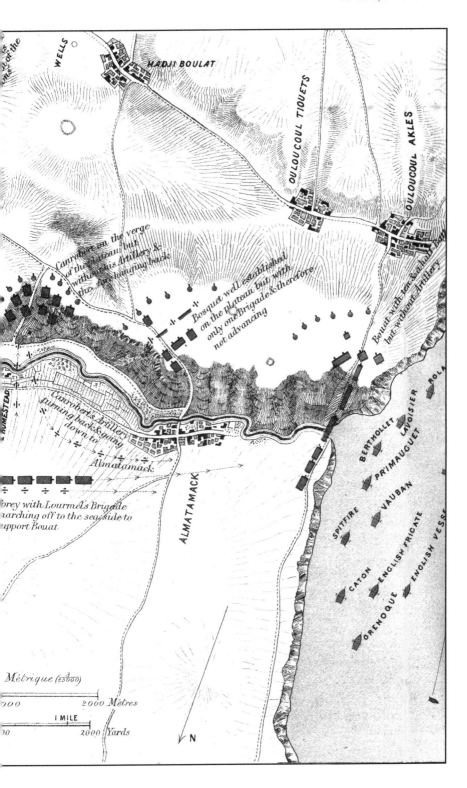

WELLS

HADJI BOULAT

OULOUCOUL TIOUETS

OULOUCOUL AKLES

Canrobert on the verge
of the plateau but
with all his Artillery &
therefore hanging back

Bosquet well established
on the plateau but with
only one Brigade & therefore
not advancing

Bouat with two Battalions
but without Artillery

ROLA

BERTHOLLET

LAVOISIER

PRIMAUGUET

HOMESTEAD

Canrobert's Artillery
turning back & going
down to

VAUBAN

SPITFIRE

Almatamack

ALMATAMACK

CATON

ENGLISH FRIGATE

ENGLISH VESSE

brey with Lourmel's Brigade
arching off to the seaside to
pport Bouat

ORENOQUE

Métrique (₂₅₀₀₀)

000   2000 *Mètres*

| 1 MILE |

00   2000 *Yards*

↙ N

enemy had been previously driven out of this ground by our riflemen. The fire was now most severe, for the enemy now fired grape at us (very appropriate in a vineyard), which, with shot and shell, whistled about us and ploughed up the ground in all directions. How any of us escaped is a miracle; our line was, of course, completely broken, owing to the nature of the ground.[3]

Away to the left of the Scots Fusilier Guards came the Coldstream Guards, amongst whom was Charles Townsend Wilson. He too described the ordeal of coming under fire from the Russian batteries:

At first, our progress was not seriously meddled with; the Muscovite being busy with Brown and Evans in advance; but, suddenly – just as we reached the gardens bordering the Alma – a murderous storm of round shot and shell broke upon us; with the view of allowing the first bitterness of the outburst to expend itself, the troops crouched, for a few moments, behind the embankments of the vineyards, and the blackened ruins of the village; but the virulence of that diabolical artillery was no short lived spurt; so, onwards, through thick and thin. Right through the tangled shrubs tear the glorious battalions, they plunge into the river, they sprawl up the steep slippery banks on the other side, they are floundering through another vineyard, interspersed with fruit trees, and intersected with deep dry ditches; all the while, the air swarms thicker and thicker with projectiles. We are in a very hell, nothing to be heard, save the humming of shells, the whiz of round shot, the rattle of grape and canister. The trees crash, and split around, the ground is torn up under our feet, our comrades are beaten down.

During those terrible moments, the conduct of the soldiers was wonderful; scarcely a man of them had ever seen a shotted musket fired before, except at a target, and yet, they looked in the conjuncture as cool, as self-possessed, as if 'marking time' in an English barrack-yard. Indeed, at this point of our advance, I observe many fellows munching the grapes that hung in clusters on every side. The tumble down of mess-mates only gave rise to the quiet observation, 'There goes old Tom,' 'Our Dick's done for.' What a true nobleman does the Briton stand forth, when the tug of war, or adversity comes!

The bearing of the field officers' horses was likewise remarkable. Fright had so effectually tamed their vices and caprices, that, in this danger, they were the most manageable of animals; for instance, I observed a little fury of a mare notorious for inherent bitterness of temper, following her master (who had dismounted after crossing the river) through all the intricacies of the orchard, with the docility of a pet spaniel.[4]

Advancing with Wilson and the Coldstreamers was William McMillan:

We halted on a beautiful plain before reaching the river Alma and we loaded our rifles and deployed into line, then advanced. The Light Division extended in skirmishing order. We had not got far before the Russians open fire on us with the big guns. Their shots came rolling along we could see them coming so we opened the ranks and let the shot go through. The mounted officers were on the lookout even the Duke of Cambridge see one coming, he sing out Lookout my boys there is another shot coming, so we done as before, opened the ranks and let it through. About this time I saw the first man wounded carried to the rear. He belonged to the skirmishers. We now advanced till we came to the river and had to get across it in the best way we could. I happened to cross at a pretty shallow place only took me up to the hips. The Russians opened the most dreadful fire of musketry, they had just got the range of us when we came to the river. I was very thirsty and would have been glad to have a drink out of the river but we had no time to wait. After we crossed the river we came into a vine plantation and the grapes were just about ripe and plenty of them. I stooped down to take a bunch to quench my thirst and at the same time I was stooping there was a grapeshot came from the Russians and dropped at the same place close to my head. I dropped the grapes and advanced as quickly as possible.

On the banks stood a village which was on fire, every house in it. This was done by the enemy to annoy us. Between the river and the hill were some gardens, and vineyards etc and they were full of Russian troops. Besides every available point on the hill being covered in artillery and infantry, there was redoubts and batteries at every point, entrenchments thrown up and every possible means had been taken to make a strong resistance. There was about 48 thousand of the Russians entrenched around the heights to oppose our advance on Sevastopol. We had to take these heights before we could proceed any further. So we set to work and at 1:30pm the first gun was fired by our artillery which was taken up by the French on our right. There began a bloody fight, our artillery advancing as opportunity afforded. The Light Division advanced and cleared the enemy out of the foot of the hill. All this time we were on line just out of reach of their cannon we could see the enemy beautiful. Our artillery was too much for them they soon silenced the enemy's batteries. We then advanced and supported the 2nd Division in going through a vineyard. In crossing the vineyards the bullets fell like hell and ever so many of our men were wounded. We got to the foot of their hill where we got out of the fire for a few minutes and got formed.[5]

One Russian shell after another came flying into the ranks of the Guards and it was actually something of a relief to them when General Airey, the quartermaster general, came galloping up with orders for the Duke of Cambridge to get the Guards forward in support of the Light Division. De Lacy Evans also rode over, urging an immediate advance, and soon the Brigade of Guards was on the move again, advancing towards the river and plunging through the water, with Campbell's Highland Brigade on their left. George Higginson, of the Grenadier Guards, described the advance:

We reached the river bank without serious loss, but we found the centre of the bridge broken, and the men could only cross in file over a plank hastily thrown by the Engineers. I forded a little further up, the river being about 20 yards broad, greatly varying in depth. While engaged in forming our line under the shelter of the bank, Colonel Hood beckoned to me from the centre of the battalion and said, 'Hamilton has lost his horse; you will therefore ride on the right to the line; and mind it will be *at your peril* if you take an order from anyone so long as you see me sitting on this horse.' He then proceeded to align the companies, as carefully as the shelter of the bank would admit; the line being complete and under control, he then gave the order to advance, which was passed rapidly by each captain. As we reached the summit of the bank we came under withering fire which, although fortunately it was aimed far too high, would have been sufficient to arrest the progress of men long familiar with the sound of shot, shell and musketry. Encouraged, no doubt, by the check they had effected on the advance of the Light Division, the Russians had formed a line in

advance of their breast-work, and were thus able to resist our attack
with vigour; but after a volley from the front rank, our Grenadiers
began their slow and steady advance, the rear rank firing what the front
rank loaded. For it must be borne in mind that we still lived in muzzle-
loading days, and that the ramrod and percussion cap could not be
handled with the rapidity of a magazine rifle. Before long the advance
line of the enemy began to fall back on the breast work, a movement
which encouraged us to press forward as rapidly as we could without
losing our compact formation.[6]

The sight of the tall bearskinned Guards, resplendent in their scarlet coats as
they advanced, must have been truly spectacular, with the kilted Highlanders
on their left, their pipes skirling. The contrast between the two could not have
been greater.

Meanwhile, in the Great Redoubt up on the Kourgane Hill, the tired but
victorious men of Codrington's mixed force were resting, seeing to their
wounded and preparing the position for defence in anticipation of a Russian
counter-attack. They were also looking round anxiously for support. Then, on
the slopes above them a large force of infantry appeared, stirring the British
from their labours and causing the officers to call their men to arms once more.
At first there was some confusion, then a tense wait whilst the men levelled
their rifles and prepared to open fire. The large mass continued coming down
towards them at a good pace, the front ranks with charged bayonets. And then,
with hundreds of British fingers twitching on the triggers of their rifles, and
with the men of the Light Division ready to blaze away, someone, somewhere,
shouted, 'The column is French! The column is French! Don't fire, men! For
God's sake, don't fire!' Despite this, a ragged fire opened up from the British
ranks, but as the word flew back and forth a bugler from the 19th sounded the
ceasefire, a call that was picked up by other buglers who then sounded the call
to retire, much to the mystification of the majority of both officers and men in
the redoubt. Any doubts were removed, however, when the call 'Retire' was
sounded again, at which the confused but obedient British troops began to fall
back, leaving the Great Redoubt to the mass of infantry approaching it.
Unfortunately, the column wasn't French; it was Russian.

Some four battalions of the Vladimirsky Regiment had been waiting
patiently in the hollow, its mounted officers watching the fight on the slopes
below them. The men themselves stood all this time in battle order, under fire
from stray British bullets. Soon afterwards a shell exploded beneath regimental

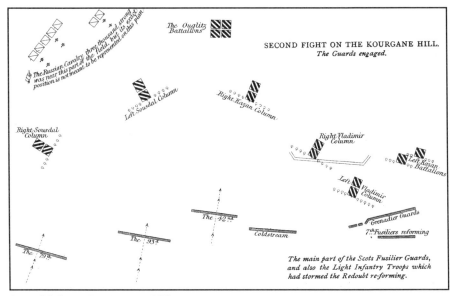

Second fight on the Kourgane Hill.

aide-de-camp Lieutenant N Gorbunov's horse, sending him crashing to the ground. As he lay there he saw another officer, Colonel Kovalyov, hit by a British bullet, which smashed into his Cross of St George. A brother officer, N A Naumov, carried his commander away from the battlefield, but the wound was a mortal one. The officers and men of the Vladimirsky Regiment were curious to examine the Minié bullets – they called them 'thimbles' – which were taking such a toll on them. Gorbunov later recalled:

> During our long stay in battle order it was evident that the order of our columns of attack must have been known to the enemy because the battalions' flanks were shelled. We didn't fire a single shot in reply, but many of our officers, mainly company commanders, were killed. Our blood began to run quicker; there was the horror of the endless victims, and, finally, the approaching enemy – all these electrified us so much that as soon as we heard the order the battalions began to advance immediately as if on parade.[7]

The attack by the Vladimirsky Regiment was destined to become one of the great feats of Russian arms, but arguments raged as to who actually led it. Generals Kvitsinsky and Gorchakov both claimed the credit. It mattered little at the time, of course. What was important was that the British had to be driven from the redoubt, and driven from it quickly. The Russians advanced slowly and steadily, with their front ranks charging their bayonets. Codrington's men were already pulling back, although many remained to open fire on the Russians. The British fire from the redoubt was answered by the Vladimirsky Regiment, with the 33rd in particular suffering. Here and there small groups of British soldiers, convinced that the call to retire had been sounded in error, held their ground and returned fire, but the momentum was well and truly with the Vladimirsky Regiment, which swept forward and retook the Great Redoubt, killing, wounding or capturing all those who attempted to dispute the position with them.

Once the redoubt had been secured the Vladimirsky halted. It is said that a lack of artillery support forced them to do so. After all, there was just a single gun remaining in the redoubt, the one which had been taken by Heyland of the 95th. The gun captured by Captain Bell had already been removed. Perhaps it was the lack of guns that caused the halt, or, possibly, it was the sight that greeted them upon their arrival at the Great Redoubt. For, coming up at pace from the river were the Brigade of Guards and, on their left rear, Sir Colin Campbell's Highland Brigade. Captain John Alexander Ewart was with the 93rd Highlanders when they began their advance:

> And now came our turn. Lord Raglan had made up his mind to get to the earthwork, and the 1st Division was ordered to storm. Up we all jumped in an instant, and Guards and Highlanders went at the river. At the spot where my own company crossed, the water was tolerably deep, and came up to about my breast; however, I was soon over, and giving my kilt a shake, got my men rapidly re-formed. The regiment then advanced, as before, in line; but the Russians had now got their eyes upon us, and at once opened fire, the guns from the earthwork on their extreme right crossing with a heavy musketry fire from the regiments who were lining the heights opposite to us. One shell knocked over three or four of the light company under Gordon, which was next to my own; but on we went rapidly to the front. A Russian rifle regiment was one of those firing at us, and poor Abercrombie, who was a few paces to my right, was shot through the heart, one of my own sergeants being about the same time shot through the body, and one of my corporals, a fine young lad, in the stomach. The whistling of the balls was something wonderful; one broke the scabbard of my claymore; and MacGowan, who

commanded the company on my right, got a ball through his kilt. Had we paused, we should have suffered a heavy loss; but nothing could exceed the impetuosity of our men, and on we dashed, getting at last a little shelter as we ascended the hill. It was tolerably steep, but we at last reached the summit, and then for the first time got a close look at the Russians, who were in column.[8]

The Brigade of Guards was commanded by Major General Henry Bentinck, and consisted of the 1st battalions of the Coldstream Guards, under Colonel Arthur Upton, and the Scots Fusilier Guards, under Colonel Sir Charles Hamilton, and the 3rd Battalion Grenadier Guards, under Colonel Frederick Hood. All three battalions were deployed in line, from left to right in that order. The order to advance was, naturally enough, greeted with cheers by the Guards, who had been subjected to long-range Russian artillery fire since halting at the enclosures on the north bank. The advance of the Grenadier Guards on the right took them towards the bridge over the Alma, whilst the Coldstreamers, away to the left, were forced to cross the Alma three times, on account of the bends in the river. The Scots Fusiliers occupied the centre of the Guards' line, and it was they who were the first to feel the blast of the Russian guns. Russian round shot came bouncing in thick and fast, knocking over Guardsmen like skittles and reducing the bodies in most cases to a bloody pulp. And yet, even at times such as these, the officers of the Guards could still find time to enjoy a joke or two, as Lieutenant John Astley later recalled:

A big shot came bounding along and passed through the centre. A capital chap, named George Duff, who was our best wicket-keeper, was just in front of me, and I sang out to him, 'Duff! You are keeping wicket, you ought to have taken that.' He turned, and, smiling quietly, said, 'No, sir! It had a bit too much pace on. I thought you were long stop, so I left it for you.' ... the shot and shell kept whizzing and whistling over our heads, and the dirt sent flying every now and again as the shot struck, and some poor fellow to the right or left would be carried to the rear. Now we got up for the last time and marched down to the corner wall – no running for its shelter, mind, but as cool as lettuces. By this time the skirmishers were nearly through the vineyards, and we got the order to advance, and over the wall we went. I gave one or two fellows a hand up, and the balls did whistle like 'old

Billy'. We were now in the vineyards, and pushing our way through the tangled vines. Few stooped to pick the grapes; but the grape and canister made many a poor fellow double up. We reached the edge of the stream – already tinged with blood – and I saw poor Charlie Baring, who was with the right flank of the Coldstreams, tumble over. I ran up to him for a second and saw that his arm was broken. I cut back to my company and went into the river, but it was only up to my knees. There was an old pollard willow lying half across a stream in our track, and, curious to say, some of the men would try to cross the water by its aid, so as to keep their legs and feet dry. We crossed and got under the steep bank ... where we were safe as if we were in the ditch of the Tower of London. We were getting our men nicely into their places – for the vines and the river had broken our touch; by rights we should have had time to reform, and have taken off our packs, for then we would have charged up the hill in proper form; but our Colonel, Sir Charles Hamilton, shouted to us to 'advance and support the Light Division,' who were catching it uncommon hot at this time; so we clambered up the steep bank and doubled up the hill in the teeth of a tremendous fire.[9]

The Scots Fusiliers crossed the river under fire, although casualties were fairly light. But the situation changed dramatically once they reached the south bank. Indeed, they had barely begun to emerge from the cover of the river bank than they began to come under heavy fire from Russian artillery situated on either side of the post road. One of the first up was Lieutenant the Hon. Hugh Annesley, whose cry of 'Forward, the Guards!' had barely left his lips when he was struck in the mouth by a bullet from a canister shell. The bullet passed through his jaw and shattered his teeth, but he survived his terrible wound. John Astley didn't get much farther before he too was struck down:

Immediately in front of us was one of those infernal earthworks armed with eight or nine big guns, well served with grape and canister, also a regiment of Russian riflemen, some lying full length, others kneeling, and the rest standing; but one and all taking pot shots at us as we came up the hill, and they must have been bitter bad marksmen, or else our line of two deep ought to have been annihilated. We had fixed bayonets, and I verily believe we should have driven the Ruskies out of their battery; but just at the critical moment the 23rd Welsh Fusiliers – who had been terribly cut up, and had gathered round their colours at the corner of the battery – got the order to retire, and they came down the hill in a body, right through the centre of our line, and carried a lot of our men with them.

This caused our line to waver and retire, leaving the officers in front, and just as I was yelling to our company to come back, I got a fearful 'whack' and felt as if some one had hit me hard with a bludgeon on the neck. Fortunately, I did not fall, but turned and went down the hill, feeling awfully queer and dizzy. How I got there I don't know; but I found myself standing in the river and sousing my face with water, which somewhat revived me; then one of our drummers came running up and gave me a go of brandy, and helped me through the vineyard, and there I lay down behind the wall which we had so lately crossed.[10]

Astley was out of the battle for the time being. His comrades were likewise in a bad way. Their advance up the slope towards the Great Redoubt was carried out in the best tradition, in line, as if they were on parade – and this despite the intense Russian fire, and despite the fact that they were unsupported, being several minutes ahead of both the Grenadiers and Coldstreamers. Leading the way was the Scots Fusiliers' colour party, consisting of Lieutenant Robert Lindsay, carrying the Queen's Colour, Lieutenant Arthur Thistlethwayte, with the regimental colour, and Sergeants Bryce, McLeod, McKechnie and Lane. Their main problem came when Codrington's retiring men came charging down towards them. The Guards could not return fire, of course, as Codrington's men masked the Russians, whilst they in turn received the fire aimed at the retiring British infantry as well as that intended for themselves. A group from the retiring 23rd Welsh Fusiliers hit the Guards so hard, in fact, that several men were bowled over. One man even suffered several broken ribs when he was clattered into by a fleeing Welshman. The 5th and 6th companies of the Scots Fusiliers were swept backwards whilst the others were thrown into confusion. Captain Reginald Gipps takes up the story:

Our formation already imperfect was more broken by the rush of the Light Division breaking through our ranks, nevertheless we advanced to within I should say twenty yards of the Russian

Redoubt, in our progress bayoneting those Russians who had left the shelter of the Redoubt in pursuit of the Light Division. Up to this moment we had continued to advance but now finding our flanks unsupported and masses of the enemy in our front, we halted and commenced firing, as yet we had not fired a shot, waiting for the Grenadiers and Coldstreams to arrive, well knowing their eagerness to be with us, and that a few minutes at the most would see them at our side.[11]

Taking heart from this, two battalions of the Vladimirsky Regiment began a slow advance from the Great Redoubt, intent on engaging the Scots Fusiliers. Both sides were preparing to get stuck into each other when suddenly a shout rang out, 'Fusiliers retire!' It remains a mystery who gave the order, and for whom it was intended. There is every possibility that it was intended either for Lacy Yea's fusiliers, still fighting the Kazansky away to the right of the Guards, or perhaps even the 23rd Fusiliers. Nevertheless, it was repeated and picked up by the Scots Fusiliers, the left companies of which were in total confusion, and with the Vladimirsky battalions almost upon them the Guards suddenly turned and gave way, as Gipps later recalled:

> At this moment some one (alas, who was it?) rode or came to our commanding officer and told him to give the word for us to retire and then and then only did we give way to the overwhelming masses in our front – this order was repeatedly given and retire we did.[12]

The Scots Fusiliers fell back in some disorder, much to the amusement of the other two battalions of Foot Guards, who hooted with derision, crying out, 'Who's the Queen's favourites now?', a reference to the fact that Queen Victoria is said to have favoured the regiment.

But not all of the Scots Fusilier Guards retreated, for as the Vladimirsky Regiment advanced they found a small group of bearskinned Guardsmen standing firm, in the middle of whom were Lieutenants Lindsay and Thistlethwayte, proudly and defiantly holding the regiment's two colours. The Russians stepped forward to engage them, and some severe close-quarter fighting ensued. Lord Chewton, commanding the 3rd Company, was in the thick of it, waving his bearskin above his head, crying, 'Come on, lads, we'll beat them yet and gain the battle,' before he was struck down, his leg shattered by a ball. He was quickly surrounded by a group of Russians who bayoneted him mercilessly. Lieutenant-Colonel Francis Haygarth attacked two Russians himself, trying to save Chewton. He later wrote:

> I was horribly distressed on looking back for my company to find them going down the hill, and I rushed after them shouting to them to come back as I had never heard the order to retire given. As I was cutting along I saw Chewton fall and immediately afterwards received a blow in my left thigh from a bullet, which broke my thigh and brought me down. The next thing I saw was a Russian about to bayonet Chewton, when another brute came at me and fired his musket at my head. The bullet entered my bearskin, grazed my head and made a most awful wound in my shoulder. I feared that I should bleed to death but could do nothing as I was at the mercy of the Russians. Our fellows however rallied at once and came back again and right glad was I when they marched over me.[13]

Chewton was left wounded on the ground to be horribly mauled by the Russians when they passed over him. 'Poor Lord Chewton,' wrote Astley, 'was most awfully cut about, five wounds in arms, head and leg; he was bayoneted and beat about the head as he lay on the ground with a broken thigh, and his life only saved by a Russian officer during the momentary retreat we made.'[14] Elsewhere, a fierce struggle began for the colours being proudly held aloft by Lindsay and Thistlethwayte.

Much confusion surrounds this particular phase of the battle. Indeed, Kinglake, the British historian of the war, completely overlooks the stand made by Lindsay and the men of the centre companies of the Scots Fusilier Guards. Lindsay himself always maintained the men on either side of him never gave way. Furthermore, the historian of the Scots Guards claimed it was a vital stand, for if the entire regiment had been thrown back there was every possibility that the Kazansky Regiment on their right would have almost certainly swept back Yea and the 7th Fusiliers, with the result that a huge breach would have been made in the British line.[15] There was also one final piece of evidence to support Lindsay: he was awarded the Victoria Cross.[16] Lindsay himself was extremely modest when it came to the part he played in the battle. Indeed he barely mentioned it when he wrote to his mother afterwards:

> The Battle of Alma you will, I have no doubt, hear talked of and described till you're sick of it, but it was a most glorious action, and

from the nature of the ground those engaged in it could see the whole thing. The advance of the Guards in line along the plain with a hundred pieces of cannon firing was very much admired. At the end of the plain and before mounting the heights there was a small river with steep banks to cross. Here we were enabled in some measure to reform and again advance under a tremendous fire of grape and canister to the support of the Light Division, who were being cut to pieces almost hand-to-hand with the enemy. We advanced steadily until the 23rd came back in confusion and broke our line. Here we had some difficulty in rallying and reforming under the pouring fire, and I had the good fortune to attract the attention of Bentinck and the Duke of Cambridge, who thanked me and Thistlethwayte on parade next morning before the Brigade of Guards and Highlanders. We then continued our advance and took the entrenchment, though with a loss of nearly a third of our numbers. The Russians stood with the greatest determination, and never turned till we were quite close to them. Our extreme closeness when they fired their last volley is the only way I can account for not being shot, as their balls rose and passed like hail through the colours that I carried. As it was, three out of the four colour-sergeants were killed. Hugh Drummond, the Adjutant, shot a Russian just after he had bayoneted an officer close to me.[17]

The Duke of Cambridge, on the other hand, was rather more generous in his praise for Lindsay when he met the latter's father after his return from the Crimea:

I can tell you, General, your son is a very fine fellow, a most gallant soldier among gallant men, for they are a most noble set of fellows. How we escaped has been a marvel to me. I watched him with the Queen's colours at Alma – at one moment I thought him gone, the colours fell and he disappeared under them, but presently he came out from below them, the flagstaff had been cut and the colours fell over him, but he raised them again and waved them over his head. He has my highest approbation.[18]

Lindsay was rather more forthcoming, however, following a visit to the battlefield thirty-four years later in the autumn of 1888. Walking the battlefield with his wife obviously stirred vivid memories in him, and he added more detail to his earlier account of the fighting:

The colours were well protected by a strong escort, four non-commissioned officers and eight or ten privates; one amongst them I especially remember on account of his cheery face and perfect confidence inspiring, trustworthy demeanour. Sergeant-Major Edwards always afterwards took credit for having selected Reynolds as one of the escorts to the colours, but he chose him on account of his size. I always remained Reynolds' friend, and backed him through many a trouble. When the battalion came home I was fortunate to be able to place him in an excellent situation, which he held to the day of his death.

When the colours were attacked Reynolds did some execution with the bayonet, and Hughie Drummond, who had scrambled to his legs after his horse was killed, shot three Russians with his revolver. Berkeley was knocked over at this time, and all the non-commissioned officers with the colours, excepting one sergeant. The colours I carried were shot through in a dozen places, and the colour-staff was cut into. Poor old Thistlethwayte had a bullet through his bearskin cap. As is frequently the case with troops in their first engagement, the elevation given to the Russian fire was, fortunately for us, too high for the deadly execution which might have been given to it. In my own case I neither drew my sword nor fired my revolver, my great object being to plant the standard on the Russian redoubt and my impression is that nobody was into the earthworks before I was.[19]

Whilst Lindsay, Chewton and Thistlethwayte made their stand with men of the centre companies, the rest of the Scots Fusilier Guards were driven back almost all the way to the river. John Astley was still recovering from being shot in the neck by a Russian bullet. His was a very lucky escape, as he later wrote:

I lay very still, and never took my hand off the back of my neck, where there was a tidy hole, and I bled freely. I felt no other wound, so I concluded that I had a ball in my head, and that I was not long for 'here.' My head throbbed fearfully, and when the doctor came to have a look at me he said: 'Well! What's the matter with you?' I replied, 'I've got a ball in my head and am as good as settled any time.' He rejoined, 'Not you! Let's have a look at you?' so I took my hand off the hole in my neck, and he felt about and discovered a little hole in front, where the ball had gone in; and as soon as he told me this I felt a different man, for I knew that the ball had gone bang through and out. He put some bandages round my neck, and was then obliged to hurry off to more urgent cases.[20]

The check suffered by the Guards was only momentary, for coming up on the right of the Scots Fusiliers were the Grenadier Guards, whilst away to their left came the Coldstream Guards. William McMillan later described the advance:

The 2nd Division retired on us and we advanced halfway up the heights. The hill right up to the top was covered with the enemy who showered their cannonballs down towards us but they fell short. We then advanced some distance without firing. When we were within good range we commenced firing. About this time there was an order given by some of the commanders to retire, it was supposed to be a great mistake but we did retire 40 or 50 yards. And the enemy seeing us retire came out of the rifle pits after us thinking they had beat us and I do not believe without any word of command a whole line faced about again and advanced and about this time there was a tremendous shout commenced on the right from the French and it was taken up by each division all along the line it was just like a clap of thunder. This frightened the Russians and they retired and we advanced after them and shot them down by hundreds with the Minié rifle.[21]

With them came Major Hume, of the 95th, with a small group of Derbyshire men, bringing with them their colours. These men received permission to join the Grenadiers, and so took part in the advance, as did other groups of men from the Light Division who rallied, turned and then began advancing once more towards the Great Redoubt. One of the decisive moments of the Battle of the Alma was now at hand, and Kinglake was at his descriptive best when he wrote of the advance, particularly that of the Coldstream Guards:

What the best of battalions is, when, in some Royal Park at home, it manoeuvres before a great princess, that the Coldstream was now on the banks of the Alma when it came to show its graces to the enemy. And it was no ignoble pride which caused the battalion to maintain all this ceremonious exactness; for though it be true that the precision of a line in peace-time is only a success in mechanics, the precision of a line on a hill-side with the enemy close in front is the result and the proof of a warlike composure.[22]

Nevertheless, the retirement of the Scots Fusilier Guards had left a yawning gap between the Coldstreamers on the left and the Grenadiers on the right. Beyond the Grenadiers, the 7th Fusiliers were still locked with the two battalions of the Kazansky Regiment, whilst down towards the river bank Codrington's men, the 19th, 23rd, 33rd and 95th, began to re-form, as did the Scots Fusiliers. But at this vital moment Sir Colin Campbell's Highland Brigade came storming forward away to the left of the Coldstream, passing by Buller's two battalions, the 77th and 88th, who still remained static. The 42nd were on the right, the 93rd in the centre and the 79th on the left, the three battalions advancing in echelon, right in front. It was a great sight as the long lines of British infantry went forward, supported by Sir Richard England and the 3rd Division, and by Cathcart's 4th Division. The final push for victory on the Allied left was now at hand.

Chapter 11

The Drive to Victory

The commanding officer of the Highland Brigade, Sir Colin Campbell, had seen it all before. As a young ensign he had fought at the first major action of the Peninsular War, at Vimeiro on 21 August 1808, after which he had served throughout the rest of the war, fighting at Corunna and continuing right through to the invasion of France. Those great days must have seemed an age away as he watched the fighting up at the Great Redoubt. Or perhaps it brought them vividly back to life. Campbell was also mindful of the number of men lost during a battle as a result of them falling out to carry off the wounded. Earlier in the morning he had addressed his men, leaving them in no doubt as to what he expected of them once the battle began. Sitting on his horse, he said:

> Now, men, you are going into action. Remember this: whoever is wounded – I don't care what his rank is – whoever is wounded must lie where he falls till the bandsmen come to attend to him. No soldiers must go carrying off wounded men. If any soldier does such a thing, his name shall be stuck up in his parish church. Don't be in a hurry about firing. Your officers will tell you when it is time to open fire. Be steady. Keep silence. Fire low ... Now men, the army will watch us; make me proud of the Highland brigade.[1]

Then, turning to the 42nd, Campbell said simply, 'Forward, 42nd.' And with that the Highlanders began their advance on the left of the Coldstream Guards. Waiting for them at and on either side of the Great Redoubt were four battalions of the Suzdalsky Regiment, four of the Uglitsky and four of the Vladimirsky Regiment. The Vladimirsky battalions had been buoyed by their success against both Codrington and the Scots Fusiliers, and no doubt looked to more of the same. But there was something more imposing about the advance of the British infantry now coming on to meet them. 'We were all astonished,' wrote Captain Hodasevich, a Pole serving with the Tarutinsky Regiment, 'at the extraordinary firmness with which the red jackets, having crossed the river, opened a heavy fire in line upon the redoubt.' He added:

This was the most extraordinary thing to us, as we had never before seen troops fight in lines of two deep, nor did we think it possible for men to be found with sufficient firmness of morale to be able to attack in this apparently weak formation our massive columns.[2]

The newly appointed flag lieutenant to Admiral Kornilov, Prince Bariatinsky, was another admiring Russian observer of the British advance. His horse had been wounded in the fighting on the plateau, and he watched the oncoming columns on foot. He wrote:

In the centre, a huge mass of English troops in their red tunics had already crossed the river and I could hear their blood-curdling screams as they advanced up the hill; and somewhere, far away, the sound of bagpipes. To their front and flanks their 'black riflemen' were going forward at the run. And all round the bridge were the heaps of red-uniformed English, the dead and wounded.[3]

It is likely that the 'blood-curdling screams' were, in fact, the screams of those British soldiers being hit by Russian shells, the British infantry usually coming on in a deathly silence.

As the Grenadier Guards advanced, Lacy Yea's fusiliers finally got the better of the two left battalions of the Kazansky Regiment. He had been engaged with them for some time, until the intervention of the 55th, who had been brought forward – belatedly – by Evans, along with the remaining regiments of the 2nd Division, finally turned the fight in favour of the British. The two beaten battalions of the Kazansky rallied, however, and faced up to the oncoming Grenadiers, threatening their right, whilst into the gap on their left between them and the Coldstream Gorchakov advanced, leading the two left-hand battalions of the Vladimirsky Regiment.

The 64-year-old Gorchakov was a veteran of the Napoleonic Wars and had fought during the great campaign in 1812. He was the brother of the commander-in-chief of the Army of the Danube, and was regarded as being as bad a tactician as the hapless Kir'yakov. But there was no denying his bravery, and when he joined the Vladimirsky Regiment, he did so with his coat full of bullet holes. He also arrived on foot, his own horse having already been shot from under him. When he reached the Vladimir battalions, he later wrote, which were left and forward of the epaulement, most of my staff had been wounded. My horse had been shot from under me and I had to send my aide, Major Durnov, to bring the first troops he came across. Meanwhile, in order to hold back the English, I took command of a battalion of the Vladimir – not having met any commanders as they were all wounded. The battalion started its advance, myself in front, no shot being fired. The enemy stood waiting. We had only to cover another 150 paces to close with him when again my horse was shot down; the Vladimir at once opened battalion fire.[4]

The Vladimirsky battalions tried to close with the Grenadiers, but the latters' well-drilled and destructive Minié volleys kept them at arm's length, as one of its officers, Gorbunov, later described:

> The troops of the former 6th Corps [the Vladimir] were real parade troops, famed for their military bearing, recruitment, their smartness and deep knowledge of all regulations. Our battalions, a moving iron mass, were ready to fulfil their purpose – to plunge a bayonet up to the musket's barrel, but each time we met with the deadly killing fire, and our soldiers failed to get to grips with the enemy. The failure of the repeated attacks brought our soldiers to a state of frenzy. The soldiers rushed to the attack without an order and perished needlessly.[5]

The left Vladimirsky battalions charged their bayonets once more and advanced towards the gap between the Grenadiers and Coldstreamers, but Colonel the Hon. Henry Percy, commanding the 8th Company on the left of the Grenadiers' line, quickly wheeled his company to the left and opened fire into the left flank of the advancing Russians. Percy had already been shot through the arm, but didn't consider the wound particularly dangerous, and, after bandaging it up himself, simply got on with his job. Although the rolling fire of Percy's men brought the Vladimirsky to a halt, the two remaining battalions of the Vladimirsky, along with the two right battalions of the Kazansky, now joined the fight. Thus, the two battalions of British Guards were taking on six battalions of Russians. However, the latter were encumbered by their formation, the overwhelming bulk of their firepower being locked away inside their column, unlike the British, whose two-deep lines repeated the dose given out to the French on numerous occasions forty years earlier in the Peninsula.

Soon afterwards, the Grenadiers and the Coldstream were joined in the centre by the re-formed Scots Fusiliers, and together the three battalions of Her Majesty's Guards drove on towards the Great Redoubt, firing volley after volley into the mass ranks of grey trying desperately to return the fire. Strange Jocelyn later described the fighting in front of the redoubt when the Scots Fusilier Guards went forward:

> We were then about 80 yards from their entrenchment, their men behind them, 20 and 30 deep, for they were standing on their hill and could fire over each other's heads on us. The fire for the next half hour was awful. Several old Peninsular Officers – General Brown amongst others – said he never saw heavier; and yet through it all I was most miraculously preserved. 10 of my brother officers were down, and I lost one third of my Company. One of our colours had 24 bullets through it, and the Staff of it shot away, which will give you a pretty good idea of what it was like. The Guards had the post of honour and we took one of their guns.[6]

Campbell's Highlanders were also coming upon the scene on the left of the Guards, with the re-formed men of Codrington's brigade – along with their additions – and with Yea's fusiliers. It was an unstoppable host. But still the Vladimirsky stood. There were numerous instances of bravery on both sides, particularly when the two sides closed with each other. Gorchakov himself fought as a private soldier. Indeed, for his bravery at the Alma he was made a patron of the Vladimirsky Regiment. Elsewhere, Gorbunov recalled the bravery of a grenadier from the Vladimirsky who fought like blazes in front of the Great Redoubt. In the hand-to-hand fighting, he wrote,

> a tall, brave corporal of the 1st grenadier company, Bastrykin, distin-guished himself. He was a native of the Yaroslav province. I saw how he was surrounded on all sides, but took his musket by the barrel and hit his enemies' heads with the butt, defending himself and clearing the way.[7]

The commanding officer of 16 Division, Kvitsinsky, was himself wounded in the leg. As he ordered the troops in the second line to move in support of the Vladimirsky he was struck again by a rifle bullet in the same leg, whilst a third wounded him in the arm. It was a critical moment, as Kvitsinsky himself later wrote:

The English advanced in three columns and threatened to turn my right flank, and the French were coming up on my left; the French battery deployed against my left wing [presumably Toussaint's battery, of which more later] began to rake the Vladimir. I then decided that my aim must be to save the regiment and its colours and not the guns ... I put out a screen of skirmishers under Lieutenant Bresmovsky, but then my horse was struck down and I was wounded in the leg. As I was being carried off on a stretcher made of rifles I was hit yet again by a bullet which smashed my arm and rib.[8]

Once again, the colours being proudly borne by the British regiments came in for special attention from the Russian infantry. Lieutenant Colonel A Rozin later recalled:

Many people saw the desperate, or rather the frantic, bravery of a soldier of the 1st grenadier company, called Zverkovsky, among a group who were running forward during the battle to try and seize an English flag. I can still see now his tall, strong figure as, having thrown away his musket and broken bayonet, he snatched a musket from the hands of a dead enemy soldier and began lashing out with the butt at those English troops who were attacking him until his lion strength at last finished. He fell after being struck down by a blow to the head. I was a witness to that frightful but grand scene and I pitied from my heart that this courageous man would never receive a much-deserved Cross of St George. How surprised we were when, three days later, Zverkovsky suddenly returned to the regiment, not alone but with some lightly wounded comrades. Zverkovsky explained that at night, after the battle of 20 September, and being refreshed by cold dew, he regained consciousness and found himself in captivity. He incited the other wounded, which were able to stand, to escape. They took advantage of the drunken state of some English soldiers and broke through their line. Of course, he was awarded with the Cross of St George.[9]

Whilst the fight raged in front of the Great Redoubt, the Highland Brigade came up on the left of the Guards, the 42nd leading the way, with the 93rd and 79th in echelon away to their left. Ahead of these three battalions were no fewer than twelve Russian battalions: the two right battalions of the Kazansky, four of the Suzdalsky and four battalions of the Uglitsky Regiment which lay in wait higher up on the slopes above the Great Redoubt; in addition to these, the two right battalions of the Vladimirsky Regiment peeled away from the Great Redoubt, bringing themselves up on the left of the two right Kazansky battalions which lay directly in the path of the advancing 42nd. The problem was, of course, that the twelve Russian battalions were still in column, whereas Campbell's Highlanders were deployed in their two-deep line, in which formation every rifle could be brought to bear.

The 42nd, under Colonel Cameron, were just about to open fire when, for the umpteenth time in the day, a staff officer suddenly appeared, crying, 'Don't fire! They're French!' Fortunately, the wily Highlanders chose to ignore this ridiculous order. 'Na, na, there's na mistakin thone deevil,' one Highlander is reputed to have said as he sent a Minié ball flying into the Russian column. The 42nd opened fire on the two right battalions of the Kazansky and the right Vladimirsky battalions without halting. The fire ripped into the Russians who, in their confined formation, could reply only with a fraction of the firepower being unloaded into them. But as Campbell, whose horse had been hit twice, peered through the smoke he could see another Russian column heading towards him from his left. It was the two left battalions of the Suzdalsky Regiment who were coming on at a pace, heading directly for the 42nd's exposed left flank. But then, right on cue, the 93rd, 'mad with warlike joy', came storming forward to the left of the 42nd. The 93rd, not one of Wellington's old regiments, but one which had been given a good drubbing at New Orleans on their last major outing, were eager to get into the action, and Campbell was forced to ride over and see to their dressing, which had become somewhat disorganized. Campbell calmly got the 93rd to dress their ranks whilst under fire from the Russians. In fact, a third shot brought his horse down, and he was forced to mount the horse offered to him by his aide-de-camp, Shadwell, although a groom brought Campbell his second horse soon afterwards.

Once the 93rd were correctly formed Campbell returned to the 42nd – who had also halted – and together they continued their advance, firing as they went. Finally, the two battalions of Highlanders reached the slope where the Kazansky, Vladimirsky and now the Suzdalsky battalions waited for them. A tremendous firefight ensued, with Russian officers and NCOs being forced to manhandle their men in order to make them stand firm in the face of the storm of British lead being fired into them. John Ewart, of the 93rd, later wrote:

We at once opened fire, the men firing by files as they advanced. On getting nearer, the front company of the Russian Regiment opposite to us, a very large one, brought down their bayonets, and I thought were about to charge us; but on our giving a cheer, they at once faced about and retired. Just as I was encouraging my men to follow them, waving my claymore over my head, up galloped Sir Colin; 'Halt, ninety-third! Halt!' he shouted in his loudest tones, and we were at once stopped in our career. It was perhaps as well that he did so, as the whole of the Russian cavalry were on the Russian right, and at no great distance from us. I had noticed them directly we had descended the height, and looked behind for our own cavalry, but they were there, and luckily, not over the river. Lord Raglan had denied leave, sent a staff officer with an order for the cavalry to cross by the bridge; and if this had been done, they would have come up at the proper time. Unfortunately Lord Cardigan had commenced crossing of the ford, which caused some delay.[10]

Both the 93rd and 42nd were enjoying the better of the fight until, once again, yet another Russian column was seen approaching towards the open left flank of the 93rd. This column consisted of the two right battalions of the Suzdalsky Regiment who came pushing on in order to join their left battalions, now engaged with Campbell. It was a critical moment for Campbell, and the Russians were coming on, relishing the prospect of catching the two Highland battalions in the flank. 'But, some witchcraft, the doomed men might fancy, was causing the earth to bear giants.'[11] And so it seemed. For, just as the 93rd had come up in time to cover the left of the 42nd, so it was the 93rd's time to be saved, this time by the 79th, who came driving forward against the right flank of the Suzdalsky as it passed their front heading towards the 93rd.

Whilst moving across the front of the 79th, the two Suzdalsky battalions were hit by a tremendous fire unleashed into their flank by the Camerons, who had little trouble in dispersing the Russians. Caught by such a devastating fire, the two right battalions of the Suzdalsky soon melted away in disorder, whilst almost at the same time the two left battalions of the same regiment finally broke under pressure from the 93rd. With no friends fighting on their right, the two battalions of the Kazansky and the two Vladimirsky battalions had little option but to fall back:

Then ... there was heard the sorrowful wail that bursts from the heart of the brave Russian infantry when they have to suffer defeat; but this time the wail was the wail of eight battalions; and the warlike grief of the soldiery could no longer kindle the fierce intent which, only a little before, had spurred forward the Vladimir battalions. Hope had fled.[12]

The three Highland battalions were now up, abreast of each other, rolling over the ground held previously by the Russians. They had put in a tremendous effort to clear away a vastly superior number of Russian infantry, their task being made easier by the unwieldy formation which hampered the Russian battalions. But what an effort it had been, and now, standing triumphant upon the slopes of the Kourgane they allowed themselves the loud, deserved cheers which rang out along the hillside. Their supports, Cathcart's division, were still some way off, but the experienced Campbell knew the job was done. Even so, there still remained four battalions of the Uglitsky Regiment that had watched the fight from the upper slopes of the hill. They looked on in frustration as their comrades ran back in disorder, many of them even trying to halt the flight, but to no avail. Finally, and rather belatedly, the Uglitsky themselves tried to enter the fray, advancing downhill a little distance to attack Campbell. But it was no use. Shaken and astonished by the sight of the dense Russian

Continuation of the second fight on the Kourgane Hill.

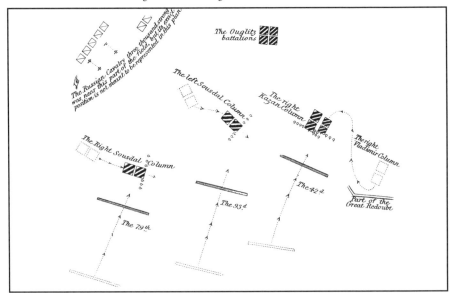

columns being flung back by two thin red lines, their advance was little more than a token gesture, and when Campbell's men opened fire again the Uglitsky quickly turned and began making their way from the field. The Uglitsky also suffered from the fire of Maude's and Brandling's horse artillery, six guns in all, which came up courtesy of Lord Lucan to support Campbell.

The triumph by Sir Colin Campbell's Highland Brigade completed the victory on the British left and centre, for the battered and bruised Brigade of Guards had finally got the better of the Russians at the Great Redoubt. It had been an extremely hard fight, but between them the Guards, along with Codrington's men, the 19th and 95th, had driven the Russians from the area in and around the Great Redoubt, and now stood cheering themselves hoarse on the slopes of the Kourgane, those cheers, it is claimed, audible over a mile away. George Higginson later recalled the moment when the victory was finally won:

> It was here that I came upon Sir George Brown, sitting on his grey horse absolutely indifferent to the hail of musketry which filled the air, and watching the relief and support which we were going to give to the detached fragments of his – the Light – Division. In a loud, encouraging tone he exclaimed, 'Go on! Press on! The day is yours!'
>
> Halting for a moment by his side, I noticed a heavy column of the enemy moving rapidly down to reinforce the hesitating troops defending the breast-work, and pointed out our danger to the general, for the fold of the ground prevented our men from seeing the threatening danger. The general replied, 'Don't you get excited, young man. I tell you the day is yours; press on!' Sir George, being short of sight, had not seen the approaching column. Our apprehension, however, was speedily relieved, for Turner's troop of Horse Artillery galloped up on our right, wheeled half-left, and, with their custom speed and accuracy, threw shot and shell into the advancing columns. I could see the Russian commanding officers waving their swords and encouraging their men, but to no purpose, the columns turned and fled.
>
> Meanwhile our line advanced with firm and impressive regularity until it came within fifty yards of the breast-work. The word 'Charge!' rang out; the line broke into a run, and, bounding over the parapet, our Grenadiers flung themselves on the few Russians remaining inside. The guns had already been removed by the Russians; only one was left for a trophy. Our ranks were re-formed, under the stern orders of our

colonel, and in a few minutes we stood again in column, prepared for any movement or adventure. But it was soon evident that our enemy had had enough; the army which Prince Menshikov had led the Emperor to believe held an impregnable position was in full retreat, after a battle which had lasted less than four hours. The victory was complete.[13]

The retreat of the Russians from the Kourgane forced General Kvitsinsky into pulling back the guns covering the post road, and thus the way was then left open for Pennefather and Adams, still fighting on either side of the road to continue their advance. This was made easier by the support given to them by two guns from Turner's battery that Lord Raglan had brought forward to join him on the knoll from where he had watched, somewhat dangerously exposed, most of the fighting. Turner's gunners disabled one Russian gun and blew up an ammunition wagon, which was scattered to the winds in spectacular fashion. De Lacy Evans' 2nd Division, less those who had gone off with Codrington, were now pouring up the lower slopes on the eastern side of Telegraph Hill, covered by Turner's guns, whilst away to their right the French continued to drive home the Allies' advantage. The closing stages of the battle were now fast approaching.

Chapter 12

End of the Battle

Ever since he had ordered forward Bosquet's troops just after midday, Marshal Saint-Arnaud had watched with a mixture of anxiety, pride and relief, as the Allies sought to establish themselves on the heights to the south of the river Alma. It was difficult to see what was happening to his own men owing to the lie of the land, whilst away to his left the British troops were shrouded in gun smoke. Saint-Arnaud, in fact, had done quite a remarkable job considering just how ill he was. In fact, he had barely a few days to live, but he was all activity on the afternoon of 20 September, organizing his troops and sending them into action. General Forey was sent to support Canrobert with one of his brigades, the other being dispatched to fight on the extreme right of the French attack. He then sent General d'Aurelle to support also, and after a brief reconnaissance of the river, Colonel Beuret was splashing across the Alma at the head of the 39th Regiment. Once across, the men threw off their packs and set off in double quick time, heading towards the telegraph station. All along the heights French troops had struggled to establish themselves in the face of heavy Russian fire, but as more and more of them gained the plateau, and with the eventual success of the British to the east, Russian resistance had begun to crumble. The 1st Zouaves and 1st Chasseurs, along with the 2nd Zouaves, were exposed to a particularly heavy fire, forcing them to take shelter, until two batteries of artillery under Commandant Boussinière came up to support them. But the fire of four Russian guns continued to cause casualties amongst them, whilst a heavy column of Russian cavalry suddenly appeared, hovering menacingly.

What was more of a mystery was the exact whereabouts of Kir'yakov's column of eight infantry battalions. Despite some accounts that have them disappear along with Kir'yakov at an early stage of the battle, it appears that the column was, nevertheless, still present and very threatening during the latter stages of the battle. Indeed, these eight battalions were brought forward against the advancing head of Canrobert's division once again, as they had apparently been earlier in the afternoon. However, on this occasion they had not bargained for French artillery, which quickly began to pour shot and shell into their confused ranks. Indeed, Kir'yakov himself claimed he was shelled by French ships, as he could not see where the firing was coming from. In fact, the guns had been deployed in some dead ground from where it was difficult for the Russians to see them. Whatever the case, the columns were sent reeling backwards in retreat, allowing Canrobert to continue his advance. Octave Cullet was with the 20th Ligne when they finally felt the tide of battle turning in their favour:

> In front of the battalions of the 20th Ligne and the 22nd Léger dense masses of Russian infantry made a pronounced movement to the rear. We went up in columns but now deployed to fight; we moved across the old Russian camp of huts made of straw, from where we had some respite from the enemy fire.
>
> Our elite companies of riflemen opened a deadly fire; on our right, the twelve pieces of artillery under Commandant Bertrand, covered by the 19th Chasseurs, fired a mass of shells and rockets into the masses of the enemy infantry; the ground was covered with Russian corpses. We advanced slowly; the intricacies of the ground caused many balls to rebound over our heads; our losses were almost none.
>
> On our left, where we were on the highest point of the heights, we had a grand view of the advance of the English army. It advanced in a tight mass, across difficult ground and under the deadly fire of the Russian army and their powerful artillery. The ground was strewn with dead and dying, but nothing could stop our intrepid allies; they continued their advance at an ordinary step, coolly, and without any fear, clearing in their path the 12-gun redoubt, which was vigorously defended, and continued on as if on parade until they reached the plateau, which was covered with Russian corpses; like us, they forced the enemy back, the Russians beginning to retreat from the right to the left, all along the line of battle.[1]

With the Russians in this part of the battlefield now pulling back, Colonel Cler, commanding the 2nd Zouaves, took it upon himself to charge the telegraph station. Cler raised himself in his saddle and, turning to his men, cried, 'Follow me, my Zouaves! To the tower! To the tower!'[2] The 2nd Zouaves were followed instantly by the 1st Zouaves, the Foot Chasseurs and the 39th Ligne, under Beuret and d'Aurelle:

Pointing out to them, then, the unfinished, octagonal tower, intended for a telegraph station, which stood upon the highest point of the enemy's line, the colonel cried out to his gallant fellows, 'Follow me, my Zouaves, – forward upon that tower!' and, as he spurred his horse in that direction, they all dashed after him, at the *pas de course*.

The 1st Zouaves did the same; the two regiments arrived, side by side, at the foot of the tower, and quickly made themselves masters of it, in spite of the resistance offered by two companies of skirmishers, armed with heavy rifles, who had been placed there to defend it.

But the enemy's reserves, extended *en echelon* to the right and left, so as to cross their fire over every inch of the ground lying in front of the tower, were posted immediately behind, and on either side of it. Between them, the 2d Zouaves, and the battalions of the first line under the orders of General Canrobert and Colonel Bourbaki, then began a close and deadly combat, all the more desperately fought, for its being known to both officers and men, that here lay the key to the enemy's position, and the very heart of the battle.

Colonel Cler, who had been the first to reach the foot of the tower, seized the eagle of his regiment and planted it upon the scaffolding, amid the cries of *Vive l'Empereur!* Orderly Sergeant Fleury, of the 1st Zouaves, who managed to get on top of the upper range of scaffolding, sustained the flag in this position for a moment or two, but soon fell a lifeless corpse, struck down by a grape shot in the head. The colours of the 1st Zouaves were quickly seen floating side by side with those of the 2d regiment; and had hardly been raised there, before the colour-staff was cut in two by a shell.

On the arrival of a brigade of the reserve, under command of General d'Aurelles, Lieutenant Poitevin, colour-bearer of the 39th of the line, seeing the glorious place occupied by the colours of the 1st and 2d Zouaves, rushed forward in advance of his battalion, and planted those of his own regiment upon the tower, – and as he pressed the colour-staff close to his heart to hold it up, he had his breast torn open with a round shot, and paid with his life for the performance of this act of generous daring.

The struggle around the tower, was a fierce and sanguinary one – but lasted only a short time. Prince Mentschikoff, seeing the key of his position in the hands of the French, was at length compelled to beat a retreat. The enormous mass of cavalry and infantry, assembled upon this part of the field of battle, accordingly retired in good order under cover of its artillery, which continued to sweep the space around the tower with an unceasing fire.[3]

The fighting intensified, and even Canrobert was knocked down by the fragment of a Russian ball that struck him in the shoulder. He was carried to the telegraph station unconscious, but was revived soon afterwards. By now, the French Army was well and truly established on the plateau, pressing on despite the receding Russian fire. The Turks were up also, supporting them. Even Saint-Arnaud was on the plateau, congratulating his generals for their efforts. Boussinière's artillery had moved to support them also, with Toussaint's battery opening fire on the left flank of the Russians directly opposing the British attack at a range of about 400 yards. Indeed, this artillery fire frequently goes overlooked in the majority of British histories of the Alma battle, but there is little doubt it gave De Lacy Evans' division, and, in fact, the whole of the right of the British attack, vital cover during the latter stages of the battle.

Saint-Arnaud's troops were on the plateau in strength and in possession of Telegraph Hill, their artillery pounding away at the left of the Russian Army, whilst the British in their turn occupied the Kourgane. There was no option for Menshikov but retreat. As soon as the general retreat began, the commander of the Volynsky Regiment, Colonel A Khrushchev, was ordered to cover the retreating army. The commander of artillery, Major General L Kishinsky, placed thirty guns ahead of the Volynsky, its right flank being protected by the hussar brigade and its left by the Cossacks. All these were fresh troops who had taken no part in the battle. After Kishinsky's guns opened fire, the Allied pursuit stopped. It was a painful retreat for the Russians, not only from a morale point of view, but from a human perspective also. One Russian eyewitness wrote:

> The sight was so painful and distressing that a man of a weak and nervous disposition could easily go mad. Indeed, it was impossible to watch with indifference the hundreds of mutilated soldiers, gasping for breath, who dragged themselves almost unconsciously after their comrades, letting out terrible, unbearable cries at each step. But it was an inevitable consequence of the war. Some soldiers had several wounds, six or seven, in all parts of body, mainly from rifle bullets. Fatal inflammations and infections quickly set in. Also, the soldiers

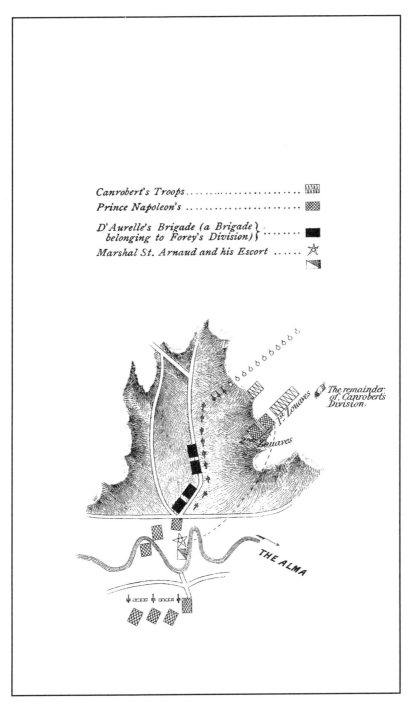

Canrobert's Troops..........................

Prince Napoleon's ....

D'Aurelle's Brigade (a Brigade belonging to Forey's Division) ....

Marshal St. Arnaud and his Escort ......

Advance of the eight battalions against Canrobert, I.

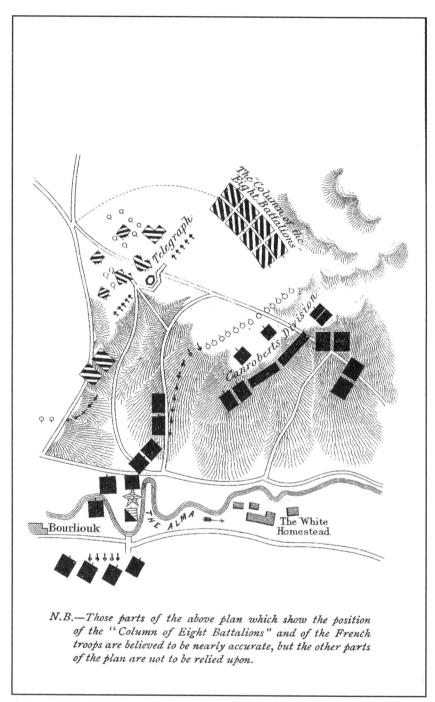

N.B.—*Those parts of the above plan which show the position
of the "Column of Eight Battalions" and of the French
troops are believed to be nearly accurate, but the other parts
of the plan are not to be relied upon.*

Advance of the eight battalions against Canrobert, II.

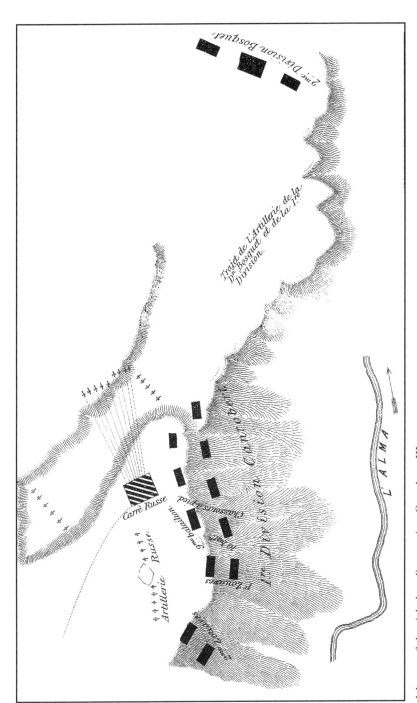

Advance of the eight battalions against Canrobert, III.

were parched with thirst, but there was neither water nor help. A retreating army doesn't leave behind it doctors, medical attendants and carriages. The wounded had to take care of themselves. The flaps of coats and ragged shirts were used as bandages. They were pleading with the passing soldiers for help but they used the last spark of life to reach their friends.[4]

Here again there is much conflict and confusion regarding the course of events from the Russian point of view. Kir'yakov was and still is alleged to have abandoned the position on the left of the Russian Army without orders and at a premature stage of the battle. Menshikov's chief of staff, Vunsh, accused Kir'yakov of performing a disappearing act shortly after the French attack on Telegraph Hill, adding that he was not seen again until the army reached Sevastopol, to which Kir'yakov responded somewhat unconvincingly in the Russian press. Captain M I Enisherlov, of the Uglitsky Regiment, writing about the battle four years later, said that only Kir'yakov himself could throw any light on the 'strange withdrawal'.[5] To his credit, Kir'yakov did actually comment on the sequence of events that led to the retreat and his part in it. Writing in 1856 he recalled the events that followed after he had withdrawn the Moskovsky and the Minsky regiments from the fire of the French ships and from the French infantry and artillery that had established themselves on the plateau. He also cited the Russian infantry's failure to stand in the face of such a hot fire from the Allies:

> Besides, the withdrawal of different parts of our front line back up the hill at different periods of time could easily have been turned into a retreat, imperceptibly both for the troops and for the commanders. Only this circumstance can explain why the retreat began, for it was never ordered. As to the fighting that went on in the intervals between the withdrawal of the troops and the full retreat from the position, it could be said that it consisted of separate actions by various units in order to support and rescue their comrades. Thus, on the right flank the Vladimirsky Regiment rescued the battery in the redoubt and the Chasseurs Regiment of His Imperial Highness Great Duke Mikhail Aleksandrovich, while in the centre the Borodinsky Chasseurs Regiment advanced and covered the retreat of No. 2 light battery of the 16th Brigade. On the left flank the Moskovsky and Minsky regiments pulled back from the fire of the enemy's ships under cover of No. 12

horse battery and No. 3 battery of the Donskaya reserve, which were advanced, these regiments having lost up to 1,600 men and being absolutely disordered.

It is obvious that, once the coordination between the actions of our troops disappeared the battle degenerated into individual actions by the regiments; none of the commanders involved in the fighting with their units could know and see what was happening at the other points on the battlefield. As the reserves were involved only at the beginning of the battle, there was no opportunity either to restore the unity in commanding or to change the direction of the battle.

It was impossible to leave the left flank exposed to the French cross-fire; there was no time to wait for the orders because our troops on the right flank were already retreating. That is why I gave orders to withdraw the left flank and formed all the troops of the left flank on both sides of the high road, behind the height where our main reserve (Minsky and Volynsky) had initially stood. Having established that the right flank was in full retreat and in order to coordinate the movement of my wing with its movement, I further withdrew the Moskovsky, Minsky, and Tarutinsky regiments and the reserve battalions of the 13th Division, formed them on the next height and put up to thirty guns on the position (the Donskaya No. 3 Battery and the No. 4 and 5 light batteries of the 17th Division) in front of the infantry. To the left of the batteries there stood two hussar regiments of Duke Maximilian Leihtenbergsky and Saxen-Weimarsky that were sent to me to cover the retreat. The enemy's infantry and cavalry were clearly seen in great masses on the position where our right wing and its reserve had been initially drawn up.

The enemy did not pursue us. After remaining some time on this second position I ordered the infantry to go towards the Kacha to where the troops of the right flank had withdrawn. Four guns of the Donskaya Reserve No. 3 battery and the cavalry covered the retreat. At nine o'clock in the evening the troops of the left wing, save for the Borodinsky Chasseurs of His Imperial Majesty's regiment, arrived at the Kacha and crossed the river in darkness. As for me, I went to report to the commander-in-chief and reached His Serenity's tent at twelve o'clock at night.

It is clear from the description I have given above that the artillery and the cavalry that covered the retreat of the left wing of the infantry were on the left wing of the Alma position as a result of the natural progress of the battle. Then there is the debate on what flank began the retreat – right or left; it is to be solved by the Borodinsky Chasseurs of His Imperial Majesty's regiment. This regiment stood in the centre and although it formed a part of the left wing, it helped No. 3 light battery of the 16th Brigade to retreat from its position on the right wing. That is why the Borodinsky were not under my command either during the battle, or during the whole day of 20 September. On retreating towards the Kacha I saw to the left and very far ahead of the right flank column a battalion in white arriving. As to the Borodinsky, they joined the left wing column only the next day, on 21 September.

I could give more evidence that the left flank did not begin the retreat but, in fact, covered the retreat of the right wing. But I will limit myself to what I have said already.[6]

Meanwhile, the withdrawal from the field continued. Captain Hodasevich, with the Tarutinsky Regiment, watched whilst the Vladimirsky Regiment fought to hold back the advancing British infantry:

In the centre, while we were retreating, the regiment of Vladimir advanced to the support of those already engaged. It deployed into columns of battalions, and charged with the bayonet without any assistance from artillery, though there were still two batteries in reserve that had not fired a shot. It was received with great firmness by the English troops, and after a fearful struggle, in which it lost half its men, forced to retire in confusion. This proves that our Generals had a very poor notion of military tactics, for to send a regiment to the charge without previously having weakened the enemy by artillery is contrary to all rule.

Prince Menshikov showed a great deal of personal courage; four officers of his suite were killed near him by the fire from the fleet while he remained unmoved. But for a Commander-in-Chief courage is not the only quality required; in fact it is a part of his duty not to expose himself, unless absolutely necessary, to the enemy's fire.

We remained on the hill a short time, above the position the army previously occupied, when the Major commanding the battalion decided that we must retreat. Skirmishers were thrown out while we went to the right about and retired thirty yards, when we again came to a halt for five minutes, only to see that our army was utterly routed and beaten out of an almost unassailable position. The retreat then began in earnest; a few minutes afterwards we became exposed to a cross fire from the English and French batteries, and on all sides the men cried out 'To the right!' 'To the left' to avoid the shot, and in one place they broke into a run. We had the greatest difficulty to keep our men in order. At one time I was obliged to threaten to cut down the first man who should break out of the ranks, and was unfortunately obliged to keep my word with one man. It must, however, be said that the men of the 6th Corps were all young soldiers, as this corps has always served as a depot for the four first corps, and frequently for the 5th and 7th Corps. ... In our regiment there were men who did not know how to load their firelocks; and when a man does not know how to use his arms, of course he would not have much confidence in himself when he hears shot, shell, and rifle-balls about his ears.[7]

The situation for the Russians was now dire. British and French artillery were pouring shot and shell into the retreating ranks of Menshikov's army. Indeed, the Uglitsky Regiment, covering the retreat of both the Vladimirsky and Kazansky regiments, suffered terrible casualties from British artillery fire as they melted away to the south. All was confusion in the Russian ranks. They had been driven from a strong position by troops they had considered to be vastly inferior to themselves, whilst many of their officers were, according to some Russian accounts, by now drunk and incapable of maintaining discipline. In all, it was a desperate situation that needed to be exploited by British cavalry. Indeed, Captain Hodasevich wrote:

We retreated in disorder across the valley that divides the heights of the Alma from those of the Katcha, and on the latter heights we by some strange accident halted and formed into order of battle. I here saw the enemy's cavalry descend into the valley, and cut off retreating stragglers, for the most part wounded men. We remained on the second line of heights about ten minutes in fear and trembling, as we expected the enemy would have followed, and we knew that our only safety was in showing a bold front while the greater part of the army continued to retreat in disorder. We then continued our retreat. Here most of us began to draw our breath more freely, and to thank Heaven we were safe for that day at least, for we could no longer hear the balls whistling about our ears. Here I asked the commander of the battalion wither we were going – I was ashamed to ask whether we were retreating, or rather running, for such it was but the Major did not know; he had no orders where to go.[8]

And yet, just at the moment when Lucan's cavalry ought to have been sent off in pursuit of the retreating Russians, Lord Raglan decided that 'the cavalry were not to attack'. Initially the British cavalry had in fact been sent forward. Lord Cardigan went off with half of his cavalry escorting the British guns on the right, whilst Lord Lucan advanced with the remainder to escort the guns on the left. Lucan, riding in front with a squadron of the 17th Lancers, actually managed to cut off a sizeable number of Russian stragglers, whilst a troop of the 11th Hussars did likewise. Amongst the latter was RSM George Loy Smith, who wrote about the brief pursuit in his diary:

On arriving at the brow of the opposite hill, before us was a vast plain. In the distance could be seen the Russian Army in full retreat, with many stragglers. We now sent out pursuers to make prisoners of all that could be overtaken. A number were brought back – most of them unwounded. One (a Pole, not wounded) appeared rather glad he was taken. The ball part of the grenade of his helmet had been shot through, which I appropriated and now have in my possession. Sergeant Bond, during the pursuit, received a bayonet wound in the face from a prisoner he had taken who pretended to surrender, then treacherously made a point at him. Bond would have cut him down, but an officer galloped up and told him to spare the scoundrel. At this moment it was perceived that a swarm of Cossacks were rapidly approaching, so that the pursuers had to retreat and this Russian escaped. It is singular that Bond was the only man of the cavalry that was wounded, and not a single horse – although we had, during the day, at three different times been exposed to a cannonade – and once been under rifle fire.[9]

There were, in fact, easy pickings to be had by Lucan's cavalry if they had been allowed to press on. Indeed, some Russian officers thought that, had the pursuit been pressed home with the vigour it demanded, barely 15,000 of them would have made it back to Sevastopol. In the event, Lord Raglan decided not to risk his cavalry, but keep them instead in his now famous 'bandbox'.

Naturally, both Cardigan and Lucan, already enraged by their lack of activity during the day, were astonished by the recall, which also involved freeing their prisoners. It was too much for them. Not only had they watched motionless whilst the infantry held sway all day, but now they were being denied the opportunity to turn a hard-earned victory into a fully-fledged rout. We can almost feel the hand of Wellington again here. We know just how much Raglan looked to Wellington during their long years of working together. Like Wellington, Raglan had seen for himself how British cavalry had come to grief on a few high-profile occasions in the Peninsular War. Indeed, Wellington developed a great distrust of his cavalry between 1808 and 1815. Now, forty years on, was that same distrust put upon his old, faithful servant, Raglan? Perhaps.[10]

Nevertheless, Cardigan got his cavalry forward to sweep the remnants of the Russian Army from the field, not that too many remained behind, save for the dead and wounded. Albert Mitchell, of the 13th Light Dragoons, was with his regiment as it advanced towards the close of the battle. His account also reveals the sense of irritation felt by the cavalry at not having done anything to help win the battle for the Allies:

> We were now ordered to cross the river at a ford, that having to pass down a narrow lane between stone walls, it took some little time to get across, during which time a field battery that was posted on the enemy's right tried its utmost to sweep the lane along which we were advancing, but luckily for us they had neglected to cut down the trees at this part (which they had done lower down the river). Their shot fell among the trees, in some instances cutting them asunder. One large tree was cut in two just on my right a few yards before I arrived at the river. As we were at a gallop we had no time to let the horses drink. They wanted water very much, but we could not stay for that. As soon as the battery found we had crossed they limbered up and retired, followed by the cavalry, who made no attempt to check our advance.
>
> We ascended the hill at a gallop in column of troops. Many poor fellows we passed begged for assistance, but we could not stay to render any, and after gaining some distance farther up we saw to what a fearful extent the enemy had suffered. His dead were lying by scores, and we could also see that our own poor fellows had suffered terribly. There were Guardsmen, Highlanders, and Light Division men in great numbers killed and wounded. We pushed on in haste, expecting to be

called into play on the top of heights.

We soon arrived there, and then what a sight! Our divisions were in line on the crest of the hill hurrahing, and throwing their caps in the air. We took up the cheer, and I shouted with the rest, when a troop leader, looking sternly at me, said: 'What are you shouting for? We have done nothing to shout for yet.' He said the same to several others; so we gave it up, and left the cheering for those who had won a victory.

The enemy, who were now in full retreat, had by this time got some distance across the plain, which was pretty level for two or three miles. Yet there were great numbers of stragglers between us and his rearmost troops. With a view to the capture of these we were moved out of the front, and many of them were driven in prisoners. As soon as the enemy saw how we were employed he brought some guns into action, but did not open fire on us. Among the prisoners we found many quite drunk, which we were not surprised at after a little while, for there were two large barrels of spirits as well as some empty ones. The spirits were destroyed as soon as possible, as some doubts existed as to whether they might be poisoned. At any rate that is what we were told by the officers.

There were hundreds of firelocks lying about in all directions, as well as knapsacks, and even their coats, jackets, and belts; thus showing how eager they were to lighten themselves as much as possible for a run. As for small-arms ammunition, the whole field was strewn with it. It appeared as if they had sown it broadcast.[11]

William McMillan's regiment, the Coldstream Guards, had halted on top of the heights from where they had a great view of the Russian retreat:

They retreated up a valley in such a confusion as no person ever saw. Our artillery galloped on up the hill and opened fire with grape, every shot we could see whole lanes swept through them. They went as fast as their legs could carry them. We could not get any further after them with any effect, so we halted and had an hour's rest. I looked about me for a little time not having any time before and all on their hill where the enemy had been entrenched and on the ground and they had retreated over, there were hundreds of them lying killed and wounded.[12]

The French, too, felt somewhat irritated by the lack of an effective pursuit, and wondered what price they might pay for it during the coming days and weeks. In the meantime, they congratulated themselves on a first victory in the Crimea and on a job well done:

> Our contact with the Russian rearguard lasted one hour; the enemy did not appear any more other than in black lines on the horizon. Our brigade returned to the battlefield, and we opened our ranks so as not to step on the corpses of the enemy; our soldiers bent down at each step to share their water with the poor Russian wounded.
>
> For the majority of us, we had received our baptism of fire; our soldiers showed the usual French dash, the élan and qualities of even the oldest troops. Because of the smoke we could not see what was going on far away on other parts of the battlefield.[13]

Captain Fay, Bosquet's aide-de-camp, was likewise pleased with the way the day had gone but also felt that chance for complete victory had slipped away:

> On our left, the English finally started to appear, who were less shaken than us, having been under fire of the riflemen and the Russian batteries for only one hour and a half. As they crossed the bridge, they met serious opposition, which they met with their usual firmness and resolution, but they were not able to turn the right of the Russian line which was too firmly established. However, after the removal of the Telegraph, the English batteries, united with those of our reserve, caused the retirement of this part of the enemy army, which had appeared to be withdrawing to Bakchi Seraï. As the English cavalry had difficulty, said one of them, with the passage of the Alma, it was too late to charge, and we regretted not having any on our side with which to turn the retirement of the enemy into a rout and to collect the fruits of victory, while perhaps pushing as far as Sebastopol and taking their artillery and baggage. Not being able to pursue the enemy, we were obliged, for around four hours, to bivouac on the battlefield, having inflicted, in this first meeting, only a moral failure, since their army was withdrawn almost intact, and in rather good order.[14]

The Russian Army continued its retreat. There was much criticism from Russian officers of Menshikov and of his arrangements for such an eventuality, not that he appears to have considered this likely:

And soon our line (on somebody's 'wise' command) began to retire while the first line there began a bayonet charge. This was doomed to failure, the men being sacrificed to the enemy in order to secure the flight of the rest of the army. Tired, exhausted, and battered, the men, not wishing to surrender, were forced to leave the heights and to take flight.

They were running, but to where? Nobody knew because, whether out of pride, short-sightedness or inexperience, His Serenity [Menshikov] had not even fixed a line of retreat in case such was necessary. Nevertheless, everybody and everything was running instinctively along the road to Sevastopol. At the time, the enemy's rifles and artillery were causing great devastation in the crowded ranks of the fugitives. So many officers, so many soldiers were killed at this time.

Not more than 10,000 of ours held their position during seven hours this day. Our artillery covered a large area with the bodies of our enemies, and if His Serenity had been more skilful our men would have remained in their positions, and to retain the battlefield would have been very advantageous to us. But God was merciful to us; we haven't lost any colours and only three damaged guns were taken by the enemy.[15]

It was at such chaotic times as these that the army surgeons came under most pressure. It was bad enough trying to treat the wounded during the battle, but when the Russians finally gave way and retreated the strain was simply too much for them. This account from one such Russian army doctor only serves to illustrate the almost impossible task they were faced with. It also highlights the great mistake committed by the Allies in not following up their victory sooner:

But the enemy, having driven us from the heights, was content with firing at the retreating soldiers from their position. During the next two days, they were celebrating their victory over the Russian vanguard. That mistake rescued our army from total destruction and Sevastopol from being captured! Indeed, who could have believed that Russia left only a fraction of the army to defend the Crimea and protect the Black Sea fleet whilst we had an army of more than a million? Who should be blamed? What might have happened had not the enemy made such a bad mistake? It's terrible to think what might have happened! Be that as it may, our defeated army has not been in Sevastopol for nine days and it took three days for the men to catch their breath, recover themselves and come to their senses and to realize the defeat had not been a dream but a bitter reality!

The first dressing station was established two versts from Burliuk, between the hills. But as soon as we began to operate on the wounded, we came under fire from the ships out at sea, forcing us to move the station back. But we did not remain here long either because the enemy, having taken our position on the heights, began to fire on us, and far too accurately! Having dressed eighty officers and men from different regiments, I, with my ambulances, moved off again but with difficulty and it was not until eight o'clock in the evening that we reached the fugitives at the Kacha.

It was a terrible picture! Hundreds of wounded, having just left the field of battle, and having become separated from their retreating regiments, asked us, with pleading gestures, bloodcurdling groans and howls of despair, to take them to our ambulances and wagons which, however, were already full. What could I do for them? All we could tell them was that other regimental ambulances were following us and they would take them. One soldier was dragging himself along, having lost a hand, and having been shot through the stomach. Another had just one leg and his jaw smashed. Another's tongue was ripped out, his body covered with wounds, and the unfortunate wretch showed he wanted water only with pained expressions. But where could we get it from? From the Alma to the Kacha there was not a single stream! So many groans, so many complaints, so many prayers for death I had to listen to! One after another used the last of his strength, straining themselves in order to avoid being taken by the enemy, where he might, in fact, have found better care![16]

The Russian medical services were evidently overstretched and chaotic, as is often the case with a beaten retreating army. But although things were bad, the situation was barely any better on the Allied side, and the need to tend the wounded obviously entailed a delay. Ironically, this was the very thing that prevented the Allies from an effective pursuit on 21 September and, consequently, saved Sevastopol.

Chapter 13

Victory and Defeat

Despite the failure to follow up and pursue the retreating Russian Army, the Battle of the Alma was a resounding victory for the Allies. The position which Menshikov assured the czar could be held for weeks had been taken within just a few bloody hours. But it had been taken at a great cost to both British and French, to which the countless dead and wounded bodies lying about the field testified. Indeed, the last time the British Army had slumped down exhausted after such an action in Europe was the night of 18 June 1815. Charles Townsend Wilson, of the Coldstream Guards, left one of the most vivid descriptions of the immediate aftermath of the battle:

> No sooner was the British Grenadier allowed to pile arms, and 'fall-out,' than he acted nobly – worthy of himself. He went mercifully among the poor moaning, bleeding Russians (remarkably fine young men, by the bye) giving them drinks of water out of his own scantily filled bottle. Having done thus charitably, the hero proceeded to look after his own interests, to make an inspection, verily, of the cowhide knapsacks so liberally scattered about; and well pleased was he to find them comfortably furnished. Every 'Rooshian kit' contained a long thin roll of black rye bread, carefully enshrined in a canvas envelope, just like a petrified black pudding – prog most uninviting to the eye – a good cotton shirt, a pair of drawers, flannel belt, hold all, complete 'housewife,' and some leather for mending boots, &c. But of all the personal property lately appertaining to the enemy, their serviceable Russian leather boots took our men's fancy the most. In every direction you observed Jack, Tom, and Harry, unceremoniously, but wisely, trying on these excellent moveables, and, as soon as fitted to their liking, flinging away their own used up 'bluchers.'[1]

However, it was sometimes a risky business for a British or French soldier to walk amidst the Russian wounded, particularly if they stopped to help and give aid, as they were not always repaid in kind, as Timothy Gowing, of the Royal Fusiliers, recalled:

After the enemy had been fairly routed, I obtained leave to go downhill. I had lost my comrade and I was determined to find him if possible. I had no difficulty in tracing the way we had advanced, for the ground was covered with our poor fellows – in some places sixes and sevens, at others tens and twelves, and at other places whole ranks were lying. 'For these are deeds which shall not pass away, and names that must not, shall not, wither.'

The Russian wounded behaved in a most barbarous manner; they made signs for a drink, and then shot the man who gave it them. My attention was drawn to one nasty case. A young officer of the 95th gave a wounded Russian a little brandy out of his flask, and was turning to walk away, when a fellow shot him mortally; I would have settled with him for this brutish conduct, but one of our men, who happened to be close to him, at once gave him his bayonet, and dispatched him. I went up to the young officer, and finding he was still alive, placed him in as comfortable position as I could, and then left him, to look for my comrade. I found him close to the river, dead; he had been shot in the mouth and left breast, and death must have been instantaneous. ... In passing up the hill I had provided myself with all water bottles I could, from the dead, in order to help revive the wounded as much as possible. I visited the young officer whom I saw a shot by the wounded Russian, and found he was out of all pain: he had passed into the presence of a just and homely God. The sights all the way were sickening. The sailors were taking off the wounded as fast as possible, but many lay there all night just as they had fallen. Dear reader, such is war.[2]

Lieutenant George Peard, of the 20th Regiment, was likewise very wary of the unpredictable wounded Russian soldiers:

The wounded Russians received the greatest kindness from our men, who gave them water, biscuits, and everything they possessed. They even lent them their pipes, for which they generally were most grateful. Sometimes, however, these kindnesses were offered to men who, though in great agony, refused with a sullen shake of the head to accept them. These were dangerous fellows; and I believe it is too true that one of our men was fired at by a man to whom he had offered some water. The body of a poor Russian officer was lying near our camp; he had two medals and a miniature of a lady in his pocket. He had evidently been killed by a shell, as his head was dreadfully disfigured. I thought the Russian private soldiers, with very few exceptions, ugly-looking fellows, and they almost all seemed to me to have fat, pale faces, devoid of intellectual expression.[3]

Charles Townsend Wilson continued to describe the battle field after the fighting had ended:

No words of mine can convey an adequate idea of the field of battle, on the morning of the 21st. The slopes, whereon the second and Light Divisions had breasted an awful fire, and won immortal fame, were literally ploughed up with cannon shot, and sodden with blood. The weltering quick and the mutilated dead, of friend and foe, lay cheek by jowl; here, the headless trunk of what lately was a soldier of our 7th Fusiliers, there, a groaning Russian shot through both thighs; in another place, a horse in his last agony 'fretting fetlock deep in gore.' While intermixed with corpses, were hundreds of muskets, knapsacks, camp-kettles, helmets, and shakos; everywhere you heard shrieks, deep moans, scraps of prayers, and the never-ending cry, 'Water! water! water!'

Men who had been shot through the heart, remained in the very attitudes in which they received their mortal hurts; thus, you had but to set one corpse on its legs again, to have a statue in clay of the soldier in the act of ramming down a cartridge; another body presented the posture of taking aim, and so on, through all the sections of the platoon exercise. But the most striking of the victims of instantaneous death, which I came across, was a young Russian rifleman – he could not to be more than 16 years old at the outside – appeared kneeling amid the havoc, with his hands clasped, and his great glassy blue eyes turned heavenward – the ball must have smitten the lad as he prayed! That rigid form, the sun beaming on its waxy brow, and round about, a ghastly huddle of defaced carcasses, shivered arms, heavy shot, shell splinters, all smeared with clotted gore, composed a picture that haunted me for many days.[4]

Another Guards officer, George Higginson, was ordered by his commanding officer, Colonel Hood, to return across the battlefield in order to look for any dead or wounded comrades who had fallen prior to crossing the river:

My errand took me across the battlefield, which presented a scene that not even the 60 years which have since elapsed can obliterate from my memory. As I turned back towards the Russian entrenchment, which was the chief object of our contest, the very atmosphere seemed to be tainted with an inexpressible odour of bloodshed. The unnatural attitude of the dead and the contorted movements of the wounded gave rise to feelings which it needed all one's resolution to control. Almost the first among the dead whom I recognised was poor little Harry Anstruther [of the 23rd Welsh Fusiliers], his red coat and shirt thrown back, disclosing the bullet wound which had struck him in the heart. Only two days before he had found me lying prone on the grass writing a hurried letter to my people at home, and throwing himself down beside me, asked for a slip of paper on which to write a few lines. I have reason to know that the dear little lad expressed in those hurried lines the conviction that he should meet his death in the approaching fight. His elder brother had been invalided home while we were in camp at Varna.

Riding on a little further, I met a litter carried by four bearers of the Scots Fusilier Guards, conveying to the ship for embarkation Frank Haygarth, he looked so pale and exhausted from the fearful wounds he had received that as I bent over him and heard his half whispered, 'Goodbye, Hig!' I little thought that for many long years afterwards we should talk over together events of the campaign in which we had shared the opening scene. Before reaching the river bank I met another litter, also carrying to the shore a grievously wounded soldier whom I recognised by the cap which lay upon his prostrate form, as a private in the Guards. As he turned his face towards me I saw his lips moved, and in the belief that he had some message to convey to his friends at home, I halted the bearers and bent over my saddle to listen. With a faint attempt at a smile he simply said, 'I think, sir, they'll say we did our duty today.' Nothing more! I signalled to the bearers to proceed, and reflected as I rode forward how much true nobility may lie beneath a rough draft of a private soldier.[5]

William McMillan of the Coldstream Guards, promoted corporal the following day, recorded the aftermath in his diary in his own inimitable style:

We piled our arms and a great many of us went down to the river for water. It was an awful sight to see, some with their brains blown out, others shot through the body and in the agonies of death. Some wounded in the limbs and crying for mercy, some fainted through pain and dying quietly. And to hear the groans indeed it was most awful. In going downhill through the dead and wounded our men took a canteen each from off the Russians knapsack of them that was dead and they soon found out where Russians carried purses and money. We were allowed to take what we wanted from the dead. They had very good clean linen shirts which suited us very well. Well we got down to the river and got plenty of water. In coming up the hill amongst the dead and wounded the poor fellows asked us water which we gave them. One officer gave one of our drummers his gold watch for a drink of water. We got back in time to fall in, the battalion went on to another hill and bivouacked for the night. Halted close to one of the Russians Commissary. There was plenty of hay and black bread. So we lit our fires and made a little coffee and I can assure you I did not sleep any that night. A good many of us sat round the fire and was talking about the battle. I took off my socks to dry at the fire and someone was good enough to take them away so I never had another pair of socks throughout the winter. Well when it became light the next morning I got up to look about me. The first thing I saw was a Russian's head lying close to me, it had been blown off by our big guns and many others lying dead had been shot by a sniping.[6]

John Astley, of the Scots Fusilier Guards, was still recovering from a neck wound which left him, naturally, somewhat dazed. He wrote home two days later whilst on board the battleship *Sanspareil*:

Hepburn, Ennismore, and I stuck together, and here we are, in a fine ship, with every comfort and kindness. I do not know what we shall be done with yet. Bulwer of ours is here, shot through the hand, and poor Charlie Baring of the Coldstreams with his left-arm taken off at the socket. We had nine fellows put hors de combat: Colonel Haygarth, one through the leg, and when on the ground at a fearful wound which has taken off the top of his shoulder. Poor Lord Chewton, most awfully cut about, five wounds in arms, head, and leg; he was bayoneted and beat about the head as he lay on the ground with a broken thigh, and his life only saved by Russian officer during the momentary retreat we made. Colonel Berkeley, leg broke, but doing well. Annesley, shot through the cheek and mouth, and jaw cut about; he cannot eat or speak, but doing well. Buckley, a ball in the nape of his neck, extracted behind the shoulder blade. Gipps, a bayonet wound in his hand, but not much hurt; doing well. Dalrymple, a spent ball on the knee, also doing well – making eleven officers hit out of twenty-nine. The Brigadier, two Majors, and the Adjutant had their horses shot under them, and bullets through their bearskins.

Poor Horace Cust [Coldstream, attached to the Staff] was killed; he had his thigh broken by a round shot, and died from exhaustion after amputation. The Coldstreams did not suffer near so much as we did, through not being in front of the battery.[7]

Sir Edward Colebrooke had come ashore the day after the battle to take a look at the battlefield:

The road to the field could be traced by the line of wounded that were making their way to the shore, some carried on stretchers, others (French) limping on with difficulty. I pushed on for the scene of the English struggle, and passing the village crossed the river by the bridge, and ascended the hill which led to the Russian redoubt. The scene of the fiercest struggle lay to my left, and the ground was thick with the slain. I could not resist the temptation of entering the redoubt, but the sight of the dying and dead around me was sickening and I quickly passed on. The first bodies I had fallen in with on the other side of the river were covered by their cloaks, but as I advanced this became impossible, and they lay as they fell, many of them stiffened and contorted. The wounded were propped up and were waiting their chance of removal. A considerable number of Russian dead lay outside the work, mixed with our men. Groups of officers and men were scattered about, eagerly discussing the events of the previous day, or examining the bodies of the fallen. The work which covered the Russian artillery was formed of earth thrown up from the rear, and was scarcely three feet high. It gave cover to their artillerymen and a body of infantry that lined it; but it offered no obstacle to our advance. It was pleasing to observe the pity with which our people looked on the wounded Russians; one of them, shocked at the coarse stuff a young lad had by him, handed over his biscuit from his scanty store, whilst others tried to comfort them with the words, 'Doctor, ship,' which they supported as much as they could by signs. I gladly passed on from scenes of misery I could not alleviate, and after visiting the hill carried by the Highlanders, I passed the valley (about a mile in breadth) to the opposite ridge, where I found the first and second

Divisions, and asked after friends. I sat a short time with Sir D. Evans, whose wound I had heard of; and with Sir C. Campbell, who described to me the part his brigade had taken in the action. When he saw the struggle on his right in front of the batteries, he pushed, he said, for the height which turned and commanded the redoubt.[8]

In all, British losses were put at 26 officers and 19 sergeants killed, and 73 officers and 95 sergeants wounded. Of the rank and file, 308 were killed and 1,444 wounded. French losses are not so easy to determine. Indeed, when Lord Raglan read Saint-Arnaud's dispatch and accompanying casualty list he was more than a little surprised. Officially, the French suffered 1,343 killed and wounded. Raglan, however, thought that 60 killed and 500 wounded was nearer the mark, based upon Saint-Arnaud's own figure of just three officers killed.[9] One is tempted to suggest that, with the fighting on the plateau being nowhere near as bitter as on the Kourgane, Raglan may well have had a point. After all, he had spent six years in the Peninsula with Wellington reading exaggerated and often absurd casualty reports.

The battle highlighted the problems that existed between the French and British command, for although the French appeared willing to act in a spirit of comradeship, Raglan was still very suspicious and uneasy about his French allies. The intervening years between the end of the Napoleonic Wars – and certainly since the death of Napoleon Bonaparte in 1821 – and the Crimean War had gone some way towards smoothing the way for Anglo-French cooperation, but Raglan could never forget that it was these very same allies who had taken his right arm off at Waterloo. Whilst he was willing to entertain their ideas and plans, and go to great pains to keep them happy, he was, nevertheless, careful to play his cards as close to his chest as possible. The British Army was his to command, and he would do so as he saw fit, and not how the French wanted him to.

As for the Russians, things were more serious. Their losses were tremendous – 145 officers and 5,600 other ranks were recorded as casualties. The newspaper *Russian Invalid* put the figure at 1,752 killed, 2,315 wounded and 405 'shell-shocked'. Amongst the dead there were 45 staff and chief officers, including four wounded generals: the commander of the 16th Infantry Division, Lieutenant General Kvitsinsky, and one of its brigade commanders, Major General Shchelkanov; the commander of the 17th Regiment Major General Goginov; and the commander of the Moskovsky Regiment, Major General Kut'anov. But, more harmful to the Russian cause was the damage done to the soldiers' morale. Their confidence in the commanders and in their own abilities to send the invaders back into the sea was severely shaken. Furthermore, there was little now between the Allies and Sevastopol, the defences of which were far from ready to withstand a siege.

Meanwhile, the business of tending to the wounded – as well as burying the dead – went on. The dead were buried in pits close to where they had fallen after all reusable equipment had been removed. The Russians were buried together in their own mass graves, as were the British and French, separated in death as they had been in life. The wounded, in the meantime, were collected and either seen to on the battlefield or in rear of it, or were carried off to the ships waiting offshore. George Lawson was a surgeon with the 3rd Division:

> The scene after the engagement, going over the field, and looking after the killed and wounded, is a sight not to be described. Many of the poor fellows had to be on the field all night, not being able to get them off that evening. There was plenty of work for the doctors.[10]

Lawson also relates that a field hospital had been established about half a mile in rear of the battlefield:

> Here the marquees were pitched that had been brought in the reserve wagons – consisting of six country cards or 'Arabas' (it's all that could be obtained for this purpose) – such bedding and comforts as these sufficed to carry were unpacked, and the medical officers exerted themselves zealously in affording aid. The wounded of the 1st Division were all collected and got under cover in some houses in a vineyard near the scene of the action the same evening; but as night fell soon after the battle ceased, and it became intensely dull, many men who had fallen on the more distant and broken parts of the field, were unavoidably left to the following morning, when strong fatigue parties were sent out to collect the remainder of the wounded and to bury the dead. A farmhouse in the village that had escaped the fire was taken, the whole yard littered down deep with hay, and here this latter portion of the wounded, as they were brought in, were placed – their hurts attended to, nourishment given to them, and they were sent down as speedily as possible to the beach, a distance of three miles, for conveyance to Scutari. The whole of the British wounded and many Russians were thus disposed of by the evening of the 22nd.[11]

Despite the poor conditions in the dressing stations after the battle, the wounded soldiers still managed to put a brave face on their predicament. These anecdotes were just a few that were published in a contemporary French book on the war:

> An artilleryman, a native of Paris, had both his arms blown off when loading his gun. He was taken to an ambulance. On the way, he met his captain, who said he was sorry to see him so badly 'rearranged.' The artilleryman replied, 'I am only annoyed that they did not leave me with one with which to eat my soup.'
>
> A soldier of the 19th regiment received a ball in the shoulder, and was taken to an ambulance, and addressing the surgeon said: 'Major, give me the ball. I want to return it to the Russians who lent it to me. What belongs to Caesar, give to Caesar.'
>
> One doctor prepared to operate on a Zouave who had had his arm smashed by a Russian shell. The doctor proposed using chloroform. When the Zouave asked what it was the doctor explained it would deaden the pain during the operation and ease his suffering. The Zouave dismissed this suggestion, adding that such measures were for women. The Zouaves do not need any chloroform! Just allow me to smoke my pipe while you cut away! The arm was removed without the man uttering a single word of complaint, nor any sign of pain in his face. Instead, he smoked his pipe quietly until the arm was cut off.[12]

The battlefield itself was a shocking sight. The dead and wounded lay thickly on the ground. This was particularly so around the Great Redoubt and on the slopes leading to it, testifying to the bitterness of the fighting. The correspondent of *The Times*, William Russell, wandered the battlefield afterwards, and was particularly interested in the discarded Russian weapons and equipment:

> Every one of the enemy had a loaf of black bread, and linen roll containing coarse broken biscuit or hard bread like oil cake. Though some other troops had been at the armour for a couple of days, no bones were found about the ground. The ground was in a most filthy state. After battle came removal of the wounded and the burial of the dead.
>
> The Russian dead were all buried together in pits, and were carried down to their graves as they lay. Our parties on the 21st and 22nd buried 1,200 men. The British soldiers were buried in pits. Their firelocks, and the useful portions of their military equipment, were alone preserved.

The quantity of firelocks, great coats, bearskin caps, shakos, helmets and flat forage caps, knapsacks (English and Russian), belts, bayonets, cartouch-boxes, cartridges, swords, exceeded belief; and round shot, fragments of shell smeared with blood and hair, grape and bullets, were under the foot and eye at every step. Our men broke the enemy's firelocks and rifles which lay on the ground. As many of them were loaded, the concussion set them off, so that dropping shot never ceased for about 40 hours. The Russian musket was a good weapon to look at, but rather a bad one to use. The barrel, which was longer than ours, and was polished, was secured to the stock by brass straps, like the French. The lock was, however, tolerably good. The stock was of the old narrow Oriental pattern, and the wood of which it was made – white-grained and something like sycamore, broke easily. From the form of the heel of the stock, the 'kick' of the musket must have been sharp with a good charge. Many had been originally flint-locked, but were changed to detonators by screwing in nipples and plugging up the touch holes with steel screws the cartridges were beautifully made and finished, the balls being strongly gummed in at the end, but the powder was coarse and unglazed, and looked like millet-seed; it was, however, clean in the hand, and burnt very smartly. The rifles were two-grooved, and projected a long conical ball. The ball was flat at the base, and had neither hollow cup nor pin; its weight must exceed that of our Minié ball. These rifles were made by J. P. Malherbe, of Liege. The bayonets were soft and bent easily. Some good swords belonging to officers were picked up, and weapons, probably belonging to drummers or bandsmen, exactly like the old Roman sword, very sharp and heavy. Some six or seven drums were left behind, but nearly all of them were broken – several by the shot which killed their owners. No ensign, eagle, standard, or colour of any kind was displayed by the enemy or found on the field. Our regiments marched with their colours, as a matter of course, and the enemy made the latter a special mark for the rifles. Thus it was so many ensigns, lieutenants, and sergeants fell.[13]

Like the majority of the Allied troops, Octave Cullet, of the French 20th Ligne, spent the night on the battlefield amidst a very mixed atmosphere:

The night was passed in sadness, for the joy of the victory was, alas, tempered by the close vicinity of the ambulances, where the dead and dying were piled up. The Russians were mixed with ours; we gathered them up without distinction, without preference.

On the morning of the 21st, General Thomas was carried off on a stretcher by soldiers of the 20th Léger. He was surrounded by the officers of his brigade who said their goodbyes; he expressed his regret that he had to leave us at the beginning of a glorious campaign.

The day passed in transporting the casualties on cacolets [mules with panniers] which went down the valley from the Alma, and to the shore where boats waited to take them to Constantinople. Sometimes we buried the dead in isolated pits, sometimes in the deeper ones when the bodies had accumulated on the same spot.[14]

With the battle won and arrangements for the collection, treatment and transportation of the wounded well under way – not to mention the burying of the dead – it was vital that the Allied commanders pressed home their advantage and set about pushing on to Sevastopol. After all, were not the Russians scattered and decisively beaten? Some of the British divisional commanders seemed to think so. Indeed, when George Paget, of the 4th Light Dragoons, was inspecting the battlefield afterwards with the commander of the 4th Division, Sir George Cathcart, the latter commented, 'Ah! Those fellows have had such a dressing, that they will never meet us in the open again.'[15] It was absolutely vital that the Allies made for Sevastopol, which lay relatively unprotected just a few tantalizing miles to the south. Indeed, the fortifications on the Severnaya, the suburb on the northern side of Sevastopol, were considered to be virtually non-existent, save for a large star fort, and it was believed that even that had yet to be armed by the Russians. And even as the Battle of the Alma was being fought, defences were being hastily thrown together around the southern side of Sevastopol. A swift move south by the Allies would surely bring about the capture of Sevastopol, and with it a quick end to the war. After all, the destruction of Russian's great naval base on the Black Sea was the object of the game.

Sadly, it was not to be, for when the sun came up on the morning of Thursday, 21 September, both British and French armies claimed they were in no condition to advance. It is remarkable that, despite appreciating full well the need for a swift advance south, both Raglan and Saint-Arnaud refused to move. In another moment of apparent distrust and finger-pointing, each commander blamed the other. Saint-Arnaud claimed his men were exhausted, that their packs had been left behind in the rear and that the French soldiers went nowhere without them. The French, in fact, blamed Raglan and the British for the delay. Two days after the battle Saint-Arnaud wrote to his brother:

The English are not yet ready; and I am detained here, as at Baltchick, and as at Old Fort. It is true, however, that they have more wounded than I, and that they are further from the sea.[16]

The French historian of the war, Bazancourt, was rather more pointed:

The English, intrepid and indefatigable in action, appear not to understand the vast importance of a day, or an hour of delay, in a warlike situation. They either know not how to hurry themselves, or will not do it. 'I have lost fewer men than they,' writes the Marshal, 'because I have been more rapid. My soldiers run; – theirs march.'[17]

It was certainly the case that the British wounded did indeed have to be transported 3 miles or so from the battlefield to the beach and from there to the ships waiting to take them back to Scutari. But this still does not excuse the lack of an immediate advance. After all, did not the Duke of Wellington have his army on the march towards Paris less than a day after defeating Napoleon at Waterloo, and all this after a battle that made the Alma look like a skirmish? Charles Townsend Wilson was certainly very mystified by the decision to delay the pursuit:

Why Menschikoff was not followed up on the morning or noon, at latest, of the 21st, is a mystery. With the exception of the light division and a brigade of the second, neither our own nor the French forces had suffered very materially; the troops too were in highest spirits, and, from the colonel down to the fifer, cried aloud for marching orders. Some declared the illness of St. Arnaud, unquestionably a bold and enterprising soldier, to be the cause of our inertness. Others attributed the halt to a merciful regard for the sick and wounded. Now, we are at this moment without means of judging whether the former opinion to be correct or no; but surely we ought not to think so poorly of our superiors, as to believe them to have been paralysed by the motive set forth in the second supposition. Does not history teach rapidity of movement in war to be the mainspring of ultimate triumph? For example, look at that immortal campaign of 1796, which annihilated five armies, and wrested from Austria the humiliating peace of Campo Formio. To what are we to attribute such astonishing results, except to genius and activity, without a pause? Had Napoleon tarried three days on the bloody field of Montenotte, what must have happened? Why, his little army would have been crushed by the vast masses converging upon it from all sides. France would have been invaded. The tricolour of the Republic would have been trampled under the abhorred German hoof. Take the same conqueror's marvellous campaign of 1814. Contrast his unvarying success with the uniform failure of his lieutenants. Consider how he overcame everywhere, while they were beaten everywhere. But why pursue the subject further? No one denies that audacity, promptitude, and brains, usually carry the day, even against odds.

'Then you are abandoning the wounded to their fate, for leaving the dead to bury the dead,' some may exclaim. God forbid! The fruits of victory might have been plucked without recourse to the cruel alternative of neglecting the victims of strife. A few seamen and marines from the fleet, together with the battered Light Division could put the dead decently out of sight, tended the hurt, and placed them on shipboard, while the mass of the Anglo-French hunted Menschikoff.[18]

Octave Cullet was frustrated by the delay but knew exactly who was to blame for it:

The army was impatient to continue on its way. Everyone understood that if we gave the enemy time they would strengthen their new position and we would lose all the advantages we had gained from the first victory. Alas! We were forced to take into account the slowness of our allies. It was impossible to do justice to the firmness and bravery of the English army; but we could not help noting that it was through their slowness it was their fault that we lost two days at the Old Fort, that at the Alma, the four hours' delay made it impossible to execute the Marshal's plan and that at this moment the success of the campaign depended on the speed of our advance. If, in accordance with his plan, the Russian army had been turned on its right with the same vigour that Bosquet's division had shown on the left, who can say what might have happened if, when attacked frontally by our impetuous troops, they had found their right and rear attacked by the whole English army during their retreat?[19]

Whatever the reason, and whoever was to blame, the fact remains that vital time was lost in not marching south towards Sevastopol on 21 September. What consequences this would have for the Allies would soon be seen.

Chapter 14

Aftermath

Hindsight is the most powerful weapon in the arsenal of an armchair general. It is easy, looking back over the years, to consider the various 'what ifs' of any battle or campaign. Indeed, the Crimean War was to throw up what would prove to be one of the most studied and controversial episodes in British military history, namely the Charge of the Light Brigade. The Battle of the Alma similarly has its own 'what ifs', even if they are far less controversial. The problem with 'what ifs' is that they simply didn't happen, and therefore any discussion of them rarely yields anything useful. The great American historian Jac Weller, writing in his classic study of the Waterloo Campaign, *Wellington at Waterloo*, said whenever he read a sentence that began with 'if' or 'had' he flinched like a recruit firing a rifle for the first time.[1] Such exercises may be useful in staff colleges, Weller added, but they have little place in the serious study of military history. And we are inclined to agree with him.

Some may consider what might have happened if Menshikov had moved his cavalry against Raglan's exposed left flank during the British advance, or what problems the French might have encountered had the Russians blocked up the passes leading up to the plateau on which the fighting on the Russian left took place. They might even consider what might have happened had the Russians decided to oppose the landings on 14 September. But none of these events happened and therefore they are not really worth discussing.[2] As historians, we can seriously consider only those events which did happen, analyzing performances by armies and individuals, their mistakes and their successes.

If mistakes were made at the Alma, they were certainly made by the Russians, and by Menshikov in particular. Russian leadership at the Alma was almost non-existent, from Menshikov downwards. The Russian commander-in-chief appears to have come from the Wellington school, inasmuch as he was reluctant to delegate any responsibility to anyone. Wellington, of course, was singularly brilliant and almost unique in terms of his style of command, and it would take an equally brilliant commander to adopt his style successfully. Sadly, Menshikov was not in the same league. Hence on 20 September, he tried to be everywhere at once, which he found impossible. As a result, his commanders had no idea what the Russian plan was, not that there ever appears to have been one anyway. It was simply a case of barring the way to Sevastopol by deploying his troops on the heights to the south of the river Alma and hoping for the best. That was all. As one Russian officer wrote afterwards:

> Before the battle there was total disorder within the army. Neither the troops nor the commanders (even the corps commander) knew what the plan was for the forthcoming battle. They did not know if the battle was being fought in order to stop the enemy once and for all or whether it was simply a delaying action in order to gain time for a retreat to the next defensive position to slow down the advance of the allies. Such a situation made it impossible to act with intent and did little for the presence of mind or confidence of the troops.[3]

Menshikov was criticized for the deployment of his troops, although this is somewhat harsh. Perhaps he was guilty of not deploying more troops on his left flank to oppose the French and stop them from gaining the heights. The problem was, of course, that the Allies had powerful guns out at sea which were capable of shelling anything within a few hundred yards of the shore. Thus, it is understandable that Menshikov did not wish to expose his men to such punishment. It was a tough call and, as events were to prove, he got it wrong. The deployment of his troops in the centre and on his right appears to have been adequate, but no matter how good the deployment there was always the possibility that the attacking troops would be simply too good, and so it proved. Indeed, the Russians were genuinely surprised by the bravery and tenacity of the British, who, they had been led to believe, were masters of the sea but were poor when fighting on land, and it is easy to imagine their feelings when the long red lines came on towards them. The Russians traditionally fought in columns, and so it came as quite a shock to them when they appeared unable to stop the thin, weak-looking lines. Given the fact that the Russians, and particularly the senior commanders, were well aware of the capabilities of the British infantry – the Napoleonic Wars still lived in their memories – this should not have come as a surprise.

To their great credit, individual Russian regiments fought extremely well. Chief among them was the Vladimirsky Regiment, which sent the regiments of Sir George Brown's Light Division tumbling from the Great Redoubt after its initial capture, whilst the Kazansky Regiment performed well against Yea's Fusiliers. There were, in fact, feats of distinction performed all the way along the front, but many were in isolation and were unsupported. Where advantages were gained, such as those by the Vladimirsky Regiment, Menshikov – or, for that matter, any other senior officer – was unable to take real advantage of it and press it home. Thus, the British were able to re-form and come on again.

But it was not only Menshikov and the Russians who demonstrated a lack of tactical know-how. On the British side, too, Raglan showed why he was a poor choice as commander-in-chief. After forty years of service in the shadow of the Duke of Wellington, the Alma was his first, and somewhat belated, opportunity to take command of an army in the field. And like everything else he did in the Crimea, Raglan allowed the dead hand of the duke to descend upon him once more. His old chief once said that he got greater exertions from his men when he was on the spot, and so Raglan, having first issued the most basic of all plans – there was no turning movement, just a straightforward frontal attack – took himself off and tried to ape the duke.

The problem was that Raglan placed himself in a position not to the immediate rear of the advancing British troops, from where he would have been able to bring direct command over his men – which is where Wellington was always to be found – but on the southern side of the Alma, almost within the Russian positions themselves, effectively cutting himself off and preventing himself from exercising any personal influence on the battle. Raglan's bravery was never in doubt, and he can never be accused of shying away from the heat of battle. The problem was his positioning. Thus, the most important events on the battlefield, as far as the British were concerned, were largely brought about as a result of command and control exercised locally by divisional, brigade and regimental commanders. This was not a mistake in the sense of the word, certainly not a crucial one – victorious commanders may make errors but they only become crucial errors if they lose[4] – but it certainly demonstrated a lack of judgement on Raglan's part, as well as his shortcomings as a commander-in-chief.

The performance of the French commander-in-chief, Saint-Arnaud, is more difficult to analyze; after all, he was extremely ill at the time of the battle and had only a few days to live. He had far greater recent experience of war than Raglan, and yet it could be argued that his own plan similarly lacked imagination. However, unlike Raglan, Saint-Arnaud had very little room for manoeuvre, given that the sea lay immediately to his right whilst the British were cramping him on his left. His plan of action was also largely dictated by the lie of the land in front of him, for whilst the British had good, open and relatively easy ground over which to move – even before and after negotiating the river – the French were faced with extremely difficult and almost cliff-like hills which were impossible to climb. Indeed, had it not been for the few passes that cut their way through these hills it is difficult to see how the French could have contributed to the Allied triumph. In fact, it says more about Menshikov's failure to defend these passes than about Saint-Arnaud's tactical acumen. As it turned out, the French did extremely well to cross the river, gain the passes and, subsequently the heights, and hold them in the face of Russian resistance. Despite a marked lack of coverage in English-language history books, the Alma was certainly as much a French victory as it was British.[5]

As for the British soldier at the Alma, he had shown himself a worthy successor to those who had gone before. Indeed, the men of Albuera would have been more than satisfied by the conduct of their descendants. The 7th Royal Fusiliers stood and traded volleys with the Kazansky without flinching, and the Guards had shown why they considered themselves the best of British, even allowing for the upset to the Scots Fusiliers, whilst the Highland Brigade showed once again why the Scottish soldier was still something to be feared. There was a great deal of inexperience amongst both the commanders and the men themselves, and mistakes were undoubtedly made, many of them, however, stemming from misinterpretation of bugle calls, another consequence of fighting alongside erstwhile foes. But when the time came for them to get stuck into their enemies they were not found wanting. The French soldiers, too, showed they lacked nothing of the passion and élan that had swept their ancestors to countless victories across Europe decades before. And, it should not be forgotten, it was barely six days since the Allies had set foot in the Crimea. It was still an extremely early stage of the war. Both British and French were still feeling their way.

Tactically, there was nothing new in the way the Battle of the Alma was fought. In fact, the Duke of Marlborough would have had little trouble in commanding the British Army on 20 September 1854, for nothing had changed in the 150 years since he led his men to victory at Blenheim in 1704. Nor would Wellington himself have been surprised by anything at the Alma; his own lieutenants did exactly the same as he had done forty years before. The Russians, too, stood and fought as they had done at Borodino and Leipzig. In fact, the claim that the Crimean War was the first of the modern wars is something of a mistake. There was certainly nothing new at the Alma, no modern innovations, no startling tactics. The Allies, and in particular the British, came on and fought in exactly the same way as they had done for the past 150 years. True, their weapons had changed – the 4th Division, however, was still armed with a smooth-bore musket, albeit a percussion one – but there was nothing modern about the Battle of the Alma. All of the commanding officers looked back to the old days, to the Napoleonic Wars, and, indeed, would continue to do so for the remainder of the war. Perhaps the Alma should be more correctly called the last of the old battles.

Despite the lack of a rigorous pursuit of the beaten Russian army, the Allies had won an important victory. How important it was can be gauged simply by considering the consequences of a defeat. With no obvious line of retreat, with no reserves and with no means of supply save for the ships out at sea, the Allies would have been faced with the alarming and potentially disastrous prospect of a re-embarkation. This was a hazardous operation at best, but with a Russian army in pursuit the consequences do not bear thinking about. As it was, the victory on the Alma allowed the Allies to establish themselves in the Crimea and move on to the business of attacking Sevastopol.

As for the Russians, the defeat at the Alma came as a major shock. Months had passed in expectation of the prospect of war and, consequently, preparations should have been made to meet the invaders. It was bad enough that the British and French had been allowed to land unopposed. This, however, was not seen as so bad a setback, given the strength of the Alma position and the confidence expressed by Menshikov in holding it and being able to throw the Allies back afterwards. Now that this too had gone terribly wrong, there not only seemed to be nothing between the Allies and Sevastopol, but the Russians' confidence in themselves – and perhaps more important, the soldiers' confidence in their generals – had been severely shaken. Czar Nicholas himself could hardly believe it when news of the defeat reached him at St Petersburg.

Nicholas had every faith in Menshikov's abilities and declaration that he could hold the position for days. We may well imagine his shock when news of the battle arrived. In fact, the Battle of the Alma was still in progress – albeit at a late stage – when Menshikov sent one of his aides-de-camp, Captain S Greig, off to Nicholas with a report of the battle. It is said that when Greig asked Menshikov what he was to report to the emperor, Menshikov simply pointed at the retreating detachments of Russian troops, saying, 'Report what you see yourself.' The young officer was so affected by the sight of retreating troops and large numbers of wounded, that he was still shaking when he arrived at St Petersburg on 27 September to deliver the report. Having listened to Greig's report, Nicholas, stunned and somewhat taken aback, cried bitterly and, seizing Greig by the shoulders, began to shake him repeatedly, asking him,

'Do you understand what you are saying?'[6] An official from the Russian ministry for war, D Milyutin, later recalled:

> September 27th was a very sad day for our society. Captain Greig came as a courier from Prince Menshikov with a sorrowful message of an unlucky end to the battle. His brief report didn't have any details of the battle's progress. Prince Menshikov left his aide-de-camp to tell his own story, for he was an eyewitness of the battle. It was clear that the Czar was eager to hear the details of the first meeting between his army and the Allies. But the impressionable aide-de-camp was so shocked with images of battle, in which he took part for the first time, that even after the seven days' galloping he couldn't get rid of the impression, and described the battle in such an unattractive and offensive light that the Czar grew angry, rebuked him and sent him off to bed to sleep.[7]

Not long after Greig's arrival in St Petersburg, Menshikov's couriers arrived to deliver his own account of the battle, in which he intimated that his men had not fought well, a version that was initially believed by the czar. It is a sad reflection of Menshikov's own abilities as a commander that he should have to try to put the blame for the defeat on the Russian soldiers in order to cover up his own shortcomings. His chief of staff, Vunsh, later presented the czar with a more accurate account of the battle, but not before Nicholas was writing of the 'want of courage on the part of the troops'.[8]

By trying to shift the blame onto the private soldiers, Menshikov was doing them a great injustice. Indeed, they had fought extremely hard at the Alma but with outdated weapons which left them at a great disadvantage on the battlefield. Indeed, several Russian accounts speak of casualties being inflicted by Allied rifles from a range which they themselves had no hope of matching. They simply had to stand there and take it. Only when the Allies closed with them were the Russian infantry able to hit back, and even here they seemed to have been constrained by Suvorov's old adage about the bayonet being more effective than a bullet. This was all very well, but in order for the Russians to use their white weapons they had to get in close, something that only the Vladimirsky Regiment managed to do to any effect.

The disastrous news of the defeat at the Alma was withheld from the Russian people for days, and it was not until the first week in October that word of the disaster began to filter out onto the streets. When it did, the people took it badly. Indeed, one of the great Russian historians of the war, Eugene Tarle, considered the news of the defeat at the Alma to have produced a far worse reaction in Russia than anything else during the entire war. 'Neither Inkerman nor the Chernaya Rechka nor even the final assault and the fall of Sevastopol, though this latter event was far more important than the Alma, produced a more depressing effect.'[9] Perhaps this reaction was simply the result of Russian overconfidence – or rather overconfidence by Menshikov.

But despite the trauma of defeat, not all the Russians were in a state of panic. At least one group of officers were entertained by some ladies from Sevastopol who appear to have been far from panic-stricken by the news of the battle:

On 21 September at dawn, our regiment started off for Sevastopol and by one o'clock in the afternoon had reached the southern side of the town. Upon halting, some ladies from Sevastopol, wearing funeral dress, visited us and entertained us at a splendid and pleasant breakfast. We hardly had time to answer their many questions; they were sorry at the outcome of the battle the day before, and for the wounded that we carried with us. These patriots politely invited us for dinner, gave us their addresses and servants and then left.

But we were not able to enjoy the hospitality of the citizens of Sevastopol again, for soon afterwards we received an official invitation from Vice-Admiral Kornilov to have dinner on the ship *Konstantin*. During the dinner the captain of the ship and his officers asked us many questions about the Alma battle. Whilst we were being entertained by our hosts, the lower ranks were entertained by the ordinary sailors. In the evening we were ordered to take up a position near Sevastopol. Here orders were issued regarding those officers who were wounded at the Alma battle; General-Major Zhabokritsky was appointed to command the 16th Division in place of General-Lieutenant Kvitsinsky, and Colonel Rakovich as commander of our regiment in place of Kovalyov.

The next morning I went to visit Sevastopol. The town was full of feverish activity. Some of the citizens were packing their belongings on carriages, hurriedly but without panic. There were no signs of despondency or hopelessness for the future.

The sailors were crossing the streets in different directions. One could see intensive activity on the shores of the harbour and on the ships, but everything was done correctly and carefully, and in good order, all with the same objective: to save Sevastopol.[10]

In Britain, meanwhile, news of the Allied victory at the Alma was received with great joy. Dispatches from Raglan were sent off to Stratford de Redcliffe at Constantinople, who in turn relayed the news by means of telegraph to the British consul in Belgrade on 23 September and directly to London on 25 September. The news was received in London on Thursday, 28 September, and began appearing in newspapers on Saturday, 30 September. The *Moniteur*, published in Paris, carried Saint-Arnaud's dispatch on Monday, 2 October. In London, the lord mayor received the news at Mansion House at nine o'clock in the evening, whereupon he immediately summoned members of his household and set off for the London Tavern, where the new members of the Corporation were enjoying a good dinner. The civic trumpeter sounded his call, whereupon a crowd of 'eager spectators soon surrounded the group, upon whose identity a flickering light was thrown by the bull's-eyes of half a dozen policemen's lanterns.'[11] That essential and most valuable chronicler of the day, the *Illustrated London News*, carried full reports of the battle and how it was received in its edition of 7 October, complete with reports of the celebrations and firing of guns at the Tower of London that took place on the morning of Monday, 2 October. The following week's edition carried the announcement of Saint-Arnaud's death, as well as various engravings of the battle, poems and full reports from Lord Raglan, as would subsequent editions during the next few weeks.

The great irony of the edition of 7 October carrying news of the Battle of the Alma was that it also carried a report about the 'alleged capture of Sebastopol'. Reports had been received from a variety of places, including Odessa, Vienna and Bucharest, stories that had been repeated in Paris, claiming that Sevastopol had fallen to the Allies on 25 September. One report, published under the heading 'Decisive Intelligence', ran as follows:

> We have received from our Correspondent at Vienna (by Submarine and European Telegraph) the following despatch:
> 'On the 23rd Fort Constantine was destroyed by the Allies, and Fort Alexander taken. On the 24th, all the redoubts and forts around Sebastopol, all the batteries, and the Arsenal, were in the hands of the Allies. The flags of the Allies were hoisted on the tower of the Church of St. Vladimir. It is believed that the day on which Prince Menschikoff surrendered at discretion was the 26th. It is said that the remainder of the Russian fleet is safe in the hands of the Allies. The Turkish army will at once cross the Danube into Bessarabia.'[12]

The report was supported by several other accounts, although it also came with a statement from the Duke of Newcastle expressing caution to the British public. He was totally justified in his caution, for the reports were, of course, false. How different the course of the war might have been had the reports proved true, and had Sevastopol indeed fallen on 25 September 1854. Think of it: no Balaklava, no Inkerman, no terrible winter, nor any Florence Nightingale. How different British history would have been. But the reports proved a false dawn. They were totally without foundation.

As events were to show, the delayed Allied advance following the Battle of the Alma gave the defenders of Sevastopol valuable time to improve the town's defences. These were weak and were vastly different from the sort of walls which protected many a European city. They were certainly weaker those which the Allied armies had been used to dealing with during the Napoleonic Wars. Nevertheless, they were enough to prevent the Allies from launching an all-out assault once they arrived at Sevastopol. The arguments still rage as to whether the Allies should have attacked the moment they arrived at Sevastopol on 27 September. How different the outcome of the Crimean War would have been we will never know, but there is little doubt that many of the senior British commanders always felt that an immediate assault would have swept the Allies into Sevastopol without too much difficulty. Indeed, when Raglan ordered the siege train to be brought up, Sir George Cathcart, commanding the 4th Division, is reputed to have said simply, 'But my dear chap, there's nothing to knock down.' And thus it was that the Allies settled down to besiege Sevastopol, a town which would finally fall on 8 September 1855, but only after an epic defence by the Russians which would cost thousands of lives and last for no fewer than 349 days.

By the time Sevastopol fell – and even then it was only the southern side of the town that was abandoned by the Russians – the Battle of the Alma was becoming a very distant memory. Three more major battles were fought in the Crimea – Balaklava, Inkerman and the Chernaya – whilst the assaults on 18 June and 8 September 1855 were equally bloody affairs. But by then the heroes of the Alma and, indeed, Inkerman had long since gone, taken mainly by sickness and disease and by a terrible, harsh winter. Instead, Sevastopol was assaulted by a very different breed of soldier. Gone were most of the old sweats, to be replaced by 'boys who had been walking in the streets of London or down the quiet country lanes of England only a few weeks previously.'[13] Even Raglan was dead, carried off by disease on 28 June 1855, whilst Saint-Arnaud died just a few days after the Battle of the Alma. Menshikov was gone too. He was still very much alive – he died in 1869 – but he was removed from command following the debacle at Eupatoria in February 1855.

Gone also were the days of British and French soldiers resplendent in their red and blue uniforms, colours flying proudly overhead and their drums and bugles beating and blaring loudly as they advanced in long lines. Instead, there was almost a year of trench warfare, and a bitter existence in the camps on the Sapoune Plateau to the south of Sevastopol, all of which was so carefully recorded in sepia by Fenton and Robertson. There were midnight battles, fighting in the trenches, and terrible conditions as the men slogged their guts out in awful, energy-sapping circumstances, digging their way towards the walls of the town.

The Battle of the Alma was as much a soldier's battle as Inkerman, fought on 5 November. Bereft of any real direction from above, the crucial decisions at the Alma were made at brigade and battalion level with the private soldier, as usual, giving his all for queen, country, czar and emperor. As we have noted, the Battle of the Alma was very much the last of the old battles, certainly for the British Army, for never again would long red lines be seen advancing on a European battlefield. It is also notable for being the first and last time the Foot Guards were seen attacking on a battlefield whilst wearing their red coats and bearskins. Like Inkerman, where they were firmly on the back foot and wearing greatcoats, the Alma demonstrated how ridiculous it was to ask a man to fight wearing this impractical, beautiful but utterly inappropriate mode of head-dress. And it is to one of these bearskinned Guards officers that we turn for one of the last tributes to the Allied soldiers who won the battle:

> The Alma was a soldier's battle – a direct attack by lines on ordnance defended heights, which Menschikoff (as the officers made prisoners avowed) expected to maintain against all comers for three weeks at least. With the exception of Bosquet's brilliant stroke at the enemy's left, there was but little manoeuvring. It was all hammer and tongs; 'pluck,' perseverance, the Minié, and the *carabine a tige* did the business. Great honour, then, to the ranks of the Allied armies. Great honour to the English 'private,' and the French *fantassin* who, despite mountains, water, heavy guns, drove forty thousand veterans, like chaff to the wind, in little better than four hours.[14]

But perhaps the greatest compliment to the Allies was paid by a captured Russian officer who, when offering up a reason for the Russians' failure to hold the Alma position, said simply, 'they expected to meet men, not devils.'[15]

Chapter 15

The Battlefield Today

In 1855 an English lady published a book, *The Crimea: Its Towns, Inhabitants, and Social Customs*, recounting her nine years' residence in the Crimea. The writer – sadly anonymous – lived for some time close to the river Alma and left a beautiful description of what was to become the battlefield fought over on 20 September 1854:

> From Simpheropol, until we reach the banks of the river Alma, the country is very uninteresting and thinly peopled. A solid stone bridge is thrown over the river, and here, on every side, all is smiling, rich and luxuriant.
>
> Orchards and vineyards follow one another in never-ending succession, and the snug-looking dwellings of their owners, nestling among the trees, give one the idea of comfort and plenty. These orchards, containing sometimes several thousand trees, planted in lines about thirty feet apart, are the principal sources from whence the proprietor derives his income ... The vineyards on the banks of the Alma produce grapes which are very pleasant and good for the table, but make a very inferior sour wine. It is sold at a very low price to wine merchants, who concoct of it something which they sell as south coast wine, but which I need scarcely tell you, is anything but palatable.
>
> The Khans of the Crimea are said to have had their summer residence on the banks of this delightful stream; and on one little hillock, apparently surrounded by a kind of moat, there has evidently been a Kiosque, to which an ascent by stairs still remains. It is here that the Tatars believe that a black horse guards a hidden treasure, and many go the length of asserting that they have seen it occasionally. I, however, have sojourned often near the spot, and have never been favoured by a sight of the phantom.[1]

Today the visitor to the banks of the river Alma might have more martial-looking phantoms in mind, the ghosts of those who died fighting there in 1854.

The place certainly has an aura and an eerie feel to it, but then so does many a bloody battlefield. The battlefield of the Alma has not altered that much since the description above, the main change being the absence of the vineyards and the stone walls that once lined the northern bank of the river and which gave shelter to many a British soldier during the battle. As the English writer noted above, the country from the north to the Alma is 'uninteresting', being largely open fields and vineyards. Only to the east does the scenery become more interesting.

It is relatively easy nowadays to journey to the Ukraine, once part of the old Soviet Union. Visa restrictions were lifted in 2005 and regular flights take travellers in and out of the capital of the Crimea, Simferopol, flying via Istanbul, Kiev or Frankfurt, for example.

A good place to start is, of course, the landing beaches at Kalamita Bay. It is quite remarkable that the two Allied armies were allowed to land on this relatively narrow stretch of beach without being opposed. From here it is an easy journey south for a few miles, whereupon the visitor will come across the scene of the first fight in the Crimea, at the river Bulganak. Most visitors will probably cross the river without knowing it, for today it is little more than a tiny stream, dribbling its way beneath the main road to Sevastopol. There are certainly no heights to the south of the 'river', and it is not easy to pinpoint the exact scene of the action, particularly as a rather large village has sprung up there today.

The Alma, on the other hand, is far more rewarding. A few miles to the south of the Bulganak the heights come into view, stretching out to the west as far as the sea. Upon first seeing the heights a sense of anticlimax is understandable, as the hills look nothing like those depicted in so many of the contemporary (and not so contemporary) pictures. They certainly look nothing like those in the 1968 film *The Charge of the Light Brigade*. In fact, the heights, at least those which faced the British troops, are nothing more than a range of long, sloping, but somewhat deceptive hills stretching down to the river. The heights facing the French, on the other hand, certainly are formidable, and if it were not for the narrow passages that cut their way through the cliffs it is difficult to see how the French could have gained the plateau.

A small bridge stands today at the village of Almatamack, allowing the visitor to follow in the footsteps of Bosquet's men, amongst others, as they wound their way up onto the heights to start the slow driving in of the Russian left. Once on top, the ground is everywhere covered with extensive vineyards. The important thing here, however, is to appreciate the problem faced by

Menshikov when deploying his troops, for the whole area is devoid of any real cover, and the troops would have been exposed to the fire of the Allied fleet standing offshore. Otherwise, it is a useful exercise to walk along the plateau to get the Russian view. Indeed, it is easy to imagine the massed ranks of French troops standing out in the fields to the north, preparing to attack.

Away to the east across the main Sevastopol road lies the British sector. It is a useful exercise to stand to the north in the positions taken by the British before they began their advance towards Burliuk. The village was, of course, set on fire during the battle, causing great problems for the 2nd Division in particular. Looking at the ground to the south of the village today, and considering the lack of room the 2nd Division had back in 1854, it is possible that the village was rebuilt farther to the north after the war. Lying about 600 yards or so from the river there surely must have been room for the 2nd Division to re-form after passing through the smoke. Contemporary maps also appear to suggest the village was much closer to the river back in 1854. Perhaps it was indeed built further north after the war.

Having walked down the road towards the modern bridge (the original one has long since gone), the visitor is inevitably drawn to the large white stone obelisk standing away to the left of the road. This marks the site of the Great Redoubt. But before going to visit the monument, it is well worth walking out into the fields to the north of the river to get a British infantryman's perspective on the attack. There is no sign today of any stone walls or vineyards mentioned in so many accounts. Instead, there is nothing but scrub covering what, in winter, turns into an icy flood plain.[2] Nevertheless, it is easy to imagine coming under fire from both the Russian skirmishers lining the banks of the river and from the guns in the redoubt. There is an isolated grave here, marking the last resting place of Horace Cust, an officer of the Coldstream Guards who was serving on the staff at the time of the battle.

The river Alma itself has changed since 1854. In places it is possible to jump across, whilst here and there the visitor will find it easy to walk through it. However, in places it is still a formidable barrier, deep and wide. The Guards claim to have crossed the river three times on account of a bend. Whether the river has been straightened or not is unknown. It is certainly rather straight today. In fact, locals – and even the Russian author of this book – claim British maps of the battle are mainly incorrectly drawn, showing the river to have far too many bends in it.

There is no mistaking the route taken by the British infantry, however, as they advanced on the Great Redoubt. It is one of the great thrills of any trip to the Crimea to walk the line of the British attack on the Russian position. Indeed, one is struck by just how exposed they were, with no cover whatsoever, and with Russian guns wreaking havoc with grape and round shot. Every yard of ground, from the river south, was covered by fire, the Russian gunners being aided by wooden range-markers hammered into the ground. It is at this point that one realizes just how deceptive the slope is, for although it looks innocuous enough at first glance, it certainly begins to sap the energy the nearer you get to the redoubt, and all this without having to carry a rifle and equipment. By the time the British infantry reached the redoubt they must have been quite breathless, although their adrenalin probably carried them the last few yards into the position.

Today, a stone wall surrounds the redoubt, whilst low mounds are just about recognizable as being the embrasures. There are also memorials to the Vladimirsky Regiment and the 23rd Royal Welsh Fusiliers, as well as the commemorative obelisk and several mass graves, marked by huge slabs of stone. The redoubt was the scene of a major archaeological dig in 1990 during which several skeletons were found. In fact, the authors were present at a dig by the Institute of Archaeology of the Ukrainian Academy of Science in September 2007, during which the bodies of fourteen men from the Vladimirsky and Kazansky regiments were uncovered. Along with the bodies were found ammunition, the remains of boots, bags, and badges, cockades and grenades from their coats. There were also the Minié bullets that killed them. More remarkably there were the remains of a Russian drummer along with items of kit which it is hoped will help to establish his name. The bodies were reinterred in the mass graves at the Alma on 28 September 2007.

Away to the east of the redoubt can be seen the ground over which the Highland Brigade advanced, and standing in the redoubt today it is easy to imagine Campbell's men advancing. The ground has not changed at all. To the south of the redoubt lies the crest of hills from where the Allies watched the Russian retreat, and what a tempting spectacle it must have been. How different might the outcome of the Crimean War have been if Cardigan's cavalry had been launched after the fugitives?

Across the Sevastopol road and lying within the forward Russian positions is the knoll on which Raglan stood with his staff and Turner's guns as the battle unfolded before them. From here, it is easy to see why it was a bad position, particularly as he had effectively cut himself off from the rest of his army. In the event, this did not prove crucial.

A visit to the Alma inevitably ends by returning to the Great Redoubt, and by gazing out over the open slopes that lie between it and the river itself, ground which would have been covered with dead, dying and wounded British soldiers on the afternoon of the battle. It is easy to understand why Menshikov thought he could have held the position 'for weeks'. It is certainly difficult to imagine someone like Wellington being driven from it in the manner that Menshikov was. But then again, Menshikov did not know the British infantry. Indeed, when William Napier was writing of the storming of Badajoz during the Peninsular War he said the British Army bore with it an awful power.[3] Just what that power was was demonstrated fully at the Battle of the Alma.

Appendices

A Note on the Russian Regiments

1. Vladimirsky Regiment

Formed in 1700. Took part in the Great Northern War against Sweden. Was present on 27 June 1734 at the taking of Bakhchisarai, after which it withdrew to the bank of the Alma, its first meeting with this river. In 1773 under the command of Colonel A I Odoevsky it took part in putting down the Emelyan Pugachev revolt. In 1801 it took the name Vladimirsky Musketry Regiment. It took part in the Napoleonic Wars, and in particular in the campaign of 1812–14. Fought at Gorodechnya and Berezina. In 1811 it became the Vladimirsky Foot Regiment. In 1833 the Yaroslavsky Foot Regiment merged with it. At the Battle of the Alma it suffered heavy casualties and by 25 October 1854 it had less than 50 per cent of its original staff (1,724 men). For its service in the Crimean War it was awarded the Georgian banner with the inscription 'For Sevastopol in 1854 and 1855'. In 1860 General Prince P D Gorchakov became its colonel-in-chief.

2. Kazansky Chasseurs Regiment

Formed in 1700. In 1801 it became the Kazansky Musketry Regiment, and in 1811 the Kazansky Foot Regiment. In 1758 Lieutenant Colonel A V Suvorov was appointed to the regiment. During the war with Prussia the regiment took part in the battle at Tsorndorf on 19 August 1758. In 1837 it was inspected by Grand Duke Alexander Nikolaevich, the future Emperor Alexander II. During the Crimean War it was under the command of Colonel V G Gasfort, who gave his name to the hill near Sevastopol (Gasfort Hill, where the Italian cemetery was situated).

3. Moskovsky Foot Regiment

Formed on 25 June 1700. Took part in the battle at Narva on 19 November 1700, a defeat for the Russian Army. In 1704 it was with the army of Peter I during the assault on Narva, and in 1714 took part in the battle at Gangut. In 1723 the regiment was sent to the southern border of the Russian Empire to defend it against the Crimean Tatars. In 1737 it took part in the assault of the fortress of Ochakov and the occupation of Khotin. The regiment fought in the Russian-Swedish and Seven Years War, the siege of Silistria and the assault of Varna (1771–3). In 1776 it participated in the expedition to the Crimea to restore Khan Shagin-Girey to the throne, after which it served on the border of the Black Sea. In 1801 it was given the name of the Moskovsky Musketry Regiment. It took part in the Battle of Austerlitz in December 1805, and on 22 February 1811 it became the Moskovsky Foot Regiment. During the 1812 campaign it formed part of the 1st Western Army. At Borodino it defended the Bagration flèches. In 1833 the Permsky Foot Regiment amalgamated with it. At the Alma battle it suffered heavy casualties, but left the battlefield 'only when it couldn't stand any more'.

4. Suzdalsky Foot Regiment

Formed on 21 June 1701. In 1801 it became the Suzdalsky Musketry Regiment and in 1811 the Suzdalsky Foot Regiment. The famous Russian soldier Suvorov commanded this regiment from 1763 and worked out his famous training system. This was developed with the benefit of experiences gained during the wars against Frederick the Great. In November 1768 the regiment was sent from the Novaya Ladoga to Smolensk to act against the Polish rebels. It was here that Suvorov first demonstrated his outstanding military talents. He won battles at Landscrona and Stolovichi, and took Krakow (15 April 1772). This influenced greatly the outcome of the war, with the first partition of Poland being the major result. In 1837 the regiment was inspected by Grand Duke Alexander Nikolaevich. From 13 March till 27 August 1855 the regiment was present at Sevastopol, defending the second bastion. Its losses in the Crimean War were 2,099 men, including 420 lost at the Alma battle. From 1854 it was under the command of Colonel Daragan.

5. Uglitsky Chasseurs Regiment

Formed on 1 October 1708. It got the name Uglitsky on 15 April 1837. It took part in the battles in Prussia and Austria in 1805 to 1807 against the French. It also participated in the battles at Eylau and Friedland. Captain Prince Osten-Saken, the future general field-marshal, served in the regiment from 1777. In 1837 it was inspected by Grand Duke Alexander Nikolaevich. During the Alma battle the regiment was positioned in the second line of the Russian troops and was dislodged from its position by the 79th (Cameron) Highlanders. Its losses in the battle were 179 men. For its services in the Crimean War the regiment was awarded the Georgian banner 'For Sevastopol in 1854 and 1855'.

6. Volynsky Foot Regiment

Formed in May 1803 and took its name in 1811. In 1851 the future general Alexander Khrushchev was appointed as its commander. For services during the Crimean War the regiment was awarded the Georgian banner 'For Sevastopol in 1854 and 1855'.

7. Minsky Foot Regiment

Formed on 16 August 1806 as the Minsky Musketry Regiment and was sent to the western border of the Russian Empire as a reserve of the foreign army of General Benigsen. In 1806 it took part in the battles at Czarnowo, Kolozomb and Pultusk. In

1807 it was part of the 4th Division of Prince Golitsyn and fought at Eylau, where it suffered great losses. In June 1807, whilst under the command of General Prince Gorchakov, it fought on the right flank of the Russian Army at Friedland against the French corps of Lannes and Mortier. In the 1812 campaign it was part of the 1st Western Army of General Barclay de Tolly, in the 2nd Infantry Corps of General Baggovut. The regiment formed part of the 4th Infantry Division of Prince Eugene of Württemberg, and together with the Kremenchugsky Regiment formed the 2nd Brigade of this division under the command of General Pyshnitsky. The commander of the regiment was Colonel Krasavin. In the Battle of Smolensk it repulsed the attacks of Ney's corps near the village of Krasnaya. During the Battle of Borodino it was fighting from 12 till 4 pm in the centre of position near the Raevsky battery. Its commander was badly wounded, and more than a half of its officers and soldiers were killed. Because of the great losses it was reduced in one battalion and sent inland to be re-formed. On 5 December 1812 it had two battalions again and in 1814 had three battalions. It participated in the battles at Dresden and Kulm and fought on the outskirts of Paris. When the war ended it joined together with the Volynsky Foot Regiment to form the 1st Brigade of the 14th Infantry Division, part of the 5th Infantry Corps. In 1830 it took part in the suppression on the revolt in Poland.

During the Crimean War it formed part of the 1st Brigade of the 14th Infantry Division of General Moller. It took part in the battles at the Alma and Inkerman and in the defence of Sevastopol, where it was located near the 5th Bastion. It was one of the last regiments to leave Sevastopol after the town was taken by the Allied troops, forming the rearguard of the Russian Army with the Volynsky and Tobolsky regiments. At the Alma, it was positioned on the right flank of the Russian Army and was one of the last to withdraw from the battlefield. Its commander, Colonel I Prikhodkin, was badly wounded and contused, but continued to command. For this he was promoted to major-general in December 1854. His son, who took part in the battle, wrote a most impartial and sober article about the battle that was published in the magazine *Voennyi sbornik* in 1894.

8. Brestsky Foot Regiment
Formed in 1806 as the Brestsky Musketry Regiment, and was named in 1811.

9. Tarutinsky Chasseurs Regiment
Formed in 1813 from half of the soldiers of the Moskovsky garrison regiment. In 1833 the 28th Chasseurs Regiment joined it and it took the name of the Tarutinsky Chasseurs.

10. Borodinsky Chasseurs Regiment
Formed in 1813 from the other half of the soldiers of the Moskovsky garrison regiment. In 1833 the 27th Chasseurs Regiment joined and it took its name of Borodinsky Chasseurs. In 1812 the father of the famous Russian writer Fyodor

Dostoevsky served in the regiment in the capacity of a staff doctor. In 1824 one of the leaders of the Decembrists' revolt, M M Naryshkin, was an officer in the regiment. In the Alma battle the regiment was positioned in the centre of the Russian line. It fought practically without any support, save for some artillery, and during some hours of fighting repulsed several of the Allied attacks.

11. Belostoksky Foot Regiment
Formed in 1807 from three combined garrison battalions which had distinguished themselves in the defence of Danzig. Took its name in 1811. In 1813–14 it participated in the Napoleonic Wars and fought at Leipzig. At the beginning of the Crimean War it was stationed in the Caucasus and fought against the Turks near the village of Atshur. Its 5th and 6th reserve battalions took part in the Battle of the Alma. They were badly trained and even worse armed, and left the battlefield at the beginning of the battle. Its 3rd and 4th battalions proved their bravery at the assault of Kars and took three guns and four Turkish colours.

12. Hussars of His Imperial Majesty Prince Nikolai Maximilianovich Regiment (Kievsky Hussars Regiment)
Formed in 1775 from the personal staff of the Kievsky Cossacks Regiment. It took part in the war of 1812 and the Napoleonic Wars, the Crimean War and the Russian-Turkish War of 1877–8. In the Crimean War it was present at the battles of the Alma, Inkerman and the Chernaya. The commander was Major General I A Khaletsky, who also commanded the Hussars brigade. It played no active part at the Alma. It was one of the oldest regiments of the Russian Imperial Army.

13. Hussars of His Royal Highness Grand Duke Saxen-Weimarsky Regiment (Ingermanlandsky Regiment)
Formed in 1704 as the Dragoon Regiment of Colonel Unog. In 1709 it took part in the Battle of Poltava. It fought in Poland in 1733–5, the Turkish War of 1736–9, the Swedish War in 1742, the Russian-Turkish War of 1769–74 and the Russian-Polish War of 1792–4. In 1807 it fought at the Battle at Friedland where it lost one third of its officers. At the Battle at Ostrovno, during the 1812 campaign, it lost a quarter of its officers. Because of the great losses it took on the role of the military gendarmerie in the Battle of Borodino. In 1831 it took part in the suppression of the Polish revolt. In 1841 contact was made with the Dukes of Saxe-Weimar, and Karl-Alexander Saxe-Weimar became the honourable colonel of the regiment. At the Battle of the Alma it was commanded by Colonel Batovich. It played no part in the battle and withdrew from the position having suffered three casualties.

The Armies at the Alma

The Russian Army

Commander-in-chief: General Prince Alexander Sergeevich Menshikov.

16th Infantry Division (Kvitsinsky)
1st Brigade (Shchelkanov)
31st Vladimirsky Regt
32nd Suzdalsky Regt

2nd Brigade (Schonert)
31st Uglitsky Chasseur Regt
32nd Kazansky Chasseur Regt

17th Infantry Division (Kir'yakov)
1st Brigade (Kurt'yanov)
33rd Moskovsky Regt

2nd Brigade (Lachinov)
33rd Borodinsky Chasseur Regt
34th Tarutinsky Chasseur Regt

13th Infantry Division
1st (reserve) Brigade (Aslanovich)
25th Belostoksky Regt
26th Brestsky Regt

14th Infantry Division
1st Brigade (von Moller)
27th Volynsky Regt
28th Minsky Regt

6th Cavalry Division
2nd (Hussar) Brigade (Velichko)
11th Kiev Hussars
12th Ingermanlandsky Hussars

The French Army

Commander-in-chief: Marshal Armand Jacques Leroy de Saint-Arnaud.

1st Division (General François Certain Canrobert)
1st Brigade (Espinasse)
7th de Ligne
1st Zouaves
4th Chasseurs

2nd Brigade (Vinoy)
27th de Ligne
20th de Ligne
9th Chasseurs

2nd Division (General Pierre François Joseph Bosquet)
1st Brigade (D'Autemarre)
50th de Ligne
3rd Zouaves

2nd Brigade (Bouat)
6th de Ligne
7th Léger
3rd Chasseurs

3rd Division (General Prince Jérôme Charles Napoleon)
1st Brigade (Monet)
3rd Marine Regt
2nd Zouaves
19th Chasseurs

2nd Brigade (Thomas)
20th Léger
22nd Léger

4th Division (General Elie Frédéric Forey)
1st Brigade (de Lourmel)
19th de Ligne
5th Chasseurs

2nd Brigade (Aurelle)
74th de Ligne
39th de Ligne
26th de Ligne

The British Army
Commander-in-chief: Field Marshal Lord Raglan, the Hon. Fitzroy James Henry
Somerset.
1st Division (Lieutenant-General HRH the Duke of Cambridge)
Brigade of Guards (Bentinck)
Grenadier Guards
Coldstream Guards
Scots Fusilier Guards

Highland Brigade (C Campbell)
42nd Regt
79th Regt
93rd Regt

2nd Division (Lieutenant-General Sir De Lacy Evans)
Pennefather's Brigade
30th Regt
55th Regt
95th Regt

Adams' Brigade
41st Regt
47th Regt
49th Regt

3rd Division (Major-General Sir Richard England)
Eyre's Brigade
4th Regt
28th Regt
44th Regt

J Campbell's Brigade
1st Regt
38th Regt
50th Regt

4th Division (Major-General Sir George Cathcart)
Horn's Brigade
20th Regt
21st Regt
68th Regt
1st Rifle Brigade

Torrens' Brigade
46th Regt (2 coys)
63rd Regt
57th Regt (1 troop)

Light Division (Lieutenant-General Sir George Brown)
Buller's Brigade
19th Regt
77th Regt
88th Regt

Codrington's Brigade
7th Regt
23rd Regt
33rd Regt

Cavalry Division (Major-General Lord Lucan)
Light Brigade (Lord Cardigan)
4th Light Dragoons
8th Hussars
11th Hussars
13th Light Dragoons
17th Lancers

British Casualties

General Staff

Lieut. T. Leslie, Royal Horse Guards, Orderly officer to the Commander of the Forces, wounded severely; Capt. H. E. Weare, 50th Regiment, D.A.A.G., wounded severely.

First Division

Staff: Capt. H. W. Cust, Coldstream Guards, Aide-de-Camp to Major-General Bentinck, killed.

Grenadier Guards: Lieut. Col. Hon. H. Percy, wounded slightly; Lieut. R. Hamilton, wounded slightly; Lieut. J. M. Burgoyne, wounded slightly.

Coldstream Guards: Lieut. C. Baring, wounded severely.

Scots Fusilier Guards: Lieut. Col. J. H. Dalrymple, wounded slightly; Lieut. Col. C. A. Berkeley, wounded severely; Lieut. Col. H. P. Hepburn, wounded severely; Lieut. Col. F. Haygarth, wounded severely; Capt. Lord Chewton, wounded severely; Capt. J. D. Astley, wounded severely; Capt. W. G. Bulwer, wounded severely; Capt. D. F. Buckley, wounded severely; Capt. R. Gipps, wounded slightly; Lieut. Lord Ennismore, wounded severely; Lieut. Hon. H. Annesley, wounded severely.

93rd Regiment: Lieut. R. Abercrombie, killed.

Second Division

Staff: Lieut. General Sir De Lacy Evans, severe contusion, right shoulder; Lieut. Col. Hon. P. E. Herbert, 43rd Regiment, Assist. Quartermaster-General, severe contusion back of neck; Capt. Thompson, Deputy Assist. Quartermaster-General, on shoulder blade; Ensign St. Clair, 21st Regiment, Acting Interpreter, shot through right arm; Capt. A. M. McDonald, 92nd Regiment, Aide-de-Camp, wounded severely.

30th Regiment: Lieut. F. Luxmore, killed; Capt. T. H. Pakenham, wounded severely; Capt. G. Dickson, wounded severely; Capt. A. W. Connolly, wounded slightly; Lieut. and Adjutant M. Walker, wounded slightly.

55th Regiment: Brevet-Major J. B. Rose, killed; Capt. J. G. Schaw, killed; Major F. A. Whimper, wounded dangerously; Brevet-Major J. Coats, wounded severely; Lieut. G. E. Bissett, wounded severely; Lieut. E. Armstrong, wounded severely; Lieut. and Adjutant J. Warren, wounded slightly.

47th Regiment: Lieut T. Wollocombe, wounded severely; Lieut. N. G. Phillips, wounded severely; Lieut. J. C. Maycock, wounded slightly.

95th Regiment: Lieut. Col. W. Smith, wounded severely; Capt. G. J. Dowdall, killed; Capt. J. G. Eddington, killed; Lieut. E. W. Eddington, killed; Lieut. R. G. Polhill, killed; Lieut. and Adjutant J. C. Kingsley, killed; Lieut. W. L. Braybrooke, Ceylon Rifles, attached to 95th Regiment, killed; Major H. Hume, slight contusion; Brevet-Major A. T. Heyland, arm amputated; Capt. V. Wing, wounded; Capt. J. W. Sargent, wounded slightly; Lieut. A. Macdonald, slight contusion; Lieut. R. Gerard, contusion in abdomen; Ensign W. Braybrooke, wounded; Ensign J. H. Brooke, wounded in 2 places; Ensign B. C. Boothby, foot amputated; Ensign E. Bazalgette, wounded; Surgeon A. Gordon, slight contusion.

Third Division

4th Regiment: Lieut. Col. H. C. Cobbe, wounded slightly; Capt. G. L. Thompson, wounded slightly.

Light Division

7th Regiment: Capt. the Hon. W. Monck, killed; Capt. C. L. Hare, wounded severely; Capt. C. E. Watson, wounded severely; Capt. W. H. D. Fitzgerald, wounded severely; Lieut. D. Pearse, wounded severely; Lieut. F. E. Appleyard, wounded slightly; Lieut. P. G. Coney, wounded severely; Lieut. The Hon. A. C. H. Crofton, wounded slightly; Lieut. G. W. W. Carpenter, wounded slightly; Lieut. H. M. Jones, wounded severely.

23rd Regiment: Lieut. Col. H. G. Chester, killed; Capt. A. W. W. Wynn, killed; Capt. F. E. Evans, killed; Capt. J. C. Connolly, killed; Lieut. F. P. Radcliffe, killed; Lieut. Sir W. Young, Bart., killed; Second Lieut. H. Anstruther, killed; Second Lieut. J. H. Butler, killed; Capt. W. P. Campbell, wounded severely; Capt. E. C. Hopton, wounded slightly; Lieut. H. Bathurst, wounded severely; Lieut. F. Sayer, wounded slightly; Lieut. and Acting Adjutant A. Applethwaite, wounded severely.

33rd Regiment: Major T. B. Gough, wounded severely; Capt. H. C. Fitzgerald, wounded slightly; Lieut. F. Du Pre Montague, killed; Lieut. A. B. Wallis, wounded slightly; Lieut. W. S. Worthington, lost one leg; Ensign C. M. Siree, wounded severely; Ensign J. J. Greenwood, wounded slightly.

19th Regiment: Lieut. and Adjutant A. Cardew, killed; Ensign G. D. Stockwell, killed; Lieut. Col. R. Saunders, wounded severely; Major H. E. McGee, wounded slightly; Capt. R. Warden, wounded slightly; Lieut. R. Wardlaw, wounded severely; Lieut. L. D. Currie, wounded severely.

88th Regiment: Quartermaster T. Moore, wounded slightly.

2nd Battalion Rifle Brigade: Capt. Earl of Errol, wounded in hand.

Artillery: Capt. A. Dew, killed; Lieut. A. Walsham, killed; Lieut. R. H. Cockerell, killed.

Royal Engineers: Lieut. H. Teesdale, wounded severely.

Total killed, 26; total wounded, 76; grand total, 102.

Return of Casualties which Occurred in Action on the River Alma, Crimea, 20 September 1854

13th Light Dragoons: 1 horse wounded.

Artillery: 3 officers, 9 rank and file, 26 horses, killed; 1 sergeant, 20 rank and file, wounded.

Royal Engineers: 1 officer wounded.

First Division

Grenadier Guards: 10 rank and file killed; 3 officers, 3 sergeants, 113 rank and file, wounded.

Coldstream Guards: 1 officer killed; 2 officers, 27 rank and file, wounded.

Scots Fusiliers: 3 sergeants, 17 rank and file, killed; 11 officers, 13 sergeants, 1 drummer, 136 rank and file, wounded; 1 rank and file missing.

42nd Regiment: 5 rank and file killed; 2 sergeants, 30 rank and file, wounded.

79th Regiment: 2 rank and file killed; 7 rank and file wounded.

93rd Regiment: 1 officer, 7 rank and file, killed; 3 sergeants, 41 rank and file, wounded.

Total: 2 officers, 3 sergeants, 41 rank and file, killed; 16 officers, 21 sergeants, 1 drummer, 354 rank and file, wounded; 1 rank and file missing.

Second Division

30th Regiment: 1 officer, 11 rank and file, killed; 4 officers, 2 sergeants, 1 drummer, 60 rank and file, wounded.

55th Regiment: 2 officers, 1 sergeant, 10 rank and file, killed; 6 officers, 4 sergeants, 92 rank and file, wounded.

95th Regiment: 6 officers, 3 sergeants, 42 rank and file, killed; 11 officers, 12 sergeants, 1 drummer, 115 rank and file, wounded; 3 rank and file missing.

41st Regiment: 4 rank and file killed; 1 sergeant, 22 rank and file, wounded.

47th Regiment: 1 sergeant, 3 rank and file, killed; 4 officers, 4 sergeants, 1 drummer, 56 rank and file, wounded.

49th Regiment: 1 sergeant, 1 rank and file, killed; 2 sergeants, 1 drummer, 10 rank and file, wounded.

Total: 9 officers, 6 sergeants, 71 rank and file, killed; 25 officers, 25 sergeants, 4 drummers, 355 rank and file, wounded; 3 rank and file missing.

Third Division

4th Regiment: 2 officers, 8 rank and file, wounded; 3 rank and file missing.

44th Regiment: 1 rank and file killed; 7 rank and file wounded.

Total: 1 rank and file killed; 2 officers, 15 rank and file, wounded; 3 rank and file missing.

Fourth Division

21st Regiment: 1 rank and file killed.

First Battalion Rifle Brigade: 1 rank and file wounded.
Total: 1 rank and file killed; 1 rank and file wounded.

Light Division
7th Regiment: 1 officer, 2 sergeants, 38 rank and file, killed; 11 officers, 16 sergeants, 1 drummer, 151 rank and file, wounded; 2 rank and file missing.
23rd Regiment: 8 officers, 3 sergeants, 1 drummer, 39 rank and file, killed; 5 officers, 9 sergeants, 4 drummers, 139 rank and file, wounded; 2 drummers missing.
33rd Regiment: 1 officer, 3 sergeants, 52 rank and file, killed; 6 officers, 16 sergeants, 2 drummers, 159 rank and file, wounded.
19th Regiment: 2 officers, 1 drummer, 38 rank and file, killed; 5 officers, 4 sergeants, 2 drummers, 168 rank and file, wounded; 6 rank and file missing.
77th Regiment: 3 rank and file killed; 17 rank and file wounded.
88th Regiment: 4 rank and file killed; 1 officer, 2 sergeants, 14 rank and file, wounded; 1 rank and file missing.
Second Battalion Rifle Brigade: 2 sergeants, 9 rank and file, killed; 1 officer, 1 sergeant, 3 drummers, 34 rank and file, wounded.
Total: 12 officers, 10 sergeants, 2 drummers, 183 rank and file, killed; 29 officers, 48 sergeants, 12 drummers, 682 rank and file, wounded; 9 rank and file and 2 drummers missing.

Summary
Cavalry. 1 horse wounded.
Artillery. 3 officers, 9 rank and file, 26 horses, killed; 1 sergeant, 20 rank and file, wounded.
Engineers. 1 officer wounded.
First Division. 2 officers, 3 sergeants, 41 rank and file, killed; 16 officers, 21 sergeants, 1 drummer, 354 rank and file, wounded; 1 rank and file missing.
Second Division. 9 officers, 6 sergeants, 71 rank and file, killed; 25 officers, 25 sergeants, 4 drummers, 355 rank and file, wounded; 3 rank and file missing.
Third Division. 1 rank and file killed; 2 officers, 15 rank and file, wounded; 3 rank and file missing.
Fourth Division. 1 rank and file, killed; 1 rank and file wounded.
Light Division. 12 officers, 10 sergeants, 2 drummers, 183 rank and file killed; 29 officers, 48 sergeants, 12 drummers, 682 rank and file, wounded; 9 rank and file missing.
Grand total: 26 officers, 19 sergeants, 2 drummers, 306 rank and file, 26 horses, killed; 73 officers, 95 sergeants, 17 drummers, 1,427 rank and file, 1 horse, wounded; 2 drummers, 16 rank and file, missing.

(Signed) J. D. Bucknall Estcourt
Adjutant-General.
Head-Quarters, Alma River, Sept. 22, 1854.

Notes

Chapter 1. A Rupture with the Russians

1. *Annual Register* (London, 1854), 533.
2. Wellesley, Sir Victor, and Sencourt, Robert, *Conversations with Napoleon III* (London, 1934), 54.

Chapter 2. The Allies Go to War

1. Stephenson, Sir Frederick Charles Arthur, *At Home and on the Battlefield: Letters from the Crimea, China and Egypt, 1854–1888* (London, 1915), 69.
2. Higginson, General Sir George, *Seventy-One Years of a Guardsman's Life* (London, 1916), 85.
3. *Annual Register*, 132–3.
4. Higginson, *Seventy-One Years*, 85–6.
5. Ibid., 86.
6. Bazancourt, Baron de, *The Crimean Expedition, to the Capture of Sebastopol: Chronicles of the War in the East*, trans. Robert Howe Gould (London, 1856), I, 34.
7. Wantage, Harriet S, *Lord Wantage, VC, KCB: A Memoir, by His Wife* (London, 1907), 20–21.
8. Skene, James Henry, *With Lord Stratford in the Crimean War* (London, 1883), 40–41.
9. *Annual Register*, 160.
10. Russell, William Howard, *The British Expedition to the Crimea* (London, 1877), 50.
11. Wantage, *Lord Wantage*, 22–3.
12. General Order, 3 September 1854.
13. Munro, William, Surgeon-General, *Reminiscences of Military Service with the 93rd Sutherland Highlanders* (London, 1883), I, 7.
14. Astley, Sir John Dugdale, Bart., *Fifty Years of My Life, in the World of Sport at Home and Abroad*, 2 vols (London, 1894), I, 197.
15. Gowing, Sergeant Timothy, *A Soldier's Experience, or, A Voice from the Ranks* (Nottingham, 1903), 38.

Chapter 3. Across the Black Sea

1. Bazancourt, *Crimean Expedition*, I, 173.

2. Higginson, *Seventy-One Years*, 139.
3. Calthorpe, Somerset John Gough, *Letters from Head-quarters, or, The Realities of the War in the Crimea*, 2 vols (London, 1856), 130–35.
4. Wilson, C T, *Our Veterans of 1854: In Camp, and before the Enemy, by a Regimental Officer* (London, 1859), 102.
5. Hamley, Lieut. Col. E Bruce, *The Story of the Campaign of Sebastopol, Written in the Camp* (London, 1855), 15.
6. Wilson, *Our Veterans*, 106.
7. Ibid., 106–7.
8. Airey, Maj. Gen. Sir Richard, *Opening Address of Major General Sir Richard Airey, KCB., Quartermaster-General of the Forces before the Board of General Officers Assembled at the Royal Hospital Chelsea* (London, 1856), 118–20.
9. Evidence of Sergeant Thomas Dawson in *Second Report from the Select Committee on the Army before Sebastopol* (London, 1855), 249.
10. Ibid., 250.
11. Pearse, Major Hugh (ed.), *The Crimean Diary and Letters of Lieut.-General Sir Charles Ash Windham* (London, 1897), 20–21.
12. Astley, *Fifty Years of My Life*, I, 198.
13. Bazancourt, *Crimean Expedition*, I, 198–9.
14. Stuart, Brian (ed.), *Soldier's Glory, being Rough Notes of an Old Soldier by Major-General Sir George Bell* (London, 1956), 208.

Chapter 4. Summer in Sevastopol

1. Oliphant, Laurence, *The Russian Shores of the Black Sea in the Autumn of 1852* (London, 1854), 254–5.
2. The name 'Malakhov Hill' first appeared on the general map of Sevastopol in 1851 and was named after a Russian sailor, Mikhail Mikhailovich Malakhov. He began his military service in 1789 with the Black Sea Fleet. He was a boatswain, a skipper, a rigging-master. By 1827 he was a captain, after which he went to Sevastopol, where he commanded a company of sailors working in the town. He made his home in the Korabel'naya. Malakhov was greatly respected for his honesty and justice. People often went to his house, which was situated at the bottom of the hill, looking for advice, and soon it was called 'Malakhov Hill'. Malakhov had two sons, Afanasy and Iliya, and six daughters. His sons also became sailors, and both took part in the defence of Sevastopol from 1854 to 1855. *Nikolaevskii vestnik*, 9 February 1868, no. 11.
3. Oliphant, *Russian Shores*, 260–61.
4. Ibid., 260–61.
5. Hodasevich, Captain R, *A Voice from within the Walls of Sebastopol: A Narrative of the Campaign in the Crimea and of the Events of the Siege* (London, 1856), 20.
6. Ibid., 31–2.
7. Chennyk, S, *Alma: 20 sentyabrya 1854* (Simferopol, 2004), 38.

Chapter 5. The Landings

1. Cler, Jean Joseph Gustave, *Reminiscences of an Officer of Zouaves: Translated from the French* (New York, 1860), 166.
2. Stuart, *Soldier's Glory*, 210.
3. Rochet, S (ed.), *Un régiment de ligne, pendant la guerre d'Orient: notes et souvenirs d'un officier d'infanterie, 1854–1855–1856* (Lyons, 1894), 68.
4. Ibid., 68–9.
5. Russell, *British Expedition*, 86.
6. Lysons, Sir Daniel, *The Crimean War from First to Last* (London, 1895), 80–81.
7. Anon., *Les Militaires chrétiens de la guerre d'Orient* (Versailles, n.d.), 35.
8. Cler, *Reminiscences*, 167–8.
9. Colebrooke, Sir Edward, *Journal of Two Visits to the Crimea, in the Autumns of 1854 and 1855, with Remarks on the Campaign* (London, 1856), 12.
10. Peard, Lieutenant George Shuldham, *Narrative of a Campaign in the Crimea, including an Account of the Battles of Alma, Balaklava and Inkermann* (London, 1855), 36.
11. Hingle, Keith, *The Diary of Sgt. W. McMillan* (London, n.d.), 20.
12. Anon., *Sketches in the Camp and Field, being Sketches of the War in the Crimea* (London, n.d.), 55.
13. Hamley, *Story of the Campaign*, 12–14.
14. Paget, General Lord George, *The Light Cavalry Brigade in the Crimea* (London, 1881), 15.
15. Mitchell, Albert, *Recollections of One of the Light Brigade* (Tunbridge Wells, n.d.), 41.
16. Mabell, Countess of Airlie, *With the Guards We Shall Go* (London, 1933), 66.
17. Ibid., 67.
18. Rochet, *Régiment de ligne*, 69.
19. Ibid., 69.
20. Ibid., 70.
21. Mitchell, *Recollections*, 45.
22. Ibid., 46–7.
23. Rochet, *Régiment de ligne*, 70.
24. Loy Smith, George, *A Victorian RSM: From India to the Crimea* (Winchester, 1987), 99–100.
25. Mitchell, *Recollections*, 49–50.
26. Rochet, *Régiment de ligne*, 70–71.
27. Ibid., 71.
28. Peard, *Narrative of a Campaign*, 49–51.
29. Rochet, *Régiment de ligne*, 72.

Chapter 6. The Russians

1. Kukharuk, A, 'Russkaya armiya v Krymskuyu voinu', *Rodina*, 1995, no. 3–4, 22–6.
2. Ul'yanov, I E, *Regulyarnaya pekhota 1801–1855: istoriya rossiiskikh voisk* (Moscow, 1996), 131–2.
3. Volkov, S, *Russkii ofitserskii korpus* (Moscow, 1993), 59.
4. Ibid., 60.
5. De Cuistin, Markiz, *Nikolaevskaya Rossiya* (Moscow, 1990), 148.
6. Hodasevich, *Voice from within the Walls*, 21–3.
7. Gagern, F, *Dnevnik puteshestviya po Rossii v 1839* (Leningrad, 1991), 682–3.
8. *Ofitserskii korpus russkoi armii: opyt samopoznaniya* (Moscow, 2000), 85.
9. Ibid., 86.
10. Ibid., 86.
11. Hodasevich, *Voice from within the Walls*, 30.
12. Jesse, Captain William, *Russia and the War* (London, 1854), 34.
13. *Voennaya entsiklopediya* (St Petersburg, 1914), XVI, 643.
14. Durop, K, 'Takticheskoe obrazovanie armii v mirnoe vremya', *Voennyi sbornik*, 1872, no. 2, 239.
15. Ibid., 232.
16. Zaionchkovskii, P, 'Russkii ofitserskii korpus na rubezhe dvukh stoletii', *Voenno-istoricheskii zhurnal*, 1972, no. 3, 49.
17. Hodasevich, *Voice from within the Walls*, 51.
18. Panaeva, A, *Vospominaniya* (Moscow, 1986), 231–2.
19. Jesse, *Russia and the War*, 150–51.
20. Ibid., 28–9.
21. Ibid., 29.
22. Ibid., 30–31.

Chapter 7. Preparations for Battle

1. Hodasevich, *Voice from within the Walls*, 59–60.
2. Ibid., 62–3.
3. Dubrovin, N F, *Materialy dlya istorii Krymskoi voiny* (St Petersburg, 1871–4), 432–4.
4. Ul'yanov, *Regulyarnaya pekhota*, 162. Proof of this can be gauged from the amount of Russian helmets from the Crimean War bearing the number '26' now residing in British museums or featured in books. These were taken during the advance on Sevastopol when Lucan's advance guard clattered into the Russian troops leaving the town. The baggage wagons were taken and along with them those containing hundreds of helmets marked '26'. This is probably because of the practice the Russians had of removing their helmets during the march.
5. Lyashuk, P, 'Intendantstvo: iznanka kampanii v Krymu 1854–1855', *Rodina*, 1995, no. 3–4, 90–93.
6. 'Furazhnaya shapka obraztsa 1844', *Formennaya odezhda*, 1998, no. 1, 10–17.

7. *Voennaya odezhda russkoi armii* (Moscow, 1994), 190–91.

8. Ul'yanov, *Regulyarnaya pekhota*, 165–6.

9. Shirokorad, A, *Entsiklopediya otechestvennoi artillerii* (Minsk, 2000), 45.

10. MacMunn, Sir George, *The Crimea in Perspective* (London, 1935), 5.

11. Hodasevich, *Voice from within the Walls*, 64–5.

12. Cler, *Reminiscences*, 172–3.

13. Rochet, *Régiment de ligne*, 72–3.

14. Astley, *Fifty Years of My Life*, I, 209–10.

Chapter 8. The French Move First

1. Peard, *Narrative of a Campaign*, 52–3.

2. Fay, Général, *Souvenirs de la guerre de Crimée 1854–56, par le général Fay, ancien aide-de-camp du Marshal Bosquet* (Paris, 1889), 50–51.

3. Bazancourt, *Crimean Expedition*, I, 226–7.

4. Dubrovin, *Materialy*, 434–6.

5. Fay, *Souvenirs*, 51–2.

6. Bazancourt, *Crimean Expedition*, I, 232.

7. Rochet, *Régiment de ligne*, 73–4.

8. Bazancourt, *Crimean Expedition*, I, 235. As always, nationalistic pride tends to cloud judgements as to who did and did not fire the first shots of any battle. The timings of the various events at the Battle of the Alma vary by degrees, depending upon which account is read. For example, Russian accounts have Bosquet reaching the plateau at around 11 am, over two hours before Allied accounts have him even beginning his advance. We have tended to use Allied timings rather than Russian for our account of the battle.

9. Fay, *Souvenirs*, 52–5.

10. Colebrooke, *Journal of Two Visits*, 18–20.

11. Tatorskii, Pavel, 'Vosem' mesyatsev v plenu u frantsuzov', *Sovremennik*, vol. 53, 1855, 161–201.

12. Dubrovin, *Materialy*, 432–9.

13. Anon., *Militaires chrétiens*, 38–9.

14. Lyashuk, 'Intendantstvo', 92.

15. Tarle, E V, *Krymskaya voina* (Moscow, 1941–4), II, 108–9.

16. Zaionchkovskii, A M, *Oborona Sevastopolya: podvigi zashchitnikov* (St Petersburg, 1904).

17. Fay, *Souvenirs*, 55–6.

18. Ibid., 56.

19. Cler, *Reminiscences*, 175–7.

20. Fay, *Souvenirs*, 56–7.

21. Cler, *Reminiscences*, 177–9.

22. Bazancourt, *Crimean Expedition*, I, 248.

23. Kinglake, Alexander William, *The Invasion of the Crimea: Its Origin, and An Account*

of Its Progress down to the Death of Lord Raglan (London, 1863), II, 398–401.
24. Ibid., II, 400.

Chapter 9. The British Enter the Battle

1. Kinglake, *Invasion of the Crimea*, II, 297.
2. Peard, *Narrative of a Campaign*, 54–5.
3. Seaton, Albert, *The Crimean War: A Russian Chronicle* (London, 1977), 82.
4. Ibid., 83.
5. Gowing, *Soldier's Experience*, 47.
6. Lysons, *Crimean War*, 99–101.
7. Gowing, *Soldier's Experience*, 47.
8. Norcott himself was suitably irritated by Kinglake's version of events at the Alma that he wrote a letter to *The Times*. According to Kinglake, *Invasion of the Crimea*, II, 307, Codrington was left without any cover at all, a fact disputed by Norcott. See J W Fortescue, *History of the British Army* (London, 1899), XIII, 62, for his version of events.
9. Lysons, *Crimean War*, 97.
10. Kinglake, *Invasion of the Crimea*, II, 321.
11. Lysons, *Crimean War*, 98–9.
12. Fortescue, *History of the British Army*, 63.
13. Ibid., 64.
14. Kvitsinsky, quoted in Seaton, *Crimean War*, 92.
15. Gowing, *Soldier's Experience*, 47–8.
16. Kinglake, *Invasion of the Crimea*, II, 332.
17. Gowing, *Soldier's Experience*, 48.

Chapter 10. Forward, the Guards!

1. For a study of the Foot Guards between 1808 and 1815 see Ian Fletcher's *Gentlemen's Sons: The Foot Guards in the Peninsula and at Waterloo, 1808–1815* (Speldhurst, 1992).
2. Kinglake, *Invasion of the Crimea*, II, 351. Others, such as Baring Pemberton, *Battles of the Crimean War* (London, 1962), 58, have Campbell passing this memorable comment at a later time, during the heavy fighting in front of the Great Redoubt. We are inclined to believe Kinglake's timing.
3. Stephenson, *At Home*, 102.
4. Wilson, *Our Veterans*, 132–3.
5. Hingle, *Diary of Sgt. W. McMillan*, 21.
6. Higginson, *Seventy-One Years*, 150–51.
7. Gorbunova, N A, *Collection of Manuscripts, Introduced to His Imperial Highness Crown Prince (Cesarevitch) The Defence of Sebastopol by Its Defenders* (St Petersburg, 1872), I, 57–8.

8. Ewart, John Alexander, *The Story of a Soldier's Life, or, Peace, War, and Mutiny*, 2 vols (London, 1881), I, 230–31.
9. Astley, *Fifty Years of My Life*, I, 213–14.
10. Ibid., 215–16.
11. Gipps, quoted in Sir F Maurice, *The History of the Scots Guards* (London, 1934), II, 81.
12. Ibid., II, 81–2.
13. Ibid., II, 80.
14. Astley, *Fifty Years of My Life*, I, 222. Kinglake, *Invasion of the Crimea*, II, 423, would have us believe that Chewton was killed at the Alma. In fact, he died on 8 October.
15. Although regimental pride should never be discounted, it is difficult to argue with the evidence in Maurice's *History of the Scots Guards* (II, 73–5) and with eyewitnesses themselves, including Lindsay (by then Lord Wantage).
16. Arthur Thistlethwayte, who carried the regimental colour, died of disease at Scutari afterwards. Had he lived he might well have been awarded the Victoria Cross like Lindsay.
17. Wantage, *Lord Wantage*, 31–2.
18. Ibid., 32.
19. Ibid., 37.
20. Astley, *Fifty Years of My Life*, 217.
21. Hingle, *Diary of Sgt. W. McMillan*, 21.
22. Kinglake, *Invasion of the Crimea*, II, 427.

Chapter 11. The Drive to Victory

1. Kinglake, *Invasion of the Crimea*, II, 450.
2. Hodasevich, *Voice from within the Walls*, 70.
3. Seaton, *Crimean War*, 93–4.
4. Ibid., 92.
5. Gorbunova, *Collection of Manuscripts*, I, 57–8.
6. Mabell, *With the Guards*, 72.
7. Gorbunova, *Collection of Manuscripts*, I, 59.
8. Seaton, *Crimean War*, 93.
9. Gorbunova, *Collection of Manuscripts*, I, 204–5.
10. Ewart, *Story of a Soldier's Life*, I, 231.
11. Kinglake, *Invasion of the Crimea*, II, 461.
12. Ibid., II, 462.
13. Higginson, *Seventy-One Years*, 152–3.

Chapter 12. End of the Battle

1. Rochet, *Régiment de ligne*, 76–7.

2. Bazancourt, *Crimean Expedition*, I, 252.

3. Cler, *Reminiscences*, 179–81.

4. Dubrovin, *Materialy*, 184.

5. Seaton, *Crimean War*, 87.

6. Dubrovin, *Materialy*, 437–8.

7. Hodasevich, *Voice from within the Walls*, 72–3.

8. Ibid., 74–5.

9. Loy Smith, *Victorian RSM*, 106.

10. For an in-depth study of Wellington's cavalry, see Ian Fletcher's *Galloping at Everything: The British Cavalry in the Peninsular War and at Waterloo, 1808–1815* (Staplehurst, 2000).

11. Mitchell, *Recollections*, 55–6.

12. Hingle, *Diary of Sgt. W. McMillan*, 21.

13. Rochet, *Régiment de ligne*, 77.

14. Fay, *Souvenirs de la guerre*, 58.

15. Tarle, *Krymskaya voina*, II, 110–11.

16. Ibid., II, 112–13.

Chapter 13. Victory and Defeat

1. Wilson, *Our Veterans*, 138–9.

2. Gowing, *Soldier's Experience*, 49–50.

3. Peard, *Narrative of a Campaign*, 65.

4. Wilson, *Our Veterans*, 140.

5. Higginson, *Seventy-One Years*, 155–6.

6. Hingle, *Diary of Sgt. W. McMillan*, 21.

7. Astley, *Fifty Years of My Life*, 221–2.

8. Colebrooke, *Journal of Two Visits*, 21–22.

9. Kinglake, *Invasion of the Crimea* (II, 503), quotes a conversation with a French soldier who suggested the French losses were around fifty. Kinglake naturally discounted this but used it as an indication of just how light the French considered their initial losses to have been.

10. Bonham-Carter, Victor (ed.), *Surgeon in the Crimea: The Experiences of George Lawson Recorded in Letters to his Family, 1854–55* (London, 1968), 75.

11. Ibid., 76.

12. Anon., *Militaires chrétiens*, 39–40.

13. Russell, *British Expedition*, 126–7.

14. Rochet, *Régiment de ligne*, 79.

15. Paget, *Light Cavalry Brigade*, 24.

16. Bazancourt, *Crimean Expedition*, I, 270.

17. Ibid., I, 270.

18. Wilson, *Our Veterans*, 147–8.

19. Rochet, *Régiment de ligne*, 79–80.

Chapter 14. Aftermath

1. Weller, Jac, *Wellington at Waterloo* (London, 1967), xi.
2. Various 'options' books have appeared over the years, such as Hitler invading England, Wellington being killed at Waterloo, and even the Confederates having AK47s at Gettysburg. As extreme as it seems, these are no less fanciful than considering what might have happened at the Alma had the Russians used their cavalry, for example. It never happened; thus, it's not worth discussing seriously. Leave such scenarios to the wargamers!
3. Gershel'man, S, 'Nravstvennyi element pod Sevastopolem', *Voennyi sbornik*, 1894, no. 2, 270.
4. It is still astonishing to see the amount of criticism Wellington receives, even after winning one of the most decisive battles in military history, Waterloo.
5. For example, in his 32-page account of the Battle of the Alma, Baring Pemberton, in his *Battles of the Crimean War*, gives over just two brief paragraphs to the French contribution to the victory.
6. *Russkii arkhiv*, 1892, no. 8, 479.
7. Tarle, *Krymskaya voina*, II, 116.
8. Seaton, *Crimean War*, 103.
9. Ibid., 103.
10. Rozin, A, *Ocherki iz Krymskoi voiny (dnevnik ochevidtsa)* (Moscow, 1998), 197–9.
11. *Illustrated London News*, 7 October 1854, 341.
12. Ibid., 334–5.
13. Vulliamy, C E, *Crimea: The Campaign of 1854–56* (London, 1939), 323.
14. Wilson, *Our Veterans*, 143.
15. Peard, *Narrative of a Campaign*, 63.

Chapter 15. The Battlefield Today

1. Anon., *The Crimea: Its Towns, Inhabitants, and Social Customs, by a Lady, Resident by the Alma* (London, 1855).
2. When the authors visited the battlefield in the February of 2004, on one of many such occasions, the whole area was covered in snow, and the ground over which the Light and 1st Divisions advanced frozen and covered with ice.
3. Napier, W F P, *History of the War in the Peninsula and in the South of France* 6 vols (London, 1828), IV, 432.

Bibliography

Airey, Maj. Gen. Sir Richard, *Opening Address of Major General Sir Richard Airey, KCB., Quartermaster-General of the Forces before the Board of General Officers Assembled at the Royal Hospital Chelsea* (London, 1856).

Annual Register (London, 1854).

Anon., *The Crimea: Its Towns, Inhabitants, and Social Customs, by a Lady, Resident by the Alma* (London, 1855).

Anon., *Les Militaires chrétiens de la guerre d'Orient* (Versailles, n.d.).

Anon., *Sketches in the Camp and Field, being Sketches of the War in the Crimea* (London, n.d.).

Astley, Sir John Dugdale, Bart., *Fifty Years of My Life, in the World of Sport at Home and Abroad*, 2 vols (London, 1894).

Baring Pemberton, W, *Battles of the Crimean War* (London, 1962).

Bazancourt, Baron de, *The Crimean Expedition, to the Capture of Sebastopol: Chronicles of the War in the East*, trans. Robert Howe Gould (London, 1856).

Bonham-Carter, Victor (ed.), *Surgeon in the Crimea: The Experiences of George Lawson Recorded in Letters to His Family, 1854–55* (London, 1968).

Calthorpe, Somerset John Gough, *Letters from Head-quarters, or, The Realities of the War in the Crimea*, 2 vols (London, 1856).

Chennyk, S, *Alma: 20 sentyabrya 1854* (Simferopol, 2004).

Cler, Jean Joseph Gustave, *Reminiscences of an Officer of Zouaves: Translated from the French* (New York, 1860).

Clifford, Henry, *Henry Clifford, V. C.: His Letters and Sketches from the Crimea* (London, 1955).

Colebrooke, Sir Edward, *Journal of Two Visits to the Crimea, in the Autumns of 1854 and 1855, with Remarks on the Campaign* (London, 1856).

De Cuistin, Markiz, *Nikolaevskaya Rossiya* (Moscow, 1990).

Dubrovin N F, *Materialy dlya istorii Krymskoi voiny i oborony Sevastopolya* (St Petersburg, 1871–4).

Durop, K, 'Takticheskoe obrazovanie armii v mirnoe vremya', *Voennyi sbornik*, 1872.

Ewart, John Alexander, *The Story of a Soldier's Life, or, Peace, War, and Mutiny*, 2 vols (London, 1881).

Fay, Général, *Souvenirs de la guerre de Crimée 1854–56, par le général Fay, ancien aide-de-camp du Marshal Bosquet* (Paris, 1889).

Fletcher, Ian, and Ishchenko, Natalia, *The Crimean War: A Clash of Empires*

(Staplehurst, 2004).

Fortescue, J W, *A History of the British Army* (London, 1899), vol. 13.

Gagern, F, *Dnevnik puteshestviya po Rossii v 1839* (Leningrad, 1991).

Gershel'man, S, 'Nravstvennyi element pod Sevastopolem', *Voennyi sbornik*, 1894.

Gibbs, Peter, *The Battle of the Alma* (London, 1963).

Goldfrank, David M, *The Origins of the Crimean War* (London, 1994).

Gooch, Brison D, *The New Bonapartist Generals in the Crimean War: Distrust and Decision-making in the Anglo-French Alliance* (The Hague, 1959).

Gorbunova, N A, *Collection of Manuscripts, Introduced to His Imperial Highness Crown Prince (Cesarevitch) The Defence of Sebastopol by Its Defenders* (St Petersburg, 1872).

Gowing, Sergeant Timothy, *A Soldier's Experience, or, A Voice from the Ranks* (Nottingham, 1903).

Hamley, Lieut. Col. E Bruce, *The Story of the Campaign of Sebastopol, Written in the Camp* (London, 1855).

Higginson, General Sir George, *Seventy-One Years of a Guardsman's Life* (London, 1916).

Hingle, Keith, *The Diary of Sgt. W. McMillan* (London, n.d.).

Hodasevich, Captain R, *A Voice from within the Walls of Sebastopol: A Narrative of the Campaign in the Crimea and of the Events of the Siege* (London, 1856).

House of Commons, *Second Report from the Select Committee on the Army before Sebastopol* (London, 1855).

Ishchenko, N A, *Krymskaya voina 1853–1856 godov: ocherki istorii i kul'tury* (Simferopol, 2003).

Jesse, Captain William, *Russia and the War* (London, 1854).

Kinglake, Alexander William, *The Invasion of the Crimea: Its Origin, and An Account of Its Progress down to the Death of Lord Raglan* (London, 1863).

Klembowsky, Colonel W, *Vues des champs de bataille de la campagne de Crimée* (St Petersburg, 1904).

Kukharuk, A, 'Russkaya armiya v Krymskuyu voinu', *Rodina*, 1995.

Loy Smith, George, *A Victorian RSM: From India to the Crimea* (Winchester, 1987).

Lyashuk, P, 'Intendantstvo: iznanka kampanii v Krymu 1854–1855', *Rodina*, 1995.

Lysons, Sir Daniel, *The Crimean War from First to Last* (London, 1895).

Mabell, Countess of Airlie, *With the Guards We Shall Go* (London, 1933).

MacMunn, Sir George, *The Crimea in Perspective* (London, 1935).

Maurice, Sir F, *The History of the Scots Guards* (London, 1934).

Mitchell, Albert, *Recollections of One of the Light Brigade* (Tunbridge Wells, n.d.).

Munro, William, Surgeon-General, *Reminiscences of Military Service with the 93rd Sutherland Highlanders* (London, 1883).

Oliphant, Laurence, *The Russian Shores of the Black Sea in the Autumn of 1852* (London, 1854).

Paget, General Lord George, *The Light Cavalry Brigade in the Crimea* (London, 1881).

Panaeva, A, *Vospominaniya* (Moscow, 1986).

Peard, Lieutenant George Shuldham, *Narrative of a Campaign in the Crimea, including an Account of the Battles of Alma, Balaklava and Inkermann* (London, 1855).

Pearse, Major Hugh (ed.), *The Crimean Diary and Letters of Lieut.-General Sir Charles Ash Windham* (London, 1897).

Percy, Algernon, *A Bearskin's Crimea: Colonel Henry Percy VC and His Brother Officers* (London, Barnsley, 2005).

Rochet, S (ed.), *Un régiment de ligne, pendant la guerre d'Orient: notes et souvenirs d'un officier d'infanterie, 1854–1855–1856* (Lyons, 1894).

Royle, Trevor, *Crimea: The Great Crimean War, 1845–1856* (London, 1999).

Rozin, A, *Ocherki iz Krymskoi voiny (dnevnik ochevidtsa)* (Moscow, 1998).

Russell, William Howard, *The British Expedition to the Crimea* (London, 1877).

Seaton, Albert, *The Crimean War: A Russian Chronicle* (London, 1977).

Shadwell, Lieut. General Lawrence, *The Life of Colin Campbell, Lord Clyde*, 2 vols (Edinburgh, 1881).

Shirokorad, A, *Entsiklopediya otechestvennoi artillerii* (Minsk, 2000).

Skene, James Henry, *With Lord Stratford in the Crimean War* (London, 1883).

Stephenson, Sir Frederick Charles Arthur, *At Home and on the Battlefield: Letters from the Crimea, China and Egypt, 1854–1888* (London, 1915).

Stuart, Brian (ed.), *Soldier's Glory, being Rough Notes of an Old Soldier by Major-General Sir George Bell* (London, 1956).

Sweetman, John, *Raglan: From the Peninsula to the Crimea* (London, 1993).

Tarle, E V, *Krymskaya voina* (Moscow, 1941–4).

Tyrell, Henry, *History of the War with Russia* (London, n.d.).

Ul'yanov, I E, *Regulyarnaya pekhota 1801–1855: istoriya rossiiskikh voisk* (Moscow, 1996).

Voennaya entsiklopediya (St Petersburg, 1914).

Volkov, S, *Russkii ofitserskii korpus* (Moscow, 1993).

Vulliamy, C E, *Crimea: The Campaign of 1854–56* (London, 1939).

Wantage, Harriet S, *Lord Wantage, VC, KCB: A Memoir, by His Wife* (London, 1907).

Weller, Jac, *Wellington at Waterloo* (London, 1967).

Wellesley, Sir Victor, and Sencourt, Robert, *Conversations with Napoleon III* (London, 1934).

Wilson, C T, *Our Veterans of 1854: In Camp, and before the Enemy, by a Regimental Officer* (London, 1859).

Zaionchkovskii, A M, *Oborona Sevastopolya: podvigi zashchitnikov* (St Petersburg, 1904).

Zaionchkovskii, P, 'Russkii ofitserskii korpus na rubezhe dvukh stoletii', *Voenno-istoricheskii zhurnal*, 1972.

Index